Passages of Belonging

Perspectives on Jewish Texts and Contexts

Edited by
Vivian Liska

Editorial Board
Robert Alter, Steven E. Aschheim, Richard I. Cohen, Mark H. Gelber,
Moshe Halbertal, Christine Hayes, Moshe Idel, Samuel Moyn,
Ada Rapoport-Albert, Alvin Rosenfeld, David Ruderman, Bernd Witte

Volume 7

Passages of Belonging

Interpreting Jewish Literatures

Edited by
Carola Hilfrich, Natasha Gordinsky and Susanne Zepp

DE GRUYTER

Supported by the I-CORE Program of the Planning and Budgeting Committee and The Israel Science Foundation (grant No. 1798/12)

ISBN 978-3-11-073639-7
e-ISBN (PDF) 978-3-11-052551-9
e-ISBN (EPUB) 978-3-11-052349-2
ISSN 2199-6962

Library of Congress Control Number: 2018965712

Bibliographic information published by the Deutsche Nationalbibliothek
The Deutsche Nationalbibliothek lists this publication in the Deutsche Nationalbibliografie; detailed bibliographic data are available on the Internet at http://dnb.dnb.de.

© 2020 Walter de Gruyter GmbH, Berlin/Boston
This volume is text- and page-identical with the hardback published in 2019.
Typesetting: Integra Software Services Pvt. Ltd.
Printing and binding: CPI books GmbH, Leck
Cover image: Svetlana Boym

www.degruyter.com

Contents

Carola Hilfrich, Natasha Gordinsky, Susanne Zepp
Introduction —— 1

Part I

Hélène Cixous / Translated by Eric Prenowitz
Ail! – Il ne faut pas le dire – / Oy! – You Mustn't Say That – —— 8

Carola Hilfrich
The Depository of *Zugehör: Ail!* and the Soundscape of Belonging —— 48

Cécile Wajsbrot / Translated by Susanne Zepp
Vous trouverez ce livre … / You'll find this book … —— 54

Stephanie Bung
"Vous trouverez ce livre …" – Cécile Wajsbrot and the Art of Belonging —— 58

Alex Epstein / Translated by Becka Mara McKay
קיצורי דרך הביתה, חרסינה מזרח גרמנית / Shortcuts Home; East German China —— 66

Natasha Gordinsky
Smuggled Belongings: Alex Epstein's Fiction of Immigration —— 68

Almog Behar / Translated by Vivian Eden
אֲנָא מִן אַל־יַהוּד / Ana min al-yahoud – I'm one of the Jews —— 74

Yael Kenan
"The Same Words, Perhaps a Bit More Broken": Multiple Belongings in Almog Behar's "Ana Min al-Yahoud" —— 90

Part II

Ruth Ginsburg
French Scholem, or: Scholem's Purloined Letter —— 107

Shlomith Rimmon-Kenan
Belonging Destabilized: Anton Shammas's *Arabesques* —— 126

Vivian Liska
Derrida's Appurtenances: A Footnote on Language and Belonging —— 138

Susanne Zepp
De-essentialized Belonging: Poetics of the Self in Joyce Mansour and Clarice Lispector —— 150

Anastasia Telaak
Form and Language: Alejandra Pizarnik's Spatial Poetics of Un/Belonging —— 169

Sonja Dickow
Architectures of Absence: Nicole Krauss's Novel *Great House* —— 194

Part III

Masha Gessen
Introduction to Svetlana Boym's "Remembering Forgetting" —— 211

Svetlana Boym
Remembering Forgetting. *Tale of a Refugee Camp* —— 214

Sasha Senderovich
Svetlana Boym Remembers Forgetting —— 234

Notes on Contributors —— 236

Carola Hilfrich, Natasha Gordinsky, Susanne Zepp
Introduction

This volume collects contributions from members of the research group "Fields of Belonging: Interpreting Jewish literatures," founded in 2010 at the Simon Dubnow Institute for Jewish History and Culture at the University of Leipzig. We were keen to initiate an encounter between writers and scholars in order to think about questions of belonging in Jewish literatures beyond the confines of identitary essentialism – be it an essentialism of belonging, Jewishness, or literariness. Building on existing endeavors in the general Humanities (Bell 1996, Bhabha 1994, Butler & Spivak 2007, Diner 2011, Fortier 1999, Freestone and Liu 2016, Hall 1992, Harvey 1996, hooks 2008, Leon 2009, Massey 1991, Probyn 1996, Rogoff 2000), we looked at belonging and sense of place in non-identitary terms such as movement, transformation, emergence, displacement, and transgression – in short: in terms of passages. This approach was sustained by recent research in Jewish Studies of space and place (e.g., Boym 2001, Mann 2012) as well as by spatial studies of Jewish literatures (DeKoven Ezrahi 2000, Hever 2015, Miron 2010, Newton 2005, Pinsker 2010).

However, while these studies engage mainly with the classical canon of Jewish literatures in Hebrew, Yiddish, English, and German, we sought to encompass these together with the outer and more contemporary reaches of the modern Jewish canon, including texts from North Africa, Brazil, Russia, Argentina, and France. In this context, passages appear less as intermediary stages between departure and return and more as situations that suspend any teleological orientation. In this sense, we take passages not only to include movement in space (such as from one place to another) and elapsing in time (as represented in and by literature), but also to encompass a theoretical tool for literary interpretation. Such passages are no longer metaphors or merely representations; rather, they are highly concrete situations, experiences, and forces, as in Bakhtin's seminal definition of the chronotope: "In the literary artistic chronotope, spatial and temporal indicators are fused into one carefully thought-out, concrete whole. Time, as it were, thickens, takes on flesh, becomes artistically visible; likewise, space becomes charged and responsive to the movements of time, plot and history. This intersection of axes and fusion of indicators characterizes the artistic chronotope" (Bakhtin 1981, 84).

Over the years, our joint discussions produced a ripple effect in the respective works of all participants, as well as among them. The collaboration of writers and literary scholars made us aware that, while scholarly theorizations of passages of belonging must be rigorous, the literary work challenges us to remain

https://doi.org/10.1515/9783110525519-001

on the move with our theorizations. Each of the contributions to this volume meets these challenges in its own right, while all the texts reflect how deeply our lives and work are affected by what is called a post-monolingual condition (Levy and Schachter 2015, Yeldiz 2012). For us, this condition was made concrete by thinking it in the multiple passages – linguistic, geographic, generic, cultural, historical – of Jewish and literary belonging.

The volume opens with a literary section that presents works in different genres by four contemporary writers and translations and critical commentaries of these works. Taken together, these contributions suggest that we think of belonging in terms of dispossession and movement, the vulnerabilities of owing and owning, and the charged spatiality of enactments of such vulnerabilities.

Hélène Cixous's *Aïl! – Il ne faut pas le dire – / Oy! – You Mustn't Say That –* sets the stage for such literary thinking. It is a play for two characters, the octogenarian sisters Selma and Jenny Meyer, cast in a Godotian scene "on their return from Osnabrück," their native city in Germany, and preparing a *Leberhäckele* "in the kitchen, Paris." Bickering over the basics of their umlauted Jewish family dish, they are negotiating their place in an economy of the unsayable and the position in language on which it depends. Their kitchen talk unfurls onto the soundscape of a revenant and repudiated, native language, namely, *allemand*, or "German" in French. In this soundscape, the scene of belonging plays out in an unheard-of, "*aï*literated" mode, as Carola Hilfrich suggests in her commentary. She shows how the play's acoustic territory forms a sonic discourse on belonging that is "equally feverish, energetic, and participatory," focusing interpretation on the aural lexicon and range of the soundscape.

In her poem "Vous trouverez ce livre... / You Will Find This Book...," Cécile Wajsbrot reminds us of the difficulty of escaping class, violence, and other adversities as either obstacles to or markers of belonging. The "book" she writes about is an embodiment of the exigencies of the sense of place as it connects with family histories and histories of dispossession. At the same time, her poem provides social commentary and, in fact, establishes the conditions for a negotiation of both belonging and class. Thus, it serves as a reminder that the politics of poetry resides in its centrality to the construction of a political person. Stephanie Bung unravels these intricacies from a philological perspective while emphasizing the sense of "belonging" as "ownership." In focusing on the poem's expressive voice as an embodiment of radically different experiences of owing and owning, her commentary draws attention to the potential of poetic language to rethink dominant paradigms of belonging.

The first of Alex Epstein's micro-stories, originally published in Hebrew and entitled "Shortcuts Home," consists of four sentences, each of which imagines and performs another conundrum of belonging and homeliness, while the second deals with the economy of family and cultural possessions through "a little tale of immigration." Natasha Gordinsky explores how these micro-stories resist the trope of homecoming and undermine a totalizing narrative of immigration as a single and linear story. She argues that Epstein's texts epitomize, in their fragmented form, a (post-)Soviet Jewish mode of belonging, constituted by a persistent negotiation between fiction and history.

Almog Behar's "Ana Min Al Yahoud" stages the scene of identification that regulates belonging through language and nation. Shifting between Arabic and Hebrew, his story challenges the pervasively monolingual understanding of Israeli literature, and advances a view of literary belonging as both multiple and conflicted. Yael Kenan's commentary on the story focuses on the bodily and mnemonic aspects of the Arabic tongue that dwells so prominently in the protagonist's Hebrew in/of the story. She suggests that we understand the title utterance, and its reverberations in the text, as an ethical shibboleth or a linguistic site for negotiating conflicting cultural identities. Her reading significantly complicates Deleuze and Guattari's notion of minor literatures by demonstrating how Behar's hybrid language serves as a poetic and political tool for bringing together the collective and individual.

The contributions in the second section expand this critical perspective to other works of Jewish modernity and contemporaneity.

Ruth Ginsburg's "French Scholem" discusses the double dispossession of language reflected in Gershom Scholem's writings, exposing the complex dynamics of loss between his "Bekenntnis über unsere Sprache" in a letter to Franz Rosenzweig in 1926 and a later, unpublished note from his archives, entitled "Sprache." Offering the first, and a breathtakingly close, reading of Scholem's "Bekenntnis" in the context of its original language rather than its highly influential mis/translation into French, Ginsburg establishes a seminal claim on linguistic dispossession and appropriation in Scholem's work, and sheds new light on the history and politics of its translation and circulation.

Shlomith Rimmon-Kenan, in "Belonging Destabilized," presents a literary analysis of the "radical political vision" of civic belonging that underlies Anton Shammas's novel *Arabesques*, originally published in Hebrew in 1986, and read here in translation. Focusing on the structural intricacy of the novel, its alternating voices and treatment of time, place, language, and self as fundamentally othered, she calls attention to how Shammas's vision "bridges" opposed narratives within the body of Hebrew Literature. For Rimmon-Kenan, this bridging of the work of literary imagination suggests an alternate modality of complicity with the novel, in which the reader may come to "long to belong to [the] co-existence" that it envisions.

In "Derrida's Appurtenances," Vivian Liska scrutinizes the function of this synonym for "belonging" in Jacques Derrida's thought on linguistic depropriation, focusing on his extended footnote on Jewish belonging across the Ashkenazi-Sephardi and the literary-philosophical divides in *Monolingualism of the Other; Or the Prosthesis of Origin*, originally published in French in 1996. Liska argues compellingly that this footnote is the most radical and intimate moment of Derrida's monolingual performance. The textual "appurtenance," she suggests, allows him to reassert repressed, withdrawn, and rejected appartenances or belongings at another level of negotiation. Concomitantly and paradoxically, it reveals the original choreography of his own speaking on linguistic belonging and ownership in his listening to the voices of others.

Susanne Zepp's "De-essentialized Belonging" examines the strategies by which the polylingual and multicultural writings of Clarice Lispector and Joyce Mansour de-essentialize belonging. Zepp argues that both authors transform different aspects of belonging, whether their own or that of others, into complex aesthetic forms which, in their many variations and transformations, challenge the concept of the natural possession of a given language and, by extension, the concept of identity. The lieu of these transformations, in Mansour's writings, is the poetic speaker, while, in Lispector's prose, it is to be found in her experiments with first-person narratives. Zepp suggests that we understand their major formal innovations as aesthetic comments on the complexities of belonging.

Anastasia Telaak's contribution links the specificity of the poetic form to the spatial, philosophical, and linguistic dynamics of "un/belonging" in Alejandra Pizarnik's oeuvre. She portrays Pizarnik as one of the most unconventional voices in the literary (post-)modern era and situates her in the context of the multiple traditions and discourses that intertwine in her oeuvre, including Argentinean avant-garde literature, German Romanticism, French symbolism, surrealism, (post-)structuralist thought, and Jewish tradition. Her approach suggests a reading of Pizarnik's oeuvre as a simultaneous reconstruction and deconstruction of paradigmatic spatio-temporal constellations in Jewish history.

Sonja Dickow's essay explores the multiple layers, sites, and scales of an "architecture of absence" in the plot and poetics of Nicole Krauss's novel *Great House* (2010). Focusing on its inanimate protagonist, a gigantic writing desk, as witness to the chaos and violence of modern Jewish history, she reveals an aesthetics of loss and potentiality centered on the novel's figurations of absence. Her analysis zooms out to the eponymous "Great House" of Jewish literary tradition after the destruction of the Second Temple to take account of Krauss's contemporary work with the legacy of a post-catastrophic design of a space for "the mobile house of the text." It closes up on the empty and locked drawer of the novel's desk, taking it as the unhomely container of a Bachelardian "aesthetics of hidden things." Dickow's approach intertwines questions of readability and inhabitability for an analysis of Krauss's work as a potent negotiation with the historical and psychic space of contemporary Jewish literature.

The third section, with an introduction by Masha Gessen, presents Svetlana Boym's visual essay "Remembering Forgetting. In Search of My Refugee Camp," which traces and maps the myriad passages through and within the landscape of the past of a refugee intellectual. Combining archival research with interviews she conducted with former inmates of "her" refugee camp, Boym painstakingly reconstructs the topography of a forgotten place of transition. At the same time, her reflection on emigration reveals her own "emotional geography" in transition from the Soviet Union to the United States of America. Sasha Senderovich's response to Boym's essay concludes this section.

We wish to express our gratitude to Dan Diner for giving our research group an intellectual home. We thank Vivian Liska for inviting our work for inclusion in her book series, and for her unwavering support in the preparation of this volume's publication. Further thanks go to the two institutions which graciously hosted the subsequent meetings of our group, namely, Freie Universität Berlin and the *Da'at Hamakom* Center for the Study of Cultures of Place in the Modern Jewish World at the Hebrew University of Jerusalem. Ulrike Kraus and Katja Lehming provided generous editorial support at the De Gruyter Publishing House. We also thank the editors Tom Kellner, Jeremy Schreiber, Graham Shapiro and Sam Walker, as well as the translator Margaret Ries, for their precise work on the contributions to this volume. Last, but not least, we thank Svetlana Boym's parents, Musa and Yuri Goldberg, for granting us the publication rights for her visual essay.

We dedicate this volume to the memory of Svetlana Boym, who inhabited the many kinds of passages that we speak about here with fierceness, exactitude, and openness. The image we use for our cover is a photograph from a series of visual artworks in which she explores the genesis of her writing in a foreign language. Underlaying marked pages from the English translation of Jacques Derrida's *De la grammatologie* with the movement of her reading hand, Svetlana's "Touching Writing" ideally captures the cultural, affective, and epistemic intensities of belonging in the field of Jewish literatures and literary thinking.

Jerusalem, Haifa, and Berlin, Summer 2018

References

Bakhtin, Mikhail. "Forms of Time and of the Chronotope in the Novel." *The Dialogic Imagination*. Austin: University of Texas Press, 1981. 84–258.
Bell, Vicki (Ed.). *Performativity and Belonging*. London: SAGE, 1996.
Bhabha, Homi. *The Location of Culture*. London and New York: Routledge, 1994.
Boym, Svetlana. *The Future of Nostalgia*. New York: Basic Books, 2001.
Butler, Judith, and Gayatri Chakravorty Spivak. *Who Sings the Nation-State? Language, Politics, Belonging*. New York and London: Routledge, 2007.
DeKoven Ezrahi, Sidra. *Booking Passage: Exile and Homecoming in the Modern Jewish Imagination*. Berkeley: University of California Press, 2000.
Diner, Dan. Einführung. *Enzyklopädie jüdischer Geschichte und Kultur*, Vol. I. Ed. Dan Diner. Stuttgart/Weimar: J.B. Metzler, 2011. VII–XIX.
Fortier, Anne Marie. "Re-membering Places and the Performance of Belonging(s)." *Theory, Culture & Society* 16.2 (1999): 41–64.
Freestone, Robert, and Edgar Liu (Eds.). *Place and Placelessness Revisited*. New York and London: Routledge, 2016.
Hall, Stuart. "The Question of Cultural Identity." *Modernity and Its Futures*. Eds. Stuart Hall, David Held, and Tony McGrew. Cambridge: Polity Press in association with the Open University, 1992. 274–316.
Harvey, David. *Justice, Nature, and the Geography of Difference*. Hoboken: Wiley-Blackwell, 1996.
Hever, Hannan. *To Inherit the Land, to Conquer the Space: The Beginnings of Hebrew Poetry in Israel* [Hebrew]. Tel Aviv: Mosad Bialik, 2015.
hooks, bell. *Belonging: A Culture of Place*. New York and London: Routledge, 2008.
Leon, Carol E. *Movement and Belonging: Lines, Places, and Spaces of Travel*. New York: Peter Lang, 2009.
Levy Lital, and Allison Schachter. "Jewish Literature / World Literature: Between the Local and the Transnational." *PMLA* 130.1 (2015): 92–109.
Mann, Barbara E. *Space and Place in Jewish Studies*. New Brunswick: Rutgers University Press, 2012.
Massey, Doreen. "A Global Sense of Place." *Marxism Today* 38 (1991): 24–29.
Miron, Dan. *From Continuity to Contiguity: Toward a New Jewish Literary Thinking*. Stanford: Stanford University Press, 2010.
Newton, Adam Zachary. *The Elsewhere: On Belonging at a Near Distance. Reading Literary Memoir from Europe and the Levant*. Madison: University of Wisconsin Press, 2005.
Probyn, Elspeth. *Outside Belongings*. New York and London: Routledge, 1996.
Rogoff, Irit. *Terra Infirma: Geography's Visual Culture*. New York and London: Routledge, 2000.
Yeldiz, Yasemin. *Beyond the Mother Tongue: The Postmonolingual Condition*, New York: Fordham University Press, 2014.

Part I

Hélène Cixous
Ail!

– Il ne faut pas le dire –

Personnages: Selma Meyer, 89 ans: l'aînée
Jenny Meyer, 86 ans: la cadette

En revenant d'Osnabrück, Hanovre
A Paris, la cuisine.

SELMA (à Jenny)
Suis-moi. *Hack die Leber*. Encore! Cet allemand qui remonte! Hache le foie! Compris?

JENNY
Ja

SELMA
Stop! Attends que ce soit froid

JENNY
Mais *c'est* froid! J'ai attendu

SELMA
Alors hache! Je vais te dire une chose: Osnabrück, c'est fini! On ne m'aura plus

JENNY
Je ne sais pas pourquoi nous y sommes allées après cinquante ans c'est idiot

SELMA
N'écrase pas avec la fourchette. On aurait pu refuser

JENNY
J'écrase avec la machine. C'est toi qui as accepté. A notre âge on peut tout refuser

SELMA
Mettre tout sur le compte de mes quatre-vingt-neuf ans ça me déplaît. Moi je suis toujours au volant. N'écrase pas trop!

Hélène Cixous
Oy!

– You Mustn't Say That –
Translated by Eric Prenowitz

Characters: Selma Meyer, 89: the elder sister
Jenny Meyer, 86: the younger sister

On their return from Osnabrück, Hanover.
In the kitchen, Paris.

SELMA (to Jenny)
Listen to me. *Hack die Leber*. Again! That German again! Chop the liver! Understand?

JENNY
Ja

SELMA
Stop! Wait for it to cool

JENNY
But it *is* cool! I did wait

SELMA
So get chopping! Let me tell you something: Osnabrück, that's it! They won't get me again

JENNY
I don't know why we went back after fifty years it's idiotic

SELMA
Don't mash it with the fork. We could have refused

JENNY
I'm mashing it with the machine. You're the one who accepted. At our age we can refuse anything

SELMA
Blaming everything on my eighty-nine years, I don't like that. I'm still driving. Don't mash it too much!

JENNY
Laisse-moi faire. J'en ai fait du *Leberhäckele* depuis soixante-dix ans j'en ai fait!

SELMA
On m'a fait le coup plusieurs fois: « à presque quatre-vingt-dix ans vous ne pouvez pas refuser. Vous deux, nos dernières juives. Vous devez éduquer nos jeunes. »

JENNY
C'est drôle plus tu es vieille plus tu dois.

SELMA
Les deux soeurs Meyer qui les connaît à Osnabrück? Notre époque a totalement disparu.

Je n'aime pas ça, aller survivre. Je ne dois rien à l'Allemagne

JENNY
Je mets de l'ail?

SELMA
De l'ail! *Du bist ja ganz verrückt*! On n'est pas des paysans de la campagne ici! Laisse ça, je vais finir. La dernière main. Je vais te dire une chose que je ne voulais pas te dire: tout le monde est raciste, il y a au moins douze racismes, des racistes tu en trouves partout.

JENNY
Moi je ne l'avais pas remarqué

SELMA
Sur les bancs du parc dans le train, surtout chez les bouchers, tous des racistes, tu peux rien faire sans qu'il en tombe à poignées comme des cheveux dans la soupe.

JENNY
Tu me reproches de perdre mes cheveux!

SELMA
Je te reproche de ne pas porter une perruque, surtout dans la cuisine. Regarde ça, des cheveux dans le pâté.

JENNY
Let me do it. I've made some *Leberhäckele* in seventy years I've made my share!

SELMA
They've tried it on me more than once: "At nearly ninety years old you can't refuse. The two of you, our last Jews. You must educate our youth."

JENNY
Funny, the older you get the more you owe.

SELMA
The two Meyer sisters who knows them in Osnabrück? Our era has totally disappeared.
I don't like that sort of thing, to go survive for them. I owe nothing to Germany

JENNY
Should I add some garlic?

SELMA
Garlic! *Du bist ja ganz verrückt!* We're not peasants from the countryside! Leave it, I'll finish. The last touch. I'm going to tell you something I didn't want to tell you: everyone is racist, there are at least a dozen kinds of racism, there are racists everywhere.

JENNY
I hadn't noticed that

SELMA
On park benches in the train, especially at the butcher's, racists, every last one of them, you can't lift a finger without handfuls of them dropping like a hair into your soup.

JENNY
Don't blame me for losing my hair!

SELMA
I blame you for not wearing a wig, especially in the kitchen. Look: a hair in the liver.

JENNY
Au moins c'est les miens. A Osnabrück il y avait aussi cette dame chauve dans le café, tu te rappelles son nom on s'est souri.

SELMA
Frau Knoll la pharmacienne. Son mari était directeur à Theresienstadt.

JENNY
On a mangé des crêpes l'une en face de l'autre on s'est regardées et elle m'a souri. Entre chauves dames.

SELMA
On sentait qu'elle avait des difficultés à joindre les deux bouts de son budget. Mais moi j'aurais évité de lui sourire.

JENNY
C'est elle qui a commencé. Après on dit: la Juive, elle se croit fière, elle ne veut pas sourire.

SELMA
C'est pour ça. On finit quand même par sourire aux nazis et ça n'a plus de fin. Si j'avais su, je ne serais pas retournée à Osnabrück. Je n'étais pas retournée, pendant quarante ans ça ne m'a pas gênée, je pensais toujours on ne devrait jamais retourner en arrière

JENNY
On n'a pas pu faire autrement. On nous a invitées. On nous a obligées.

SELMA
Toi tu m'as obligée, comme d'habitude, dès qu'il y a une invitation, Jenny doit accepter.

JENNY
Mais c'est *toi* qui m'as écrit si je veux venir aussi.

SELMA
Je n'avais pas envie de retourner seule.

JENNY
At least it's mine. In Osnabrück there was also that bald lady in the café, do you remember her name we smiled at each other.

SELMA
Frau Knoll the pharmacist. Her husband was the director of Theresienstadt.

JENNY
We were eating crepes across from each other our eyes met and she smiled at me. One bald lady to another.

SELMA
You could see she was having trouble making ends meet. But if it had been me, I'd have avoided smiling at her.

JENNY
She started it. Afterwards they say: the Jew she thinks she's proud, she doesn't want to smile.

SELMA
That's why. You end up smiling at Nazis and there's no end to it. Had I known, I wouldn't have returned to Osnabrück. I hadn't been back, for forty years it didn't bother me, I always thought one should never return to the past

JENNY
We couldn't have done otherwise. We were invited. We were obliged.

SELMA
It's you who obliged me to go, as usual, as soon as there's an invitation, Jenny has to accept.

JENNY
But *you're* the one who wrote me if I want to come along.

SELMA
I didn't feel like going back alone.

JENNY
Et toi tu as trouvé le programme de la Mairie très intéressant. On a été au théâtre d'Osnabrück et on jouait *Die Dreigroschenoper*. Et l'hôtel tu m'as dit c'est le meilleur celui qui était sur la place de la Cathédrale. Il y a un grand buffet pour le petit déjeuner

SELMA
Moi je ne suis pas allée pour l'hôtel, ça je l'ai dit pour toi. J'ai un peu hésité. Après je me suis dit il n'y a pas de raison de ne pas tendre la main. Je ne pensais plus au passé. De toutes les façons ces gens-là ne sont plus. Ma génération a disparu.

JENNY
Il y avait le maire aussi, la femme qui était le maire c'était pas une femme qui avait fait des études, elle était très gentille, c'est pour elle qu'on n'a pas pu dire non.

SELMA
Mais ça *on ne l'a pas su avant. On n'a rien su avant.* Et maintenant si j'avais su j'aurais préféré ne pas ajouter encore une nouvelle complication à toute cette histoire qui était déjà si compliquée à cause des nazis et maintenant par-dessus le marché il y a les nouveaux juifs aussi.

JENNY
C'est fait c'est fait.

SELMA
Les problèmes ont tellement changé. Alors maintenant je ne vais quand même pas me faire du souci pour les juifs d'Osnabrück d'aujourd'hui je m'en serais bien passée de ceux-là.

JENNY
La solution c'est d'oublier, un, deux, trois.

SELMA
Oublier, oublier, oublier. J'aurais dû y penser *avant*. Laisse cette prune, il n'y en a qu'une. C'est pour Hélène. Pour toi c'est un yaourt.

JENNY
Mais j'ai déjà mangé un yaourt ce matin

JENNY
And you thought the City Hall's program looked interesting. We went to the Osnabrück theatre and they were doing *Die Dreigroschenoper*. And the hotel you told me it was the best in town the one across from the Cathedral. There's a big buffet for breakfast

SELMA
I didn't go because of the hotel, I only said that for you. I hesitated a little. Afterwards I told myself there's no reason not to extend a hand. I didn't think any more about the past. Besides those people are gone. My generation has disappeared.

JENNY
The mayor was there too, the woman who was the mayor, she wasn't someone who'd had a higher education, she was very nice, it was for her sake we couldn't say no.

SELMA
But *we didn't know that ahead of time. We didn't know anything ahead of time.* And now had I known I'd rather not have added a new complication to this whole story that was already so complicated because of the Nazis and now into the bargain there are the new Jews as well.

JENNY
What's done is done.

SELMA
The problems have changed so much. And now I'm not going to start worrying about today's Osnabrück Jews I could have done without them.

JENNY
The solution is to forget, one, two, three.

SELMA
Forget, forget, forget. I should have thought of that *before*. Leave that plum, there's only one. It's for Hélène. For you there's a yoghurt.

JENNY
But I already had a yoghurt this morning

SELMA
Mais j'ai gardé cette prune pour Hélène. Un yaourt *nature*.

Osnabrück, j'ai pensé pendant quarante ans, ça m'aurait plu d'y retourner, mais j'ai toujours été un peu réfractaire de retourner en Allemagne, après je me suis dit pourquoi penser au passé, les anciens lieux où j'étais jeune qui sait s'ils sont encore là, les juifs tous sont partis aucun n'est revenu. Après je me suis dit si je ne reviens pas qui va revenir ? Ce qui m'a toujours un peu gênée, c'est que je n'ai jamais rencontré Hitler. Quand j'étais là-bas je ne connaissais pas Hitler.

JENNY
Le maire d'Osnabrück qui est une femme nous a invitées quand même que nous ne pensons plus au passé. On n'a jamais vu Hitler, il n'y avait pas la télévision.

SELMA
Ça on n'a pas dit à Osnabrück

JENNY
Quand j'étais jeune fille, il y avait toujours un *gesunder Antisemitismus*. On avait l'habitude ça ne nous a pas dérangées. Il y avait les *juifs-acceptés*, les docteurs, les professeurs, les avocats, c'était accepté.

SELMA
Ça on ne pouvait pas dire.

Le Docteur Pelz aussi était un *juif-accepté*. Ça c'était un sage. Il était contre l'excès de médicament. Tout le monde à Osnabrück avait confiance au Docteur Pelz.

JENNY
Lui on n'a pas osé le déporter

SELMA
On a déporté sa fille, on ne s'est pas gêné pour déporter sa fille qui s'occupait du vieux Docteur Pelz comme une mère – ça on a pu dire.

JENNY
Nous n'avons pas plus souffert dans notre école. Moi *une* fois j'ai été invitée à un anniversaire. C'était la fille du marchand de sacs. Et ça ne nous a pas dérangées du tout. On n'était ni amies ni ennemies.

SELMA
But I'm saving that plum for Hélène. A *plain* yoghurt.

For forty years I thought I'd enjoy going back to Osnabrück, but I've always been a little reluctant to go back to Germany, later I said to myself why think about the past, the old places where I was young who knows if they're still there, the Jews all left not a single one came back. Later I said to myself if I don't come back who will? What's always bothered me a little is that I never met Hitler. When I lived there I didn't know Hitler

JENNY
The mayor of Osnabrück who is a woman invited us even though we no longer think about the past. We never saw Hitler, television didn't exist.

SELMA
We didn't say *that* in Osnabrück

JENNY
When I was a girl, there was always a *gesunder Antisemitismus*. It didn't bother us, we were used to it. There were the *accepted Jews*, the doctors, professors, lawyers, that was accepted.

SELMA
That's something we couldn't say.

Doctor Pelz was also an *accepted Jew*. That was a wise man. He was against excessive medication. Everyone in Osnabrück trusted Doctor Pelz.

JENNY
They didn't dare deport him

SELMA
They deported his daughter, they didn't think twice about deporting his daughter who looked after old Doctor Pelz like a mother – *that's* something we were able to say.

JENNY
We never suffered in school. *Once*, I was even invited to a birthday party. For the daughter of the bag merchant. And that didn't bother us at all. We were neither friends nor enemies.

SELMA
Nous n'invitions pas non plus, ça ne m'a pas effleurée d'inviter une Allemande.

JENNY
Et pourtant on était allemandes. Et pourtant. En été on allait à Norderney. Avant la guerre les juifs ne sont pas allés à Borkum. Tous les juifs sont allés à Norderney. Il y avait des plages où on n'est pas allés.

SELMA
Helgoland, c'était dans le Ostsee, on n'allait pas. Mais à Norderney il y en avait beaucoup.

JENNY
Il pleuvait toujours, on avait le droit de rester une minute dans l'eau. Surtout notre mère qui avait peur de la mer.

SELMA
A Norderney c'est là que j'ai appris à danser à seize ans.

JENNY
Moi je n'ai pas eu de leçons parce que juste après il y avait quand même antisémitisme et maman a pensé que je reste comme *Mauerblümchen*, parce que j'ai l'air juif, je vais faire fleur de mur. On se sentait allemandes mais on avait l'air juif.

SELMA
Moi j'étais toujours internationale.

JENNY
Il y avait toujours déjà cet antisémitisme. On avait toujours ce journal antisémite *le Veilleur d'Osnabrück, Der Stadt*wächter, dans les années avant Hitler. Et dans le journal un jour c'est écrit d'une jeune fille qu'elle a fait opérer *den Synagogenschlüssel*, la clé de la Synagogue dans le journal.

SELMA
Quoi! C'était dans le journal?

JENNY
Et c'était moi!

SELMA
Dann haben sie genau gewußt

SELMA
We didn't do any inviting either, it never crossed my mind to invite a German.

JENNY
And yet we were German. And yet. In summer we used to go to Norderney. Before the war Jews didn't go to Borkum. The Jews all went to Norderney. There were beaches we didn't go to.

SELMA
Helgoland was in the Ostsee, we didn't go there. But in Norderney there were lots of Jews.

JENNY
It rained all the time, we were allowed to stay in the water for one minute. Especially our mother who was scared of the sea.

SELMA
That's where I learned to dance, Norderney, when I was sixteen.

JENNY
I didn't have lessons because shortly afterward there was anti-Semitism all the same and mummy thought I'll be a *Mauerblümchen*, because I look Jewish, I'll be a wallflower. We felt German but we looked Jewish.

SELMA
I was always international.

JENNY
There was always already anti-Semitism. There was always that anti-Semitic newspaper, *The Osnabrück Watchman*, in the years before Hitler, *Der Stadtwächter*. And one day in the paper there's a piece about a girl who had her *Synagogenschlüssel* operated on, her Synagogue key.

SELMA
What! That was in the paper?

JENNY
And it was me!

SELMA
Dann haben sie genau gewußt

JENNY
Parle français.

SELMA
Pourquoi? Je parle allemand?

JENNY
J'étais dégoûtée. Gênée surtout. Et on ne pouvait pas se plaindre. J'avais ce grand nez et je suis allée voir le *Nasenjosef*. Un chirurgien cosmétique, le Docteur Josef pour les Nez. Il était très fameux. J'avais déjà seize.

SELMA
Je suis partie en 1930 déjà je ne voulais pas être allemande. C'est seulement en 33 qu'il est devenu *Kanzler*.

JENNY
Hitler, on a pensé que c'est seulement un an et que ça ne va pas rester. On vivait très bien avec l'antisémitisme ordinairement *gesund* comme on disait toujours.

SELMA
Avant 1930, déjà pour moi ça suffit. J'avais peut-être 17 ans je me promenais avec Mutti. Et voilà quelqu'un en passant à côté de nous qui dit ça sent l'ail. Qu'est-ce que c'est que cette stupidité?! Quand je pense à la culture que les Juifs avaient créée. Ma grand-mère lisait Goethe son contemporain et les romans de Jakob Wassermann.

Hitler un type inculte, ce n'était même pas un Allemand.

On ne savait pas ce que c'était

L'ail on n'avait jamais vu ça

JENNY
Peut-être en Pologne les juifs en mangeaient.

SELMA
Tout le monde est raciste. Les juifs étaient plus racistes que racistes avec les Polonais. Les Polonais il y avait toujours des pogroms chez eux, ils arrivaient, c'étaient des malheureux.

Ça il ne faut pas le dire – On n'a pas besoin de cracher dans sa propre soupe.

JENNY
Speak French.

SELMA
Why? I'm speaking German?

JENNY
I was disgusted. Embarrassed mostly. And you couldn't complain. I had this big nose and I went to see the *Nasenjosef*. A plastic surgeon, Doctor Josef for Noses. He was very famous. I was sixteen already.

SELMA
I left in 1930 already I didn't want to be German. It was only in '33 that he became *Kanzler*.

JENNY
Hitler, we thought it's just for a year and it won't last. We got along just fine with the normal *gesunde* anti-Semitism as we always called it.

SELMA
Before 1930 I'd had enough already. I was maybe seventeen, I was out walking with Mutti. And someone walking by us says *smells like garlic*. What kind of stupidity is that?! When I think of the culture Jews created. My grandmother used to read Goethe her contemporary and Jakob Wassermann novels.

A guy with no culture, Hitler, wasn't even German.

We didn't know what it was

Garlic? Never seen it.

JENNY
Maybe in Poland Jews ate it.

SELMA
Everyone is racist. Jews were more racist than racist. With the Poles. The Poles, they were always having pogroms there, then they'd turn up, miserable things.

That's something one mustn't say – No point spitting in our own soup.

Ils arrivaient chez nous, ils disaient nous sommes des malheureux, ils venaient au consistoire. Le consistoire leur donnait un billet de train pour la prochaine ville.

JENNY
C'est toujours les pauvres qui sont venus, on leur a toujours donné de l'argent.

SELMA
On leur a donné *des billets de train* pour le prochain consistoire!

JENNY
Ça je ne savais pas – que

SELMA
Qu'on se sente supérieurs, les Juifs allemands? Bien sûr. Les Polonais, on ne fréquentait pas. Il y avait un esprit de caste dans cette petite communauté. L'origine –

JENNY
Ah oui l'origine. Ça nous a commandé

SELMA
Les gens d'origine polonaise personne ne les fréquentait.

JENNY
Les Ehrlich?

SELMA
On ne fréquentait pas.
Les amis de classe de ma mère, ils avaient les grands magasins

JENNY
C'étaient les grandes familles

SELMA
Il y avait un autre groupe c'étaient les avocats. Ils ne se mélangeaient pas avec les commerçants.

JENNY
De toutes les façons ces gens-là ne sont plus. Il n'y a qu'à oublier.

They'd turn up on our doorsteps, they'd say we're destitute, they'd come to the Jewish Consistory. The Consistory would give them train tickets to the next city.

JENNY
It was always the poor who came, they were always given money.

SELMA
They were given *train tickets* to the next Consistory down the line!

JENNY
That I didn't know – that

SELMA
That we German Jews feel superior? Of course. We didn't mix with the Poles. There was a sense of caste in our little community. One's origin –

JENNY
Ah yes one's origin. It controlled us

SELMA
People of Polish origin? No one mixed with them.

JENNY
The Ehrlichs?

SELMA
Didn't mix with them.
My mother's school friends, they owned the department stores

JENNY
The leading families.

SELMA
Then there was another group, the lawyers. Who didn't associate with the shopkeepers.

JENNY
Anyway none of those people exist anymore. Might as well forget it.

SELMA
Frau Engers, déjà, elle n'était pas acceptée, quoiqu'allemande, elle était sans-gêne, elle parlait fort –

JENNY
Frau Engers était chapelière, je ne voudrais jamais que ma mère soit comme elle, elle était tellement différente.

SELMA
Elle se serait fait couper en quatre pour ma mère.

JENNY
Je n'aurais pas voulu qu'une femme comme ça soit ma mère. Je suis sûre qu'elle savait nager, c'était comme un homme, elle était ordinaire, ma mère, elle, était reçue dans la haute société juive partout. Mutti était amie avec les Flattauer, les Stern und Falk le grand magasin la haute volée, die Blank.

SELMA
Mais pourtant les fils ensuite ont étudié, personne n'est entré dans le commerce.

JENNY
On a toujours dit que les Juifs étaient plus intelligents que les autres et c'était vrai. *Die Levi war die Beste.* Chaque génération était encore plus intelligente. De plus en plus intelligents.

Chacun qui monte plus haut sur l'autre.

SELMA
Ma tante Else Jonas: elle pétait plus haut que son cul.

JENNY
Mais il fallait pas lui demander de faire un gâteau. Elle était *something special* parce que son frère était *Justizrat* à Köln.

SELMA
Tout ça on n'a pas dit à Osnabrück. Hitler, entre-temps j'ai vu ces films, c'est comme ça que je l'ai connu, il avait le don d'enthousiasmer les foules, ce n'était même pas un Allemand. A Osnabrück j'ai parlé l'allemand comme jamais. On s'est tout de suite fait remarquer. « Qu'est-ce que c'est cet allemand d'avant-guerre? » ils ont ri.

SELMA
Frau Engers for example, she wasn't accepted, although she was German, she had no manners, she spoke too loud –

JENNY
Frau Engers made hats, I would never want my mother to be like her, she was so different.

SELMA
She would have done anything for my mother.

JENNY
I wouldn't have wanted that kind of woman to be my mother. I'm sure she knew how to swim, she was like a man, she was common, but my mother was received in the cream of Jewish society everywhere. Mutti was friends with the Flattauers, the Stern und Falk, the department store the upper crust, *die Blank*.

SELMA
Nevertheless the sons went to university afterward none of them went into business.

JENNY
They always said Jews were smarter than the rest and it was true. *Die Levi war die Beste*. Each generation was even more intelligent. More and more intelligent.

Each one climbing higher on the other.

SELMA
My aunt Else Jonas: she'd fart out the top of her head, always trying to move up in the world.

JENNY
But you couldn't ask her to make a cake. She thought she was *something special* because her brother was *Justizrat* in Cologne.

SELMA
Those are things we didn't say in Osnabrück. Hitler, in the meantime I've seen those films, that's how I knew him, he had a way of getting crowds worked up, he wasn't even German. In Osnabrück I spoke German like never before. Right away people noticed us. "What's that German from before the war?" they'd laugh.

JENNY
On a dû tout de suite se rendre compte qu'on était deux juives. Les Allemands avaient un flair spécial pour sentir les juifs. Nous aussi nous avons un flair spécial pour sentir les juifs.

SELMA
Le racisme n'est pas seulement contre les juifs. J'ai appris là-bas qu'il y avait trois Eglises protestantes. Même chez les protestants ce n'est pas uni. En Allemagne, il n'y a plus d'antisémitisme. Peut-être ces pauvres vieilles femmes de notre génération. Mais elles ont perdu la mémoire. Elles ont toutes souffert de la guerre aussi. Il y en a qui venaient de l'Est elles ont été persécutées tantôt par les Russes tantôt par les Allemands, des gens qui venaient de Dresden ou Chemnitz. Même chez les Allemands ce n'est pas uni. On est des Ostdeutsche on nous regarde de travers.

Entre-temps j'ai vu ces films où Hitler les a vraiment ensorcelés. Je vais te dire une chose: au début il avait enrôlé surtout la pègre en 1932-33 pour empoisonner les juifs et casser les magasins. C'était pas des gens recommandables. C'est après qu'il a réussi à ensorceler toute la jeunesse. Mais je n'étais pas là, je ne sais pas grand-chose. Je suis revenue en 33 chercher Jenny.

JENNY
Déjà dans les années 20 il y avait Hitler, ça s'est développé lentement.

SELMA
Je viens à Osnabrück en 1933 où il y avait mon oncle qui était en taule à titre de Président du Consistoire Juif. Lui et quelques messieurs ils les ont mis en taule, c'est pour vous protéger ils ont dit.

JENNY
On était très patriotiques les juifs plus royalistes que le roi ils voulaient bien prouver être de bons Allemands. Même en taule on se sent allemand.

SELMA
Quand je suis revenue en 34 j'allai à Dresden où il n'y avait pas encore beaucoup d'actions. On demandait aux juifs de faire le relevé de leurs biens, couverts en argenterie et bijoux. Et une fois le relevé bien fait on les a *soulagés*.

JENNY
Mutti voulait nous acheter une machine à coudre, *la seule chose que je sais personnellement*, et mon oncle qui était directeur de la Banque Allemande en retraite à

JENNY
Right away they must have realized we were a pair of Jews. The Germans had a special flair for sniffing out Jews. We also have a special flair for sniffing out Jews.

SELMA
Racism isn't only against Jews. When I was there I learned there were three Protestant churches. Even Protestants aren't united. In Germany, there's no more anti-Semitism. Maybe those poor old women of our generation. But they've lost their memory. They all suffered in the war too. Some of them came from the East sometimes they were persecuted by the Russians sometimes by the Germans, people from Dresden or Chemnitz. Even the Germans aren't united. If you are *Ostdeutsche* you're looked down on.

In the meantime I've seen those films where Hitler really bewitched them. Let me tell you something: in the beginning he mostly enrolled the mafia in 1932-33 to ruin things for the Jews and vandalize their shops. They were not respectable people. It was later on that he managed to bewitch all the young people. But I wasn't there, I don't know much about that. I returned in '33 to get Jenny.

JENNY
Hitler was already around in the twenties, it developed slowly.

SELMA
I come to Osnabrück in 1933 where my uncle was in jail as President of the Jewish Consistory. Him and a few other gentlemen they put them in jail, it's for your own protection they said.

JENNY
We were very patriotic the Jews more royalist than the king they really wanted to prove they were good Germans. Even in jail we feel German.

SELMA
When I came back in '34 I went to Dresden where not too many things were happening yet. They asked the Jews to make an inventory of their silver and jewelry. And once the inventory was properly drawn up they *relieved* them of it.

JENNY
Mutti wanted to buy us a sewing machine, *the one thing I know personally*, and my uncle who'd retired as director of the German Bank in Essen an der Ruhr he's the

Essen an der Ruhr c'est lui qui avait placé les biens de ma mère dans son coffre *safe*. Quand il est arrivé dans son *safe* on lui dit vous pouvez ouvrir seulement en présence de la Gestapo. Si bien qu'il a renoncé à ouvrir son coffre. Et le coffre est resté fermé.

SELMA
A quoi ça a servi? C'était l'oncle qui était le sosie du Kaiser. A quoi ça a servi? Il avait un ami industriel qui lui disait moi je reste pas un jour de plus, je m'en vais. Alors mon oncle ressemblant au Kaiser, dit, se *croyant* très malin: alors vous pouvez me vendre votre concession. Il croyait bien faire une affaire. Et l'autre qui était très malin lui a vendu cette concession au cimetière. Mon oncle ne pouvait pas imaginer étant donné ses mérites, sa ressemblance avec le Kaiser et pendant la guerre 14 il avait été officier, et quand il a été déporté il ne savait pas ce qui lui arrivait.

JENNY
Les Juifs étaient plus patriotes que les autres. Plus on est juif d'autant plus allemand.

SELMA
Hitler pour moi ça a toujours été un Autrichien ensorceleur pour Allemands. J'étais toujours antimilitariste.

JENNY
L'Autriche les gens pensaient que c'était comme l'Allemagne, ça les a gênés en rien que c'était un Autrichien.

SELMA
Il devait très bien parler, hein? Moi je ne savais rien de ce type-là.

JENNY
Tu crois qu'on savait? Moins on savait plus il était enthousiasmant.

SELMA
Et même lorsque je suis arrivée en Algérie en 1936 les gens ne voulaient rien savoir. Moi je ne savais pas. Il y avait beaucoup de réfugiés juifs mais on ne savait pas pourquoi il y en avait de plus en plus. Jusqu'en 38 à Osnabrück Mutti ne s'est pas rendu compte. Si elle est partie en décembre 1938 c'est parce que le consul de France à Dresden l'a convoquée: Madame Meyer je vois que suite à votre fabrique en Alsace vous avez un passeport français, vous devriez partir. Les jeunes sont partis avant disant on reviendra quand ça sera passé.

one who stored my mother's valuables in his *safe* deposit box. When he got to his *safe* they tell him you can only open it in the presence of the Gestapo. So he gave up opening his safe. And the safe remained closed.

SELMA
What good did that do? He's the uncle who was the spitting image of the Kaiser. What good did that do? He had a friend in the manufacturing industry who told him I'm not staying one day more, I'm leaving. So my uncle who looked like the Kaiser says, *thinking* he was so smart: in that case sell me your plot. He thought he was getting a deal. And the other guy who *was* very smart sold him his cemetery plot. My uncle couldn't imagine given his merits, his resemblance with the Kaiser and during the Great War he had been an officer, and when he was deported he didn't know what was happening to him.

JENNY
The Jews were more patriotic than the others. The more Jewish you are that much more German.

SELMA
For me Hitler was always an Austrian bewitcher of Germans. I was always anti-militaristic.

JENNY
People thought that Austria was like Germany it never bothered them at all that he was an Austrian.

SELMA
He must have been a good talker, eh? I didn't know anything about that guy.

JENNY
You think people knew? The less people knew the more thrilling he was.

SELMA
And even when I arrived in Algeria in 1936 people didn't want to know anything. *I* didn't know. There were lots of Jewish refugees but we didn't know why there were more and more of them. Until '38 in Osnabrück Mutti didn't realize. She only left in December 1938 because the French consul in Dresden called her in: Mme Meyer I see that because of your factory in Alsace you have a French passport you ought to leave. The young had left before saying we'll be back when it's over.

JENNY
Je peux toujours pas comprendre que les gens sont restés jusqu'à la guerre. Mais notre cousine Elsie Jordan –

SELMA
Il y a des gens qui ont quand même eu le courage de partir plutôt que d'être molestés.

Elsie Jordan ma cousine était partie avec ses quatre petits enfants, en un mois son mari s'est préparé à l'agriculture. Je ne sais pas qui leur a dit d'aller au Brésil une fois là-bas il s'est mis à l'agriculture et il est mort au bout de huit jours.

JENNY
Mais pourquoi tu racontes celle-là? Toi tu ne l'as pas su. C'est moi qui te l'ai racontée!

SELMA
Il y a des gens qui racontent mieux.

JENNY
Elsie a écrit à Oncle Moritz d'Afrique du Sud.

SELMA
Laisse-moi parler. Il y a une autre histoire. Les Morgenstern, un chirurgien en Autriche, eux ils étaient partis avec leurs tapis de Perse –

JENNY
– et les collections d'ivoire

SELMA
– et les collections d'ivoire. Ça c'est *moi* qui te l'ai dit. Arrivé à Oran, un deux trois, il a vite appris pédicure, couper les chemises d'homme et la pâtisserie viennoise. Je l'ai connu à Oran sur un banc du jardin du « Petit Vichy ». Un juif polonais lui dit: on ouvre une boutique de tailleurs viennois à Oran et l'autre lui a bouffé tous ses sous.

JENNY
Qui?

SELMA
Le Polonais. Ensuite

JENNY
I still don't understand why people stayed right up to the war. But our cousin Elsie Jordan –

SELMA
Still there were people who had the courage to leave rather than be molested.

My cousin Elsie Jordan left with her four small children, in one month her husband retrained as a farmer. I don't know who told them to go to Brazil once they were over there he took up farming and eight days later he was dead.

JENNY
But why are you telling that? You didn't know about it. I'm the one who told you!

SELMA
Some people are better storytellers.

JENNY
Elsie wrote to Uncle Moritz in South Africa.

SELMA
Let me speak. There's another story. The Morgensterns, a surgeon in Austria, they left with their Persian carpets –

JENNY
– and ivory collection

SELMA
– and ivory collection. *I'm* the one who told you about that. When they arrived in Oran, one two three he quickly learned pedicure, cutting men's shirts and Viennese pastry. I met him in Oran on a park bench, *Petit Vichy* park. A Polish Jew told him: Let's open a Viennese tailor shop in Oran and the other guy ran through all his money.

JENNY
Who?

SELMA
The Pole. Then

JENNY
Herbert Stern a voulu faire des ceintures de cuir à Paris

SELMA
et la même chose lui est arrivée. Lui il avait fait des études de droit. Pour quelle raison

JENNY
Mais pourquoi *tu* racontes Herbert Stern qui était *mon* fiancé?!!

SELMA
Tes souvenirs c'est *moi* qui les connais. Pour quelle raison il a pensé que c'était *quelque chose* qu'on pouvait faire des ceintures de cuir?

JENNY
Un Polonais –

SELMA
Il y a un tas de flibustiers qui profitaient de cette occasion hitlérienne

JENNY
J'avais une cousine Hilde –

SELMA
toi tu étais déjà en Palestine. *Moi* j'avais la cousine Hilde, la soeur de Marga, elle était dans un camp à Gurs mais on ne savait pas ce que c'étaient les camps, je lui ai dit viens chez nous mais entre-temps on les a déportés.

On peut pas imaginer des choses comme ça. Il ne faisait pas de la publicité pour les camps de concentration. Aujourd'hui nous voyons des films de Hitler. On voit bien qu'il avait un ascendant.

JENNY
Les jeunes étaient enthousiastes.

SELMA
Les parents la bouclaient. Il était bien conseillé. J'en avais fait un pour les enfants, un petit Hitler, pendant la guerre je leur faisais des petites marionnettes. En *deux* secondes, un petit Hitler avec la moustache et la mèche, un pour *deux*. Les enfants se le disputaient, naturellement. Pour moi personnellement tout était dégoûtant, j'étais contre tous les gens qui marchaient au pas, déjà enfant j'en avais horreur

JENNY
Herbert Stern wanted to make leather belts in Paris

SELMA
and the same thing happened to him. And he had studied law. Who knows what

JENNY
But why are *you* telling about Herbert Stern who was *my* fiancé?!!

SELMA
I'm the one who knows your memories. Who knows what made him think that leather belts was something to do?

JENNY
A Pole –

SELMA
There were lots of freebooters who profited from that Hitler opportunity.

JENNY
I had a cousin Hilde –

SELMA
You were already in Palestine. *I* had cousin Hilde, Marga's sister, she was in a camp in Gurs but we didn't know what the camps were, I told her come stay with us but in the meantime they were deported.

You can't imagine such things. He didn't advertise the concentration camps. Today we see films of Hitler. You can see he had an influence on people.

JENNY
The young were full of enthusiasm.

SELMA
Their parents kept their mouths shut. It was well advised. I made one for the children, a little Hitler, during the war I made them little puppets. In *two* seconds, a little Hitler with the mustache and the comb-over, one for *two*. The children fought over it, naturally. For me personally all that was disgusting, I was against all those people who marched in step, already as a child I detested that sort of thing

JENNY
Les communistes aussi, ces rassemblements

SELMA
J'en avais horreur. Je n'ai plus du tout pensé être allemande. Ni française. Déjà quand je suis partie les chemises brunes, mettre des uniformes, marcher au pas, ça ne m'intéresse pas du tout.

JENNY
J'ai un cousin qui a été déporté pas comme juif

SELMA
mais comme communiste. Le pauvre.

Haider ça ne m'étonne pas, on a toujours dit que l'Autriche c'est des antisémites, ils sont retombés dans cette ornière

JENNY
Haider. Sauf la moustache et la mèche –

SELMA
– Ça commence par H ça finit par R. La moustache et la mèche tu as remarqué ? Chaque fois qu'on voit une photo de Haider, on remarque tout de suite, la moustache et la mèche, qu'il les a coupées. Il est bien conseillé. Tout de suite on se dit : je ne peux pas le croire.

JENNY
J'avais pas remarqué.

SELMA
Il y a des gens qui pensent au ralenti. Moi ça m'énerve que ça recommence, l'extrême droite. Les gens sont tellement idiots il y a beaucoup de gens qui ne peuvent pas supporter l'étranger. En Autriche il doit y avoir pas mal de Yougoslaves, ça y est, faut s'en débarrasser.

JENNY
Des Serbes aussi. Surtout des Moussoulmans.

JENNY
The communists too, those meetings

SELMA
I detested it. I no longer thought I was German at all. Nor French either. Already when I left, the brown shirts, wearing uniforms, marching in step, not my thing at all.

JENNY
I have a cousin who was deported not as a Jew

SELMA
but as a communist. Poor thing.

Haider doesn't surprise me at all, we always used to say in Austria they're anti-Semites, they fell back in the same old rut.

JENNY
Haider. Except for the mustache and the comb-over –

SELMA
– Starts with an H and ends with an R. Did you notice the mustache and the comb-over? Every time you see a photo of Haider, right away you notice the mustache and the hair, that he cut them off. He's got good advisors. Right away you say to yourself: I can't believe it.

JENNY
I didn't notice.

SELMA
Some people think in slow motion. It gets on my nerves all this far right beginning again. People are so idiotic lots of people can't stand foreigners. In Austria there must be quite a few Yugoslavs, that's it, they've got to go.

JENNY
Serbs as well. Mussulmans especially.

SELMA
Hitler je pense que c'est un type qui avait la folie des grandeurs comme il parlait bien les gens l'ont suivi et l'ont utilisé. Ils ont trouvé le bonhomme qu'ils cherchaient. Je sais une chose: que malheureusement, il y avait des Juifs qui –

JENNY
– Mais ça c'est pas une chose à dire ni à écrire –

SELMA
– Ni à dire, ni à écrire, malheureusement –

Faut-il dire ce qu'il ne faut pas dire? Depuis notre voyage à Osnabrück je n'arrête plus de me poser cette question. Ce qui s'est passé là –

JENNY
C'était inimaginable –

SELMA
Ou tout le contraire peut-être –

JENNY
Moi – je ne le dirai pas et je ne l'écrirai pas

SELMA
Ça ce n'est *pas moi* qui l'écrirai. Mais moi ça m'énerve quand je pense qu'il y avait des Juifs à Vienne qui disaient, des industriels, « vivement que Hitler vienne mettre de l'ordre ici, qu'il vienne », ça m'avait marquée qu'il y avait des gens assez naïfs pour penser que c'était pas pour eux qu'Hitler vienne les tuer.

JENNY
Il faisait pas de la publicité pour les camps de concentration. Mon mari disait toujours –

SELMA
– mais quand même. Laisse-moi parler. Là où il pourrait y avoir une moustache et une mèche, ça se voit tout de suite.

JENNY
Osnabrück aussi tout a changé, rien n'a changé. C'était la première fois que je revenais. Tout avait été détruit.

SELMA
I think Hitler was a guy who had delusions of grandeur since he spoke well people followed him and used him. They found the man they were looking for. One thing I know for certain: that unfortunately there were Jews who –

JENNY
– But *that's* not something you can say or write –

SELMA
– Neither say nor write, unfortunately –

Should one say what mustn't be said? Since our trip to Osnabrück I can't stop asking myself that question. What happened there –

JENNY
It was unimaginable –

SELMA
Or quite the opposite perhaps –

JENNY
As for me – I won't say it and I won't write it

SELMA
You won't catch *me* writing *that*. But it bothers me when I think that there were Jews in Prague, industrialists, who said, "It's about time Hitler came to put things in order, let's be pragmatic." It surprised me that there were people naïve enough to think it wasn't for them that Hitler was coming to kill them pragmatically.

JENNY
He didn't advertise the concentration camps. My husband always used to say –

SELMA
– But really. Let me speak. Right where there could be a mustache and a comb-over, it catches your eye right away.

JENNY
Osnabrück too everything changed, nothing changed. It was the first time I went back. Everything had been destroyed.

SELMA
Au contraire tout avait été reconstruit, c'était bon, car si j'étais revenue plus tôt j'aurais vu des traces de guerre.

JENNY
Toute notre maison a été détruite. A la place, un nouvel hôtel très chic.

SELMA
Mais la *Schwedengasse* la ruelle par où on rentrait chez nous, elle était toujours là.

JENNY
Mais la maison non!

SELMA
Ma jeunesse était tellement loin que je n'avais pas de souvenir de jeunesse.

JENNY
Mais près de la grande Cathédrale Charlemagne devant laquelle je faisais de la trottinette parce qu'il y avait du carrelage rouge –

SELMA
Elle, de la trottinette – Tandis que moi, tout de suite la bicyclette, je n'ai même pas eu besoin d'apprendre

– Assieds-toi –

On n'a pas marché parce qu'on nous a promenées parce qu'on était invitées, on n'a pas mis le pied par terre –

JENNY
On devait raconter notre histoire –

SELMA
Les deux petites vieilles. On devait jouer notre rôle. Il y avait de jeunes étudiants qui ne savaient même pas de quoi il retournait –

JENNY
C'était dépassé.

SELMA
Ça ! Je me demande si c'était *dé*passé. Est-ce qu'ils savaient une fois ce qui s'était passé?

SELMA
On the contrary everything had been rebuilt, that was good, because if I'd come back earlier I'd have seen traces of war.

JENNY
Our whole house was destroyed. In its place, a new hotel, very chic.

SELMA
But the *Schwedengasse* the little street we took to get home was still there.

JENNY
But not the house!

SELMA
My childhood was so far off I had no childhood memories.

JENNY
But near the big Charlemagne Cathedral where I used to ride my scooter because there were red tiles –

SELMA
Her: a scooter – whereas me: right away a bicycle, I didn't even need to learn.

– Sit down –

We didn't walk because they drove us since we were guests, we never set foot on the ground –

JENNY
We had to tell our story –

SELMA
Two little old ladies. We had to play our part. Some of the young students had no idea what it was all about –

JENNY
It was outdated.

SELMA
Hah! I wonder if it was outdated. Did they even know what had happened?

JENNY
On était près de la *Rathaus* il y avait un très bon restaurant. On mangeait des choses délicieuses.

SELMA
C'était la saison des asperges. Il n'y a qu'en Allemagne que tu en trouves d'aussi belles.

JENNY
On nous a fait faire une excursion

SELMA
L'ancienne synagogue avait été brûlée. Ils nous ont donné à chacune un sachet avec quelques pierres de cette synagogue.

JENNY
C'était gentil.

SELMA
Ach! Quatsch! Il restait quelques juifs, mais pas d'Osnabrück.

JENNY
Des juifs de l'Est qui ont veillé à ce qu'on reconstruise une synagogue avec un étage pour les femmes qui était vraiment très étroit –

SELMA
D'ailleurs la synagogue était vide puisqu'il n'y avait plus de Juifs. Les seuls Juifs étaient des Russes qui ne connaissaient rien au judaïsme. On les obligeait d'aller à la synagogue parce qu'il faut au moins dix personnes pour faire un office. Alors on faisait venir les Russes par force.

JENNY
Mais quand même payés.

SELMA
Après il y avait une petite réception chez le *Vorsteher* où il y avait naturellement du hareng mariné et des *Sauergurken*. Alors il y a eu cette discussion: il y avait un grand rabbin de circonscription pour tous les environs. Lui estimait, comme il y avait si peu d'hommes, qu'il fallait compter *aussi les femmes* qui viennent, comme des personnages, pour compléter la dizaine d'hommes. Mais le chef de la communauté qui s'est bombardé lui-même chef parce qu'il avait une grosse société de transports, lui il était absolument contre. Ce Monsieur-là –

JENNY
We were near the *Rathaus* there was a very good restaurant. We ate some delicious things.

SELMA
It was asparagus season. Only in Germany do you find such beautiful asparagus.

JENNY
They took us on an outing.

SELMA
The old synagogue had been burned down. They gave us each a little pouch with a few stones from the synagogue.

JENNY
That was kind.

SELMA
Ach! Quatsch! There were a few Jews left, but not from Osnabrück.

JENNY
Jews from the East who made sure they rebuilt the synagogue with a gallery for the women which was very narrow –

SELMA
Besides the synagogue was empty because there weren't any more Jews. The only Jews were Russians who knew nothing about Judaism. They obliged them to go to the synagogue because you need at least ten people to hold a service. So they forced the Russians to come.

JENNY
Still they were paid.

SELMA
Afterwards there was a little reception at the *Vorsteher*'s house where naturally there was pickled herring and *Sauergurken*. Then there was a discussion: the Chief District Rabbi for the surrounding areas was there. He figured that since there were so few men they should *also* count the women who come, to complete the ten-man quorum. But the head of the community who parachuted himself in as head because he had a big transportation business, he was flatly opposed. This Gentleman –

JENNY
Un Monsieur Gaul.

SELMA
Il *ne faut pas* mettre de nom pour Herr Gaul. On aura encore un procès sur le dos, à cause de toi

JENNY
Ce Monsieur Aul, lui, un vrai cochon –

SELMA
lui n'était certainement pas un type d'Osnabrück, une grande gueule qui a une belle femme qu'il traite comme un chien d'une façon abominable une femme malade très belle qu'il bat, il dit: « ta gueule ».

JENNY
Ensuite on nous a emmenées dans une très belle pâtisserie on devait rencontrer les anciennes élèves du lycée –

SELMA
Quand j'ai vu toutes ces vieilles femmes aux cheveux blancs, impossible d'en reconnaître une.

JENNY
Des dames très sportives, très alertes.

SELMA
A Osnabrück on ne sait pas où sont les nazis. Il y avait une que je reconnaissais. Elle nous a invitées. Une villa dans un grand jardin –

JENNY
où on a pris le thé

SELMA
Elle disait: ce n'est pas possible mon oncle ne peut pas être un bourreau, si je le crois je dois me tuer moi-même. Je ne le crois pas. Elle parlait toujours de son oncle.

JENNY
Nebbich ! Mon mari disait toujours: mais où sont passés les nazis?

JENNY
A Mr. Gaul.

SELMA
You *mustn't* put Herr Gaul's name. We'll be sued again, thanks to you.

JENNY
This Mr. Aul, a real pig –

SELMA
he certainly wasn't a chap from Osnabrück, a bigmouth with a beautiful wife he treats like a dog in a terrible way a sickly very beautiful woman that he beats, he says: "Shut up."

JENNY
Next they took us to a very beautiful pastry shop we were supposed to meet our former classmates from high school –

SELMA
When I saw all those white-haired old women, impossible to recognize a single one.

JENNY
Sporty ladies, very alert.

SELMA
In Osnabrück, you don't know where the Nazis are. I recognized one. She invited us over. A villa in a big garden –

JENNY
where we had tea

SELMA
She said: "It's impossible my uncle can't be a murderer, if I believe that I'd have to kill myself. I don't believe it." Always talking about her uncle.

JENNY
Nebbich! My husband always used to say: "But where did all the Nazis go?"

SELMA
Ton mari je ne dirai pas quelle bêtise il a faite! Revenir à Cologne!

JENNY
il *ne faut pas* le dire!

SELMA
L'être humain ne peut pas avouer un crime. Personne ne veut avouer. Ni les nazis ni les juifs. Même Hitler – Haider non plus. Tous des innocents. C'est comme pour Pinoquet.

Il ne faut pas le dire –

JENNY
Ensuite on nous a emmenées au cimetière qui était d'un entretien parfait.

SELMA
Ce Monsieur Aul j'ai appris qu'il a fait faillite, ça m'a étonnée. Un grossier personnage il disait à sa femme:

JENNY
Boucle-la!

SELMA
Quoi!! *Wie unverschämt*! A quatre-vingt-six ans! Quoi! dire ça!

JENNY
Quoi? Qu'est-ce que j'ai dit? Dis-le ce que j'ai dit!

SELMA
Tu m'as dit Boucle-la! On a quatre-vingt-neuf-ans et à cet âge on entend des cochonneries comme ça?! C'est une obscénité!

JENNY
Qui a dit: Boucle-la?!! C'est moi ou c'est Monsieur Gaul?? (elle crie) *Monsieur Gaul a dit à sa femme, Boucle-la*! A mon avis tu as la tache aveugle et sourde! Tu as toujours été imperméable quelque part.

SELMA
Personne ne t'écoute! Puisque c'est comme ça je ne raconte plus rien!

SELMA
Your husband I won't mention the stupid thing he did! Going back to Cologne!

JENNY
You *mustn't* say that!

SELMA
Human beings are incapable of owning up to a crime. No one wants to confess. Neither the Nazis nor the Jews. Even Hitler–Haider either. Innocents every one of them. Just like Pinoquet.

You mustn't say that –

JENNY
Next they took us to the cemetery which was beautifully maintained.

SELMA
This Mr. Aul I heard he went bankrupt, which surprised me. A vulgar character he would tell his wife:

JENNY
Shut your trap!

SELMA
What?! *Wie unverschämt!* At eighty-six years of age! What! And you say that!

JENNY
What? What did I say? Say it what I said!

SELMA
You told me "Shut your trap!" I'm eighty-nine years old and at such an age I have to hear smut like that?! It's an obscenity!

JENNY
Who said: "Shut your trap"?!! Me or Mr. Gaul?? [She shouts] *Mr. Gaul told his wife,* "*Shut your trap!*" In my opinion you have a blind spot and a deaf spot! You always were impermeable somewhere.

SELMA
No one's listening to you! If that's the way it is I won't tell any more stories!

JENNY
Heureusement – sa femme est morte heureusement.

SELMA
C'est malheureux qu'on doive se réjouir. Mais maintenant je pense qu'il faut quand même dire ce qu'il ne faut pas dire, à cause de cette femme si belle et qui en est morte.

JENNY
Personne imaginait que ça pouvait arriver –

SELMA
Moi, si tu n'avais pas été là je ne serais pas retournée, pour quoi faire?

JENNY
Quand nous sommes rentrés en Allemagne après la guerre, mon mari disait toujours: c'est drôle on ne sait pas où sont les nazis.

SELMA
Je me suis dit: qui suis-je pour ne pas tendre la main? Sinon – Qu'est-ce qui reste?

JENNY
Fortunately – his wife died fortunately.

SELMA
It's unfortunate it was a lucky thing. But now I think one must nonetheless say what one mustn't say, because of that woman who was so beautiful and who died as a result.

JENNY
No one imagined such a thing could happen –

SELMA
If you hadn't been here I wouldn't have returned, to do what?

JENNY
When we went back to Germany after the war, my husband always used to say: "Funny no one knows where the Nazis are."

SELMA
I told myself: who am I not to extend a hand? Otherwise – what's left?

Carola Hilfrich
The Depository of *Zugehör: Ail!* and the Soundscape of Belonging

With matchless emphasis on the force of syllables, primal roots, tongue trills, reverberation equations, screams, glissandi, and double-speak, Hélène Cixous's work or, more aptly, "the Cixous idiom" (Derrida 2006, 22), essentially calls for a resetting of the dominant discourse of literary expression and response in the field of sound. In this vein, feminist theorists (e.g., Salvaggio 1999, Cavarero 2005) and performance artists and theorists (e.g., LaBelle 2010b, Migone 2012) claim Cixous's oeuvre as seminal to an emergent sonic turn in critical thought and to contemporary experiments on voice that valorize poetic and theatrical performance. My commentary draws on these recent insights for a reading of *Ail!* – *Il ne faut pas le dire* as emblematic, perhaps even the wild heart, of "the Cixous idiom."[1] *Pars pro toto*, I take the acoustic title of this work and the unruly modulations brought about by its oral, aural, visual, linguistic, and semantic play as cues for moving into the level of the work.

"Ail!" is, simultaneously, an exclamation of the French term for garlic, a trilling howl of pain or grief, and music in its most raw and immediate expression as pure vibration. Only in French, the word for "garlic" is homophone with a dizzying specificity of sounds both beyond and within language. These include a shrill note of distress and waves of pure vibration, as well as the affect garlic evokes as the pervasively most hated – *haï* – member of the *allium* family of root vegetables; likewise, the suffix –*aille* which forms feminine nouns of colloquial or pejorative meaning, or indicates the means of an action. Terribly sharp and sublimely sonorous, "ail!" epitomizes the transitional space of the Cixousian voice between language, the body, and music.[2] It marks this space of passage as field for a shout in literature, as an acoustic territory which, cut with vibrations

---

[1] The play premiered in June 2000 at the *Théâtre de la Tempête in Paris*. A radio version was broadcast on France-Culture on December 17, 2000. The Actor's Gang Theatre in Los Angeles presented the American premiere of *Oy!* in June 2012. *Ail!* is a theatrical condensation of two books of poetic fiction from Cixous's "German works," namely, *Osnabrück* (Cixous 1999) and *Benjamin à Montaigne. Il ne faut pas le dire* (Cixous 2001), which end, respectively begin with kitchen scenes. For an analysis of the poetics of these works, see Hilfrich (2006).

[2] Perhaps most pertinent to this commentary are Cixous's earlier comments on the aural spatiality and "musical architecture" of her writing, in *Rootprints: Memory and Life Writing* (Cixous and Calle-Gruber 1997 [1994], 64–68).

and all roots audible, forms a sonic discourse that is equally frenetic, energetic, and participatory.³

The alchemic blend of information and forces in the work's title enables us to engage with the *ail*iterated soundscape onto which the Meyer sisters' kitchen talk unfurls, and to take account of the heightened aural intensity that their conversation brings into play – alliteration specified, altered, amplified, and vocalized. Interpretation is thus ingeniously set up to focus on hearing the poetic lexicon and theatrical range of this soundscape in the Meyer sisters' lines. "On their return from Osnabrück," the city of their youth in Germany, the two sisters, bickering over the basics of their umlauted family dish of a *Leberhäckele*, find themselves cast in the soundscape of a revenant language which is *allemand*, or 'German' in French. In her opening line, Selma Meyer instructs her sister Jenny, the playwright, and us to "follow," "copy," and listen to her as she hears herself talking in "that" language: "Suis-moi. *Hack die Leber*. Encore! Cet allemand qui remonte! [Copy me. *Hack die Leber*. Again! There's that German again!]."⁴

The tone of Selma's invitation to participation is misleadingly straightforward as it comes to linger among the heightened aural intensity of the soundscape. It is an intensity composed of revenant sounds, which are native to the Meyer sisters, charged and italicized by the playwright, and at various degrees of remove familiar to us (*Hack die Leber*). Their drama is that they unfurl a persistently vulnerable body onto the soundscape, as Selma's ensuing outcry suggests ("Encore!" heard as "*en corps*! [embodied!]"). They also effect an intractable auditory feedback loop that consists not merely of hearing oneself talking but of hearing oneself slide and slip "again!," by force of the scene, into a repudiated language ("cet allemand," spit out in French).

The soundscape thus creates a kinetic reflexivity of voice on the scene of the Meyer sisters' kitchen talk, a reflexivity that is distributed unevenly among

---

3 Cixous expands on this in her later *Ayaï! Le cri de la littérature* (2013), which defines literature as the field for cries pushed to music. In the Jerusalem discussion of both this work and *Ail!*, she suggested, in response to a question about the homophony of their titles, that she is "always writing the same," namely, "a genealogy of the shout in literature." My view of the Cixousian aural territory of writing owes heavily to Brandon LaBelle's seminal definition of "acoustic territories" (LaBelle 2010a, xxiv).

4 "Suis-moi" means literally "follow me," claiming Selma Meyer's lead in the kitchen scene as "the elder" of the two sisters. Eric Prenowitz's more literary translation as "copy me" (in a previous version) suggests that this injunction also authorizes the playwright to "copy" the scene. It is resonant with *Benjamin à Montaigne* (Cixous 2001), one of the poetic fictional companion texts to *Ail!*, in which the narrator, equipped with tape recorder and writing block, makes "two copies of the scene" of her mother's and aunt's kitchen talks, driven by "that unqualifiable attention" of a deliberate hearing, or "reading" (Cixous 2001, 72–73).

themselves, the playwright, and us. Only a few lines later, Selma's performative kinesthetic in *allemand* becomes itself the object of such reflection. Returning from Osnabrück, where the sisters had been invited as the city's "last Jews," and in the intimacy of their kitchen talk, Selma voices what, so regrettably, "could not be said" in response to that invitation: "Je n'aime pas ça, aller survivre. Je ne dois rien à l'Allemagne. [I don't like that sort of thing, to go survive for them. I owe nothing to Germany]."

Selma's line encapsulates the affective charge of a movement in dispossession together with the thrashings and reversals of belonging, thereby suggesting a shared aural lexicon and range. In the loaded simplicity of her words, she bespeaks the exigencies of the possibility to think dispossession with and beyond belonging, and belonging through movement and enactments of the vulnerabilities of owing and owning.[5] In the singsong murmur "*aller-à-l'Alle*" and its primal combination of sounds, her line captures the hinge moment in which the Meyer sisters find themselves. The mix, here, is an alloy of French words for motion (*aller*, to go) and spatiality (*à*, to; *là*, there) with the German root of the French name for Germany (*alle-*, all). It produces, literally *within French*, the sound of a *Lallen*, of a "babbling" of childhood and colloquial language in its German onomatopoeia, with all its historical resonance as an equivalent to repudiated language in modern Jewish culture.[6]

To this mix of affects, percepts, and sounds of belonging, Jenny suggests to add another ingredient, introducing by way of an epenthetic riff on Selma's line the possibility of *ail* to bring that volatile mix even more fully into play: "Je mets de l'ail? [Should I add some garlic?]." To Selma, Jenny's suggestion is outright offensive and "totally crazy": "De l'ail! *Du bist ja ganz verrückt!* On n'est pas des paysans de la campagne ici! [Garlic! *Du bist ja ganz verrückt!* We're not peasants from the countryside [here]!]." Her emphatic rejection reenacts "here," at the site of the sisters' kitchen talk, the true horror of garlic at the heart of the modern, urban, and bourgeois Jewish German household.[7] In an extended passage some

---

[5] Athena Athanasiou and Judith Butler discuss this possibility in a recent volume of conversations (2013). Dispossession and belonging are here the entry points to a critique of the sovereign subject in terms of the body, gender performativity, precarity, and freedom.
[6] Heinrich Graetz's *History of the Jews* (1853) famously considered Yiddish in terms of a "Lallen und Stammeln" (cited here from Matthias Richter's work on the language of Jewish figures in modern German literature (Richter 1995, 81)). See also Ruth Ginsburg's contribution in our volume for a refiguring of "Lallen" in Gershom Scholem's repudiation of modern, colloquial Hebrew.
[7] Marion A. Kaplan, in her book on the role of women and family in the making of the Jewish middle class in Imperial Germany, discusses the passionate exclusion of garlic from the consumption patterns of the modern Jewish German household in context with anti-Semitic disparagements about "Jewish garlic smell" (1991, 35). Garlic not merely epitomizes but embodies

lines later, Selma traces this to an aural experience of race on the streets of late Weimar Osnabrück, "Avant 1930 [Before 1930]." She recalls how, walking with her mother, the anti-Semitic slur "*ça sent l'ail* [*smells like garlic*]" was hurled at them. Yet, she insists, in the household of the Meyer women, who "read Goethe [their] contemporary and the novels of Jakob Wassermann," garlic was "never seen," one "didn't [even] know what it was."

"Ail" becomes thus a trope for the aural edge of racism where the external experience of place and the internal auditory voicings of family both intertwine and unravel.[8] Selma detects here the "stupidity" of racism and the violence in sounds that are slightly more subtle than screams of hate but which, in translation to French, all the more directly reveal her early exposure to it ("ail" being homophone with "*haï*," hated). She also reclaims the exclusionary patterns of consumption in the Meyer household by which the women cast their identity onto the world not in terms of race but of class, sampling and creating "culture." "Maybe Jews in Poland ate it," ventures Jenny in response, riffing on Selma's lines in a recall of garlic as key to a translation of modern anti-Semitism against Eastern European Jews into terms of Jewish German class. The *Leberhäckele* the Meyer sisters are preparing speaks in its own way to such a process, literally "polishing away" the Eastern European origins of their family dish in an umlauted, vowel-mutated, Alemannic version.

Across these hinge and eponymous moments, from the onrush of *allemand* to the affective and epistemic intensities of *aller-à-l'Alle* and to the sonic effects and aural traces of *ail? / ail!*, Selma and Jenny tenaciously negotiate their place and position in the *ail*iterated soundscape of the play. Burrowing between the languages and between the key words, letters, and strokes of the kitchen scene, their lines open the echo chamber and sound box of *allemand*. In the space of that revenant and repudiated, always double-spoken language, the scene of belonging and dispossession plays out in a deeply aural mode. The Meyer sisters hear themselves talking, listening for and seizing the wavering qualities of that language across their lines. For them, I wish to suggest in conclusion, the kitchen scene is a question of voicing *Zugehör* – a curious German word that encapsulates the dated and colloquial meanings of familial belonging and "hearing at home" (*zu Hause*

Kaplan's claim that "German Jews tried to translate anti-Semitism against Eastern European Jews into class terms" (Kaplan 1991, 35).

8 For an analysis of racialized sonic politics in modern American culture, see Jennifer Lynn Stoever's recent *The Sonic Color Line. Race and the Cultural Politics of Listening* (2016).

hören, in the sense of one's place of origin) and the modern, technical meanings of ownership and belonging together in a spatial and bodily way.⁹

The word does not appear in the Meyer sisters' conversation in *Aïl!*, but *Zugehör* plays a compelling role in *Benjamin à Montaigne. Il ne faut pas le dire* (Cixous 2001), as Cécile Wajsbrot has already suggested (Cixous and Wajsbrot 2016, 43–44).¹⁰ Here, Selma Jonas, the narrator's mother, puts the "need to belong to something in life" into terms of an irrevocable voicing of *Zugehör*, in lines that tap, in French, all the registers of this curious German word clan: "On a besoin d'appartenir à quelque chose dans la vie. [...] Chez nous on appelle ça le *Zugehör*. Tu ne peux pas annuler le *Zugehör*. Tu crois l'annuler et ta façon d'annuler est exactement dans le *Zugehör*. [One needs to belong to something in life. [...] Where we come from it is called *Zugehör*. You can't annul the *Zugehör*. You believe you are annulling it and your way of annulling is right in the *Zugehör*]" (Cixous 2001, 140).

The Meyer sisters' lines in *Aïl!* draw us directly into the performative space of this *Zugehör*. In her conversation with Wajsbrot, Cixous speaks of her German works as depositories of "a small part of this *Zugehör*" (Cixous and Wajsbrot 2016, 45). *Aïl!* is the theatrical condensation of this genealogical custodianship. With its deliberate and meticulous attention to the Meyer sisters' voicings, the play creates an archive of the soundscape of this *Zugehör*, as well as a space for the "deliberate hearing" that is reading (Cixous 2001, 73).

References

Athanasiou, Athena, and Judith Butler. "Enacting another vulnerability: On owing and owning." *Dispossession. The Performative in the Political*. Cambridge: Polity Press, 2013. 158–163.
Cavarero, Adriana. *For More than One Voice: Toward a Philosophy of Vocal Expression*. Palo Alto: Stanford University Press, 2005 [2003].
Cixous, Hélène. *Osnabrück*. Paris: des femmes, 1999.
Cixous, Hélène. *Benjamin à Montaigne. Il ne faut pas le dire*. Paris: Galilée, 2001.
Cixous, Hélène. *Ayaï! Le cri de la littérature*. Paris: Galilée, 2013.

---

9 See the entries on the "wort sippe (word clan)" of *Zubehör* and *Zugehör* in Grimm's *Deutsches Wörterbuch*, Vol. 32, columns 236 and 406, respectively.
10 Wajsbrot refers here to the 2013 workshop of our group, which included a session on linguistic dispossession in Derrida's *Le monolinguisme de l'autre* (Wajsbrot and Cixous 2016, 69). See also Vivian Liska's critical discussion of "Derrida's Appurtenances" in our volume. Intriguingly, she suggests here that the most revealing and subversive moment of Derrida's own speaking is aural when he is "listen[ing] to [...] voices from 'the other shore'" of the Mediterranean divide between Ashkenazi and Sephardi Jews.

Cixous, Hélène, and Mireille Calle Gruber. *Rootprints: Memory and Life Writing*. London and New York: Routledge, 1997 [1994].

Cixous, Hélène, and Cécile Wajsbrot. *Une autobiographie allemande*. Paris: Christian Bourgois, 2016.

Derrida, Jacques. *Le monolinguisme de l'autre, ou la prothèse d'origine*. Paris: Galilée, 1996.

Derrida, Jacques. *Geneses, Genealogies, Genres, and Genius: The Secrets of the Archive*. New York: Columbia University Press, 2006 [2003].

Hilfrich, Carola. "The Self is a People. Autoethnographic Poetics in Hélène Cixous's Fictions. *New Literary History* 37.1 (Winter 2006): 217–235.

Kaplan, Marion A. *The Making of the Jewish Middle Class: Women, Family, and Identity in Imperial Germany*. Oxford: Oxford University Press, 1991.

LaBelle, Brandon. *Acoustic Territories: Sound Culture and Everyday Life*. New York: Continuum, 2010a.

LaBelle, Brandon. "Where do sounds come from and where do they go?" (interview). http://digicult.it/digimag/issue-056/brandon-labelle-where-do-sounds-come-from-and-where-do-they-go/. *DIGICULT* 56 (July 2010b) (8 November 2019).

Migone, Christof. *Sonic Somatic: Performances of the Unsound Body*. Los Angeles / Berlin: Errant Bodies Press (Audio Issues Vol. 5), 2012.

Richter, Matthias. *Die Sprache jüdischer Figuren in der deutschen Literatur (1750–1933) Studien zu Form und Funktion*. Göttingen: Wallstein Verlag, 1995.

Salvaggio, Ruth. *The Sounds of Feminist Theory*. Albany: SUNY Press, 1999.

Stoever, Jennifer Lynn. *The Sonic Color Line: Race and the Cultural Politics of Listening*. New York: New York University Press, 2016.

Cécile Wajsbrot
Vous trouverez ce livre ...

vous qui avez des murs couverts d'étagères remplies de livres,
vous qui ne savez plus où les ranger,
vous qui êtes obligés, périodiquement, de faire place, de jeter, de donner,
   de remiser dans la maison de campagne les livres que vous avez lus et qui vous
      ont accompagnés mais que vous ne lirez plus,
vous qui regardez les vieux livres chez les bouquinistes, dans les brocantes,
vous qui avez gardé les livres de vos parents et de vos grands-parents,
vous qui collectionnez les livres pour la reliure,
vous qui les achetez sans les lire,
vous qui entreposez, entassez, amassez
   les livres comme les objets,
vous qui savez exactement l'emplacement de toute chose, la place de chaque livre,
vous qui avez tout lu,
vous qui classez par ordre alphabétique ou par sujet, par éditeur,
vous qui avez quelques centaines, quelques milliers de livres, qui en aurez bien d'autres,
vous pour qui bibliothèque est un mot naturel,
vous qui n'avez pas eu besoin de l'apprendre à l'école, d'en demander le sens – vous l'aviez sous les yeux...

   avez-vous déjà pensé
à ceux qui aiment lire mais qui n'ont pas de livres,
à ceux qui voudraient savoir lire,
à ceux qui, dans l'exil, n'ont pu prendre qu'une valise, un sac, quelques vêtements, rien,
à ceux qui n'avaient pas,
à ceux qui ont laissé des étagères pleines et qui ont fui, ont été emmenés,
   avec leur mémoire pour seule bibliothèque,
à ceux qui ont travaillé la nuit ou des journées trop pleines à faire ce qu'ils ne savaient pas faire, à apprendre la langue et réapprendre à vivre avant d'acheter leur premier livre,
à ceux dont les grands-parents, les parents ne savent pas lire,
à ceux pour qui chaque livre est gagné contre l'adversité,
à ceux qui un jour, en classe, se croyant à égalité des autres, ont entendu un professeur dire,

Translated by Susanne Zepp
You'll find this book ...

you, who have walls covered by shelves replete with books,
you, who no longer know where to place them,
you, who, from time to time, are forced to make room, to throw, to give away,
   to store, in the country house, the books you have read, which have accompanied you, but which you will not read again,
you, who look at old volumes in antiquarian bookshops, on flea markets,
you, who kept the books of your parents, your grandparents,
you, who collect books for their binding,
you, who purchase them without reading them,
you, who store away, hoard, amass
   books like objects,
you, who know where everything is placed, the place of every book,
you, who have read everything,
you, who arrange alphabetically, or by subject, by publisher,
you, who have hundreds and thousands of books, who will have many more,

you, to whom 'library' is a native word,
you, who had no need to learn it at school, to ask its meaning – for you had it in front of you...

   have you ever thought
about those, who would like to read, but do not have books,
about those, who would like to know how to read,
about those, who, when exiled, had not been able to take so much as a suitcase, a bag, some clothes, nothing,
about those, who had not,
about those, who left shelves well-stocked, and who fled, were taken away,
   with their memories as their only library,
about those, who worked night shifts, or were too occupied all day long to do what they did not know, to learn the language, and to relearn how to live, before purchasing their first book,
about those, whose grandparents, whose parents did not know how to read,
about those, for whom every book is wrested from adversity,
about those, who, one day in class, believing to be equal to others, heard a teacher say,

vous trouverez ce livre dans la bibliothèque de votre grand-père,
alors que leur grand-père était ouvrier spécialisé, travailleur à la chaîne, paysan, mineur de fond,
alors que leur grand-père avait été torturé dans une guerre civile ou une guerre coloniale avant d'avoir pu lire,
alors que leur grand-père avait été déporté, exterminé dans un camp avant d'avoir pu lire,
alors que leur grand-père était tombé pour la patrie, ou reconduit à la frontière,
   avant d'avoir pu lire,

  avez-vous pensé une fois
à ceux qui ont découvert,
   au détour d'une bibliothèque,
     que la vie n'est pas simple.

"you will find this book in the library of your grandfather",
while their grandfather was semi-skilled, worked on the assembly line, was a farmer, a miner,
while their grandfather had been tortured in a civil or colonial war, before he could read,
while their grandfather had been deported, murdered in a camp before (having learned how to read) he could read,
while their grandfather had bled and died for his homeland, or was returned to the border,
   before he could read,

   have you thought once
about those, who discovered,
   about a library,
     that life is not simple.

Stephanie Bung
"Vous trouverez ce livre ..." – Cécile Wajsbrot and the Art of Belonging

At the end of her poem *Vous trouverez ce livre*, Cécile Wajsbrot seems to be making a statement about the hardship of living that, for most people, cannot – but should – be relieved by literature. A closer look, however, reveals that this text is actually not about the civilizing function of books, or about how they might change one's life; nor is it about how important it might be to introduce anyone in the world to reading, especially those whose lives take place removed from any library. The poem's main issue lays elsewhere. From the first line, the text addresses those who believe in possessions: their houses are full of books, handed down by their ancestors, bought at auctions, from the *bouquinistes*, and in antique shops; books they may have read once, but likely never did; books they do not even have room for. The people reproachfully addressed by the poem are *possessors*, and as such they perceive space as something that can and must be filled with objects that belong to them – such as books. Yet books are not only treated as just another possession among others. They are also conceived of as spatial in themselves, and represent a *mise en abyme* of the possessor's conception of space: their owners look at them, as if they were flasks filled with wisdom – having floated in the sea of time, and drifted ashore in their very libraries. Yet, as with space – which, adopting Leibniz's sense, one must regard as a possibility for being together rather than as representing a mere receptacle – books do not simply contain wise words destined for some future generation. Neither books nor words belong to any specific person, nor are they objects one can own, store, pass on. However, in not belonging to anybody, they may create fields of belonging, which are quite similar to the previously noted definition of space. This paradoxical meaning of "belonging" – not only in the sense of possession, but also in the possibility of being together – can be grasped in Derrida's essay *Monolingualism of the Other* (1998), where he writes: "I only have one language; it is not mine."[1] By referring to the different meanings of belonging – at least when it comes to language, literature, and books – Wajsbrot's poem brings this essay to mind. Even if your language is everything to you, if you are bound to live and to die within this

---

[1] This essay was originally published, in French, as *Le Monolinguisme de l'autre: ou la prothèse d'origine* (1996).

language,² it is not *yours* in the possessor's way of thinking. Being neither *yours* nor *theirs*, language cannot define collective ownership as we tend to when considering literature in terms of nationality. The poem, as well as Derrida's essay, rejects this latter line of thinking, as does Cécile Wajsbrot's oeuvre as a whole; her language seeks to perform "belonging" as a possibility of being together. I will return to this issue at the end of my commentary, and argue that Wajsbrot believes in the civilizing task of books after all. To do so, it is first necessary to introduce the author's work and, more specifically, its relation to time and music.

Cécile Wajsbrot usually does not publish poetry. Aside from her novels she has produced myriad essays, articles, radio plays, and short stories, as well as literary translations from English and German.³ The narrative voices of her books are thoughtfully orchestrated – her radio plays even allow these voices to be performed acoustically – though the stories they tell are never neglected for the sake of abstract rhythm or pure musicality. Still, one cannot deny that music and musicality are an intriguing element in the author's universe.⁴ Her work can be described as a permanent quest for the stylistic features that enable the reader to "hear" inner voices as Wajsbrot wishes them to be "heard." *Mémorial* (2005) is a most intense outcome of this quest for appropriate effect.⁵ It is the story of a woman who – in order to unshackle herself from a traumatic past linked to her family background – travels from Paris to Kielce, a polish town from which her father and his sister fled before the pogroms that occurred in the aftermath of the Holocaust.⁶ The entire story is a dialog that unwinds within the protagonist's head, where the voices of her ancestors, remembered or imagined, as well as of

---

2 "Yet it will never be mine, this language, the only one I am thus destined to speak, as long as speech is possible for me in life and in death; you see, never will this language be mine" (Derrida 1998, 2). From this suffering eventually springs the idea of going beyond the possessive thinking by asking if anybody actually can call his language his own language: "But who exactly possesses it? And whom does it possess? Is language in possession, ever a possessing or possessed possession? Possessed or possessing in exclusive possession, like a piece of personal property?" (Derrida 1998, 17); "What I am having difficulty understanding is this entire vocabulary of having, habit, and possession of language that would or would not be one's own – yours for example" (Derrida 1998, 22). These questions obviously are to be asked – and answered – in the colonial context: „Because the master does not possess exclusively, and *naturally*, what he calls his language [...]" (Derrida 1998, 23).
3 Cf. the bibliography of her oeuvre in Huesmann (2017, 539–550) and Böhm and Zimmermann (2010, 22–25).
4 Cf. Ette (2005, 59).
5 This work has been translated into Spanish (*Memorial*, 2007) by Lucia Dorrin, and German (*Aus der Nacht*, 2008) by Holger Fock and Sabine Müller.
6 On 4 July 1946, 42 Polish Jews were killed in Kielce by Catholic inhabitants of the town. This pogrom was not noted by historiography prior to the 1980s. One year after publication of *Mémorial*, Jan Tomasz Gross dedicated several chapters to Kielce in his book *Fear: Anti-Semitism*

other ghostly figures, weave a texture that, like a net, undermines any hope of her ever being freed from the past. According to the author, the rhythm, especially the arrangement of these voices, testifies to her struggle in crafting the musicality of this composition:

> *Mémorial* se fonde sur une structure musicale, l'alternance narration/voix étant à l'image de l'alternance récitatif/chant dans un opéra ou un oratorio. Une sorte de recherche d'équivalence d'un *sprechgesang* (Wajsbrot and Dussidour, 2005).[7]

Yet even beyond this struggle, music seems to be a profound pattern of Wajsbrot's writing. Two of five novels, which are conceived as an ensemble about different artistic disciplines, explicitly address it. In *Conversations avec le maître* (2007), the protagonist remembers the time she once spent in the presence of a famous composer. In so doing, she realizes that it is almost impossible to describe the voice of someone who is dead and she wishes there were a machine to record the memory of such a voice. The music composed by the artist can be reproduced, as can the sound, rhythm and melody of his voice, if it has been recorded, yet the most intimate, personal relationship with this voice, the singular inflection it could take at singular moments, are lost or at least locked within the heads of those who knew him well. Time and music are thus closely interrelated in this novel, which, like all of Wajsbrot's stories, revolves around the fugacity of shape, the frailty of human life, particularly as regards the catastrophes of the twentieth century.[8] Just as with *Mémorial*, at the heart of *Conversations avec le maître* are the Holocaust, the Armenian genocide and Hiroshima. The *maestro* himself – who developed a theory about the endeavor of music to grasp the enormity of these events – committed suicide, leaving his work unfinished. Yet a more optimistic outcome is also possible, as discerned from the second novel mentioned above. *Totale éclipse* (2014) is the story of a photographer trying to capture both the process of vanishing and the possibility of endurance. Her pictures represent the back of the man she loves as he disappears in the streets of Paris; but she also photographs a gingko, a tree that represents survival:

---

in Poland after Auschwitz (2006, 81–166), producing a controversial debate; thereto, see also Klimowicz (2006).

7 *Mémorial* has a musical structure that is similar to the alternating voices (either speaking or singing) in an opera or an oratorio. The alternating voices in *Mémorial* (belonging either to the narration or to the characters) are supposed to be like the equivalent of a *sprechgesang*. (My translation, S.B.)

8 This not only concerns her (fictional) writing; Wajsbrot is dedicated to the question of how one (or one's family) lives after surviving a catastrophe. Recently she organized "Écrire la catastrophe: témoignage et fiction," a *cycle de rencontres*, at the Maison Yiddish in Paris (see: www.remue.net/spip.php?rubrique432); in 2016, she published *Une autobiographie allemande*, a correspondence between Hélène Cixous and herself.

> À Hiroshima, les hommes, les maisons, la végétation, tout s'était embrasé, la chaleur avait incendié, liquéfié le paysage et les radiations agissaient en silence – poursuivant leur avancée d'année en année. Dans la désolation générale, un seul arbre se dressait, vainqueur malgré ses branches nues car debout quand tout gisait, car entier quand tout éclatait. [...] les ginkgos, longuement expérimentés dans la survivance, ayant résisté, dit-on, aux cataclysmes de la préhistoire et vécu des époques que nul homme n'a connues, les ginkgos résistèrent quand tout mourait autour d'eux et furent les premiers à se couvrir de feuilles au printemps d'après la bombe. (Wajsbrot 2014, 7)[9]

These images of continuity, on one hand, and disjunction, on the other, are triggered in an almost Proustian mode by a variety of songs. The protagonist, while watching internet videos of various performances of the songs from over the years – for example Leonard Cohen singing *Famous Blue Raincoat* in 2009 in Budapest, or Joan Baez performing *Diamonds and Rust* in 2007 in Prague, in 2008 in Treves, and in 2009 in Toronto – the protagonist remembers and relives her own emotional relationship with the respective songs. Nevertheless, in the end she decides that – instead of enhancing her feelings, dwelling in the past, and compounding the soundtrack of her life – she will, from now on, live in, and listen to, purely acoustic music:

> C'est bien, je ne veux plus écouter les paroles, je veux entendre les chansons comme une musique pure, la voix comme un instrument, les mots comme des sons, je veux que rien n'ait de sens, la suppression des sentiments, des continents, je veux que rien n'existe en dehors du sentiment de vivre, la concentration sur le travail, une avancée vers le succès. (Wajsbrot 2014, 205)[10]

Unlike *Conversations avec le maître*, *Totale éclipse* combines a love story with reflections on music. While presenting starkly different stories, both novels share this musical leitmotif, seeing that music is specifically related to time. Although many kinds of artistic productions cause us to remember, and tend to settle our

---

[9] At Hiroshima, people, houses, nature, everything had burned. The landscape had been incinerated, liquefied by the heat and the radiation acted silently – proceeding year by year. In this general desolation, one tree stood upright, vanquisher in spite of his naked branches because erect when everything else was lying down, because whole when everything else was disrupted. [..] ginkgos have much experience when it comes to survival; people say that they have resisted prehistoric cataclysms and that they lived long before any human being was alive. The ginkgos resisted when around them everything else died and they had been the first trees coming into leaves in the spring after the bomb. (My translation, S.B.)
[10] It's fine, I don't want to listen to words any more, I want to listen to songs as if they were pure music, the voice as instrument, the words as strains, I want everything not to have any meaning, the obliteration of feelings, of contents, I want nothing to exist beyond the feeling of being alive, the concentration on work, the heading for success. (My translation, S.B.)

relationship with the past, music literally "takes time,", meaning that it can only be perceived diachronically; however, since music is typically more than just one tune at one time, listening to it is at once diachronic and synchronous, leading to a palpable experience of time and space. If this quality is one of the reasons for Cécile Wajsbrot to care so deeply about music, it is certainly one of her fundamental reasons to care about literature, which, like music, is an art made of time and realized in space.

In her essay *Pour la littérature* (1999),[11] the author draws the reader's attention to a metaphor that might be considered a conceptual figure of her écriture: Wajsbrot's view is that literature is to be *relief*-like. A *relief* indicates a specific shift within time and space – either in the geological sense of tectonic movement, or in the sense of an artwork, such as a sculpture, emerging from its material background. For Wajsbrot, this metaphorical shift indicates a time lag that separates information from creation, a distance that allows for reflection and perspective, a possibility to perceive things at once diachronically and synchronously, as in music. Literature also requires this temporal distance, so as to be more than mere transcription of the present:

> La durée de ce qui est saisi, la distance temporelle dans laquelle on écrit et le désir de dire autre chose que la chose qu'on paraît raconter – d'aller plus loin qu'une simple transcription – créent tout ensemble un relief qui fait du récit non pas un texte linéaire qui n'intéresse que celui qui l'a écrit et ceux qui lui ressemblent, mais un texte littéraire où l'expérience humaine s'est déposée (Wajsbrot 1999, 34).[12]

Literature differs from other forms of écriture that are more concerned with current events, such as journalism or writing one's diary. What characterizes literary texts is a *relief* caused by temporal layering, and by joining depth with linearity. This is what allows those texts to be more than storytelling – to say more than they seem to say. This is also what makes them interesting for others, for people who do not necessarily share any personal stock of life stories with the one who is writing. Consequently, the metaphor of the *relief* is also linked to an ethical concern: literature addresses not only those who are "like me." It has no preexisting peer group, nor does it necessarily function in line with

---

11 This essay has been translated into German (*Für die Literatur*, 2010) by Nathalie Mälzer-Semlinger.

12 The duration of what we are supposed to grasp, the temporal distance that marks the moment of our writing and the will to say other things than the things we seem to tell – going beyond a simple transcription –; all this creates a *relief* that transforms a linear text in which only those who resemble to the writer are interested into a literary text where human experience has settled. (My translation, S.B.)

community-fashioning. For Cécile Wajsbrot, this is not an abstract issue. Being a French writer who lived in Paris at the end of the millennium, she knew precisely what she was talking about. By noting the *relief*-like character of literature, Wajsbrot distanced herself from the literary mainstream in France. At the time, books about Vichy and the deportation of the Jewish population were not *en vogue*, and this established a specific difference between Wajsbrot's concerns and those of most of her compatriots. This does not mean, however, that she would have defined the value of literature in biographical terms, defending her right to write about her family's story. On the contrary: by not making any concession to the literary mainstream, she defended and continues to do so literature's right – or, more precisely, its task – to be different as a whole. Only when also expressing 'another concern' are literary texts able to establish fields of belonging, rather than reproducing exclusivist circles and enhancing their respective exclusiveness. Thus, if we return to the poem, there might, of course, be an echo of Wajsbrot's experience as a child, thinking of herself as the equal of her schoolmates, and learning from the careless words of her teacher that she is not. Even so, the overarching idea of this text is not biographical at all. The list of those who are different, unlike the possessors – of those who did not grow up surrounded by books, and might never find any consolation by reading them – is not an exclusive one; and if the respective people are not addressed directly by the poem, they are included or at least thought of:

[...]
avez-vous déjà pensé
à ceux qui aiment lire mais qui n'ont pas de livres,
à ceux qui voudraient savoir lire,
à ceux qui, dans l'exil, n'ont pu prendre qu'une valise, un sac, quelques vêtements, rien,
à ceux qui n'avaient pas,
à ceux qui ont laissé des étagères pleines et qui ont fui, ont été emmenés,
avec leur mémoire pour seule bibliothèque,
à ceux qui ont travaillé la nuit ou des journées trop pleines à faire ce qu'ils ne savaient pas faire, à apprendre la langue et réapprendre à vivre avant d'acheter leur premier livre,
à ceux dont les grands-parents, les parents ne savent pas lire,
à ceux pour qui chaque livre est gagné contre l'adversité,
à ceux qui un jour, en classe, se croyant à égalité des autres, ont entendu un professeur dire,
vous trouverez ce livre dans la bibliothèque de votre grand-père,
alors que leur grand-père était ouvrier spécialisé, travailleur à la chaîne, paysan, mineur de fond,
alors que leur grand-père avait été torturé dans une guerre civile ou une guerre coloniale avant d'avoir pu lire,
alors que leur grand-père avait été déporté, exterminé dans un camp avant d'avoir pu lire,
[...]

For this might be the main concern of these lines: creating fields of belonging means to value the life of those who we are not. This is what books bring to us: another perspective, induced by the experience of a life we never had nor even encountered. Sharing this perspective might not be useful in a possessor's way of thinking – for the life it has grown from may not fit into the pattern of our society, it may even have ended hundreds of years ago – yet, nonetheless, it still helps us to create bonds that lead beyond ourselves. For to free ourselves from what holds us down does not mean the rejection of bonds. It means to transform them and to create new ones with both the aid of our free will and the books we chose to read. It means to be aware of the fact that the most noble task of literature might be to express a concern for the other and the impulse for literature that accompanies it.

References

Böhm, Roswitha, and Margarete Zimmermann (Eds.). *Du silence à la voix. Studien zum Werk von Cécile Wajsbrot*. Göttingen: V&R unipress, 2010.
Derrida, Jacques. *Le Monolinguisme de l'autre: ou la prothèse d'origine*. Paris: Galilée, 1996.
Derrida, Jacques. *Monolingualism of the Other; Or, the Prosthesis of Origin*. Transl. Patrick Mensah. Stanford: Stanford UP, 1998.
Ette, Ottmar. *ZwischenWeltenSchreiben. Literaturen ohne festen Wohnsitz*. Berlin: Kadmos 2005.
Gross, Jan Tomasz. *Fear: Anti-Semitism in Poland after Auschwitz*. Princeton: Princeton UP, 2006.
Huesmann, Hubert. *Das Erzählwerk Cécile Wajsbrots: eine literarische Suchbewegung*. Tübingen: Narr Francke Attempto, 2017.
Klimowicz, Magdalena (Ed.). *Difficult Postwar Years. Polish Voices in Debate over Jan T. Gross's Book Fear*. Warsaw: The Polish Institute of International Affairs, 2006.
Wajsbrot, Cécile. *Pour la littérature*. Paris: Zulma 1999.
Wajsbrot, Cécile. *Mémorial*. Paris: Zulma, 2005.
Wajsbrot, Cécile. *Conversations avec le maître*. Paris: Denoël, 2007.
Wajsbrot, Cécile. *Totale éclipse*. Paris: Christian Bourgeois, 2014.
Wajsbrot, Cécile and Dominique Dussidour. "En littérature, il n'est pas d'autre urgence que l'urgence d'écrire…" http://remue.net/spip.php?article1107. 2005 (6 April 2018).

Alex Epstein
קיצורי דרך הביתה, חרסינה מזרח גרמנית

קיצורי דרך הביתה

בחנות לספרים יד שנייה מצאנו ספר מרופט בשפתנו. בכל העיירות כאן מטפטף גשם בלי הפסקה.
הטכנאי של מכונת הזמן התקשר להודיע שיאחר. חיינו נמשכים.

חרסינה מזרח גרמנית

אהבה, כמו מוסיקה, היא תמיד סיפור אמיתי - באביב 1980, חצי שנה לפני עלייתנו לארץ, החליט סבי להבריח מבריה״מ המועצות את אוסף הבולים הנדיר שלו (באוסף, אגב, הייתה גם סדרה בת 175 בולים עם דיוקנאות של קוסמונאוטים, כלבים ורקטות, שהונפקו משנת 57׳ ואיל׳, לכבוד תוכנית החלל הסובייטית). לשם כך החל לשלוח לקרובינו בישראל מכתבים שכתב לסבתי עוד כשנלחם בסטלינגרד ובקורסק בשנת 1944. על המעטפות הדביק בולים מהאוסף שלו.

כל שבוע שלח לפחות ארבעה מכתבים כאלה. כעבור חודשיים קילל בלבו את קארל דניץ - האדמירל שחתם על הסכמי הכניעה של הנאצים – והתיישב לכתוב לסבתי (ששברה באותם ימים את הראש איך לארוז את מערכת החרסינה המפוארת שלהם מתוצרת הרפובליקה הדמוקרטית הגרמנית) מכתבי אהבה חדשים, שמאחד מהם העתקתי את משפט הפתיחה של הסיפור הזה. בימים ההם חסר ברוסיה נייר, וסבא כתב את המכתבים על דפים שמצדם השני היו תווים בכתב ידו של שוסטקוביץ׳, שאותם מצא, לפי טענתו, בשנת 63׳ בפאתי קלינינגרד, מודבקים על גזעיהם של עצי לבנה בחורשה אגדית אחת (אבל זה כבר סיפור אחר).

לאחר שכל אוסף הבולים שוגר לארץ בהצלחה עוד נותרו לסבי דפים אחדים בכתב ידו של מחבר סימפוניית לנינגרד, וסבתא נחלצה מיד לעזרתו ועטפה בהם את הספלים המזרח גרמניים. את הצלחות ארזו כבר בנייר עיתון „פרבדה"; הספיקו לכך שלושה גליונות מאביב 1980, שאותם אני שומר עד היום, כהוכחה נוספת לאמיתותו של סיפור ההגירה הקטן הזה.

Translated by Becka Mara McKay
Shortcuts Home; East German China

Shortcuts Home

In the secondhand bookstore we found a tattered book in our language. In all the cities here it drizzles without end. The time machine technician called to say he's running late. Our lives go on.

East German China

Love, like music, is always a true story. In the spring of 1980, half a year before we immigrated to Israel, my grandfather decided to smuggle his collection of rare stamps out of the Soviet Union. (This collection included, by the way, a series of 175 stamps with portraits of cosmonauts, rockets, and dogs, issued from '57 on, in honor of the Soviet space program.) To that end, he began to send our relatives in Israel letters he wrote to my grandmother while he was fighting in Stalingrad and Kursk in 1944. He glued stamps from his collection onto the envelopes. Every week he sent at least four letters this way. After two months he cursed in his heart Karl Dönitz – the admiral who signed the Nazi agreement of surrender – and sat down to write to my grandmother (who in those days was tearing her hair out over how to pack their good china made in the Democratic Republic of Germany) new love letters, from one of which I copied the opening sentence of this story. In those days there was a paper shortage in Russia, so my grandfather wrote the letters on the other side of notes in Shostakovich's handwriting, which he found, so he claimed, in '63 on the outskirts of Kaliningrad, glued to the trunks of birches in some mythical grove (but that is already a different story). After he successfully sent the whole stamp collection to Israel, my grandfather had several leftover pages on which the Leningrad Symphony was handwritten, and my grandmother was able to make use of them to wrap her East German teacups. The plates she had already wrapped in pages of Pravda, using up three issues from the spring of 1980, which I have saved to this day, as additional evidence of this little tale of immigration.

Natasha Gordinsky
Smuggled Belongings: Alex Epstein's Fiction of Immigration

"Kizurey derekh ha-baita" [Shortcuts Home], the title story of Alex Epstein's fifth collection of stories (translated into English as *Lunar Savings Time*), presents readers with a fragment of a travelogue. However, it is not a travelogue one would expect – a text written by a tourist returning home after a long journey. Rather, it is a three-sentence story about time-travelers (a topic which holds a prominent place in Epstein's fiction). And in this story (Epstein 2010, 30), the multi-directedness of the time travelers' movement through time and space changes the very meaning of the trajectory "towards home"; for where is home, if the travelers can inhabit different time-spaces?

The narrator, or, rather, narrators – the story is told in the first-person plural – portray a brief glimpse into their perpetual journey in time, during which they are tentatively forced to stay in one dimension of time, as they are waiting for their time-machine to be repaired. It is during this stop-over that they find a worn-out book in a secondhand bookshop, written in their native language. The story does not reveal which language these time-travelers speak, or whether they speak other languages as well. Nonetheless, for the stranded narrators – monolingual or multilingual – the book from the past becomes a fictional shortcut home, a home that exists only on the pages of the book. More precisely, the concept of home becomes redefined through fiction, which functions as a time-machine, as it can imagine different forms of belonging or non-belonging while shifting between them, thereby enabling movement in time and space.

While examining the representations of homecoming in Alex Epstein's fiction, one might be surprised to find that neither the time-travelers, nor the Zen monks, nor any of the other protagonists who inhabit his imaginary worlds, including Kafka and his friend Max Brod and the quotidian lovers, ever reach home. This does not necessarily mean that home does not exist, but rather that it is not a fixed point in time and space: once the protagonists do come home, the home which they find is no longer the same. Thus, the notion of homecoming could be deferred, or even questioned altogether, since in Epstein's fictional worlds the concept of home is never stable but is in fact constantly under construction. When considering this poetic undertaking, it seems logical that in Epstein's fictions the meaning of home is usually not investigated through an autobiographical prism, as such a prism would appear to be rather limiting for such an endeavor.

This is not to say that autobiographical materials are entirely absent in Epstein's works; but unlike other Israeli writers, he undermines the limitations of the autobiographical paradigm by revising it, namely, by adding new and sometimes even contradictory elements, thereby applying to his own biography the very same poetic process which he uses for his fictional protagonists. As a result, his Russian-Jewish belonging becomes yet another topic for fictional contemplation, and not a defining or stabilizing fact in his fictive autobiography.

Born in the Soviet Union in 1971, in Leningrad, Alex Epstein immigrated to Israel with his family at the age of nine. At the age of twenty-one, after publishing a volume of poems under the telling title *Kotev Leningrad ve-shirim aherim* [Writing Leningrad and Other Poems] (1992), Epstein turned to prose – first novels and then, at the beginning of the twenty-first century, microfiction. All of his literary texts are written in Hebrew. It seems that Epstein was never concerned with the linguistic dilemma between Russian and Hebrew; according to his own account, his Russian was inadequate for writing and remained familial language of his childhood. Yet the fact that Epstein writes in Hebrew does not automatically render him an Israeli writer; rather, just as with his protagonists, the concept of his belonging should never be taken for granted.

The yearning sense of homecoming, suggests feminist thinker bell hooks, is a "search for a place to belong" (hooks 2009, 2). Epstein's fiction could be interpreted as a similar perpetual search, through the rethinking of the concept of home. At the same time, such a philosophical and aesthetic undertaking guarantees the deferring of homecoming. After careful consideration, the search for a place to belong also enables the quest for places of non-belonging, or for modes of shifting between the two. This unique self-positioning vis-a-vis the question of belonging undermines one of the grand narratives of Israeli literature, namely, the trope of homecoming.[1] In Israeli fiction, even when concepts of exile and home are not imbued with metaphysical meaning, they still seem to have an unchangeable ontological status. In Epstein's fiction, however, the concept of "home" has only an epistemological function, and it does not operate within a structure of binary thought. This perspective enables Epstein to interpret immigration in his fiction as an ongoing process of negotiation between different forms of belonging.

In the sole academic article on Epstein's writing, Adam Rovner explores the question of genre from a narratological perspective – a question that is doubtlessly essential for understanding Epstein's innovation as a writer of microfiction. Rovner argues that the genre of microfiction allows Epstein to generate

---

[1] On the trope of homecoming in Jewish literature see Ezrahi (2000).

"a shape of time that takes the form of a causal loop," and to repeatedly perform time travel, or "chronomotion." Rovner reads Epstein from a narratological vantage point, yet almost entirely overlooks the question of movement in space. However, at the beginning of his article Rovner makes an important spatial remark, putting forward a thesis about Epstein's place within the Israeli literary establishment: "Epstein likewise remains somewhat aloof from the Tel Aviv literary scene, though he is even more distant from the Russian émigré community. His work cannot fairly be said to be marked by the concerns of the latter" (Rovner 2015, 2). While the first part of the argument attests to Epstein's off-centeredness, and rightly so, the second part is particularly significant because it testifies to the complexity of Epstein's poetic endeavor. Indeed, Epstein does not employ the conventions of representing immigration that were developed over the past decade in the works of translingual writers, and by eschewing these conventions he undermines the dominant post-Soviet narrative of immigration.[2] The prevailing post-Soviet narratives are based on the "ethnic Bildungsroman": a particular variation on the genre of the coming-of-age novel, in which the protagonist develops an awareness "of his/her ethnicity and its social significance," as the American scholar Martin Japtok has asserted (Japtok 2005, 21). Instead of presenting the reader with such a narrative of immigration, at the core of which is the coming of age of a Russian-Jewish teenager – a narrative which has been written over and over again in English, German, and Hebrew by various post-Soviet writers in the last decade – Epstein seeks a new understanding of Russian-Jewish belonging[3]: whereas an ethnic Bildungsroman presupposes a certain teleological form of identity-formation as a result of immigration, Epstein's microfiction explores in fictive terms the fragmentary autobiography of an immigrant author.

How does one contemplate, in fiction, issues of the representation of immigration, and how does fragmentation encourage one to rethink the concept of home? According to Epstein, since immigration is always a process of de-localization and re-localization, not only in space but also in time, there cannot be a totalizing narrative of immigration, or a single story to be told chronologically. Perceived as an ongoing cultural and phenomenological experience, immigration can thus be represented only fragmentarily or as a series of snapshots which constitute microfictions of belonging.

These issues are reflected in a paradigmatic microstory titled "East German China," (Epstein 2011, 2) the only text in Epstein's oeuvre to explicitly address

---

2 On the concept of translingual writing, see Kellmann (2000).
3 On the construction of "Russianness" in post-Soviet novels, see Wanner (2011).

the issue of the representation of immigration. While the Hebrew title of the story leaves no doubt as to the object that lies at the heart of the story – the family's porcelain service set made in East Germany – the English translation offers a wonderfully misleading spatial equivocality. Nonetheless, the Hebrew title also contains this spatial element, for the Hebrew word "charsina" is a portmanteau whose meaning is derived from the combination of two morphemes – "cheres" [clay] and "sin" [China in Hebrew].[4] East German china is therefore an object as well as a spatial neologism. It is an artifact of everyday life, a valuable part of a family's belongings (used only on festive occasions) which can be carried to another country; at the same time, it is a sort of eccentric spatial amalgam, created in language, of two political entities that supported the Soviet regime. Thus, "East German China" should not be understood merely as an object which is metonymic to immigration – that is, as a souvenir from the Soviet past – but also as a metaphor in the most literal sense, as a mode of transportation from one place to another. East German China is a metaphoric portmanteau, a linguistic creation in fiction and a suitcase, a vessel, designed to transport and transform memories related to immigration. But then again, is not immigration itself a sort of portmanteau which creates new forms of fragmentary belongings by smuggling into the destination country different fictive and non-fictive objects?

In this microstory, Epstein presents the reader with a compressed history of the Soviet Union through the story of family objects. The text encompasses iconic events in Soviet history – the Leningrad Symphony (finished by Dmitry Shostakovich during the German siege of Leningrad in 1941), the battles of Stalingrad and Kursk (whose dates are incorrectly and mischievously ascribed to 1944), and the German Capitulation in 1945. The story also relates to post-war developments in the Soviet Union – the final stage of the Khrushchev Thaw and the closing decade of the Soviet regime. However, and in contrast to other texts by post-Soviet translingual writers, in this microstory the political and historical Soviet condition does not serve as the main topic, but rather as one of many layers of the story in which the family's belongings are immersed.

By blurring the borders between history and fiction in the narrative itself, Epstein's microstory offers a unique contextualization of the "tale of immigration." Before immigrating to Israel, the grandparents of the autobiographical narrator were concerned with the prospects of their belongings that would be transported to a new country. While East German china, which was a status

---

4 Originating in French, the word *portmanteau* (literally, a suitcase or a trunk) was first used in the linguistic sense by none other than Lewis Carroll.

symbol for certain Soviet elites, was permitted by Soviet officials to be taken abroad, the grandfather's stamp collection was prohibited from leaving the Soviet Union. The grandfather's industrious solution – to save his precious collection by sending the letters he had written his wife during World War II to friends in Israel using the stamps from the collection – causes him to eventually produce new love letters. Thus, two kinds of letters come into being: those which can be seen as historical documents, written during the war amidst the battles, and those which are new, and are therefore works of fiction. Furthermore, these love letters serve as a pretext for yet another family belonging, as Epstein's narrator adds another layer of fiction to the family tale, stating that the new letters were written on the drafts of Shostakovich's Leningrad Symphony – Leningrad being the narrator's hometown. Near the end of the story, the narrator admits that his opening line was taken from one of these letters, written on the backside of Shostakovich's notes – "Love, like music, is always a true story."

These letters, with their double layer of historical fictions, cross the border to become the first immigrants of the family. Once the entire collection of stamps is secure in its new residence, the grandmother uses the remaining pieces of Shostakovich's draft notes to wrap and pack the East German china; some of the china is wrapped in the pages of the Soviet central newspaper emblematically titled *Pravda* [Truth]. Ironically enough, in this family history the china is perceived as more valuable than even Shostakovich's notes, and yet they are also fictively smuggled into Epstein's story.

This "little tale of immigration", as it is defined at the end of the story, turns out to be a tale of the immigration of objects. Epstein's microstory suggests that immigration like china, is wrapped in many layers of stories, or, rather, in fragments of fiction and history, both true and imagined. Thus, the tale of immigration becomes a story which is protected by layers of fiction and transported in space and time. This enables Epstein to constitute a fragmented form of (post-)Soviet-Jewish belonging in Hebrew literature – a portmanteau in itself.

References

Epstein, Alex. *Kotev Leningrad ve-shirim aherim* [Writing Leningrad and Other Poems]. Tel Aviv: Akad, 1992.
Epstein, Alex. *Blue Has No South*. Transl. Becka Mara McKay. Northampton: Clockroot Books, 2010.
Epstein, Alex. *Lunar Savings Time*. Transl. Becka Mara McKay. Northampton: Clockroot Books, 2011.

Erzahi, DeKoven Sidra. *Booking Passage: Exile and Homecoming in the Modern Jewish Imagination*. Berkeley: University of California Press, 2000.
hooks, bell. *Belonging: A Culture of Place*. New York and London: Routledge, 2009.
Japtok, Martin. *Growing Up Ethnic: Nationalism and Bildungsroman in African American and Jewish American Literature*. Iowa City: University of Iowa Press, 2005.
Kellmann, Steven G. *The Translingual Imagination*. Lincoln: University of Nebraska Press, 2000.
Rovner, Adam. "The Shape of Time in Microfiction: Alex Epstein and the Search for Lost Time." *Shofar* 33.4 (2015): 111–133.
Wanner, Adrian. *Out of Russia: Fictions of a New Translingual Diaspora*. Evanston: Northwestern University Press, 2011.

Almog Behar

אַנַא מִן אַל-יַהוּד

1

בזמן ההוא התהפכה לשוני, ועם שהגיע ראש חודש תמוז נתקע לי בפה, עמוק עמוק בגרון, עמוק מן הגרון, המבטא הערבי. כך כשהייתי באמצע הליכת רחוב חזר אלי המבטא הערבי של סבא אַנְוָואר עליו השלום, וכמה ניסיתי להוציאו מתוכי ולהשליכו באחד הפחים הציבוריים ככה לא הצלחתי. ניסיתי ניסיתי לרכך את העי"ן לרכך את העי"ן כמו אמא שעשתה זאת בילדותה נוכח המורים ומבטי שאר התלמידים, אבל זרים עוברים רק קיבעו אותי במקומי, ניסיתי לרכך את החי"ת ולעשות אותה כ"ף, ניסיתי להרחיק את הצָּדִ"י מן הסָמֶ"ךְ, ניסיתי לצאת מן הקו"ף העיראקית הזאת, ולא צלח המאמץ. ושוטרים התחילו לעבור מולי ברחובות ירושלים תקיפים, התחילו להצביע עלי ועל זקני השחור באצבעות מאיימות, התחילו להתלחש ביניהם בניידות, התחילו לעצור אותי ולדרוש בשמי וּבזהותי. ואני מול כל שוטר עובר בָּר-חוב הייתי מבקש לעמוד מהליכתי ולשלוף את תעודת-הזהות שלי ולהצביע על סעיף הלאום ולומר להם, כאילו אני מסגיר סוד שֶׁיפטור אותי מאשמה גדולה: "אַנַא מִן אַל-יַהוּד, אנא מן אל-יהוד".

אבל פתאום התחילה נעלמת לי תעודת-הזהות דווקא כשהייתי נזקק לה מאוד. וכך היו עוצרים אותי השוטרים ערב ערב ובוקר בוקר כשאין בארנקי תעודה אשר תסכים לגונן עלי. אחר-כך בבית הייתי מוצא את תעודת-הזהות מגולגלת בין שני שטרות, או בכיס מחוץ לארנק היה מתגלה לי רישיון הנהיגה, כאילו ככה הוצאתי אותו בשביל איזה דבר-מה, או בתיק הגב בין מסמכים היתה נחבאת תעודת המילואים כאילו שכחתי אותה שם בלי כוונה. אבל כשהשוטרים היו נעצרים מולי לא היתה נמצאת לי ולו תעודה אחת שתספר להם על עברי ועתידי. ואז הייתי מתחיל עושה טלפונים, אומר לשוטר, תראה, רק מאתמול המבטא שלי ערבי ככה, כבד כזה, והוא בכלל לא פַלַסְטִינִי הוא עִירַאקִי, וגם אתה לא נראה לי דובר יִידִיש מן הבית, אולי למדתָ אותה באחד המקומות החיצוניים, ובכלל, אולי גם לסבא שלךָ היה מבטא כמו שלי, ותשמע, אני מתקשר לחברים, חברים שלי, תשמע איזה מבטא יפה יש להם, עברית כמו שצריך לדבר עברית, בלי שום מבטא, ואם אלו חברי אז מי אני.

Translated by Vivian Eden
Ana min al-yahoud – I'm one of the Jews

1

At that time, my tongue twisted around and with the arrival of the month of Tammuz the Arabic accent got stuck in my mouth, deep down in my throat. Just like that, as I was walking down the street, the Arabic accent of Grandfather Anwar of blessed memory came back to me and no matter how hard I tried to extricate it from myself and throw it away in one of the public trash cans I could not do it. I tried and tried to soften the glottal `ayyin, the way my mother had in her childhood, because of the teacher and the looks from the other children, but strangers passing by just rooted me to the spot; I tried to soften the pharyngeal fricative het and pronounce it gutturally, I tried to make the tsaddi sound less like an "s" and I tried to get rid of that glottal Iraqi quf and pronounce it like "k," but the effort failed. And policemen started to head assertively towards me on the streets of Jerusalem, pointing at me and my black beard with a threatening finger, whispering among themselves in their vehicles, stopping me and inquiring as to my name and my identity. And for every passing policeman on the street I would want to stop walking and pull out my identity card and point out the nationality line and tell them, as if I were revealing a secret that would absolve me of tremendous guilt: "Ana min al yahoud, I'm a Jew."

But suddenly my identity card started to vanish precisely when I was very much in need of it. And thus, every evening and every morning the police would arrest me without anything in my wallet that would agree to protect me. Then at home I would find the identity card rolled up between two NIS 20 bills, or in my pocket outside my wallet I would find my driver's license as though I had taken it out for some reason, or in my knapsack among the papers my military reserve service card would appear as though I had forgotten it there unintentionally. But when the policemen stopped in front of me I couldn't find any document at all that would tell them about my past and my future. And then I would start to make phone calls, telling the policeman, look, it's only since yesterday that my accent has been Arab like this, heavy like this, and it isn't even Palestinian, it's Iraqi, and you don't look to me like you spoke Yiddish in your parents' home yourself, maybe you learned it somewhere outside, maybe your own grandfather had an accent like mine and listen, I'm calling friends, my friends, listen to what a beautiful accent they have, Hebrew as Hebrew should be spoken, without any accent, and if these are my friends, then who am I.

אבל החברים האשכנזים שלי פתאום לא היו עונים לי בכלל, לא היו שומעים לתחינת צלצולי, ורק לעת ערב או ביום המחרת היו מתקשרים אלי חזרה, שואלים לרצונותי ומסרבים לזהות את קולי. ואני הייתי נותר לעמוד מול השוטרים לבד, מתחיל להתקשר לחברים החֲלַבִּים והטְרִיפּוֹלִיטָאִים והתּוּנִיסָאִים שלי, אומר, אלה אולי אין להם עברית מושלמת, אינה צחה כל-כך, אינה כפי שעברית צריכה להיות, אבל בכל זאת טובה היא משלי. והם היו עונים מיד, לא מתמהמהים למשמע הצלצולים, ופתאום גם להם נעשה מבטא ערבי כל-כך כבד כל-כך, והם בדיוק היו שומעים ברקע איזה עוד פתלתל או קָאנוּן עיקש, והם היו מברכים אותי "אַהֲלַן בִּיךּ" ומכנים אותי "יָא חַבִּיבִּי" ושואלים אותי "אַשְׁלוֹנַךּ" ונפרדים ממני ב"סַלַמְתַךּ", ומה יכלו השוטרים, איך יכלו להאמין לי, אחרי שכל חברי זנחו אותי כך, שאני בן ישראל ולא בן ישמעאל. ואז היו בודקים אותי באיטיות, מפשפשים בבגדי, עוברים על פני גופי עם גלאי המתכות, מפשיטים אותי בשתיקתם היסודית ממילים ומחשבות, מחפשים עמוק בשכבות כסויות עורי את טינתי, תרים אחר חגורות נפץ, חגורות נפץ בלבי, ששים לנטרל כל חפץ חשוד. וכשהיו השוטרים ניצבים עלי בזוגות ונתארכה בדיקתם כמה רגעים, היה אחד אומר לשני תראה הוא נימול, הוא באמת יהודי הערבי הזה, ושני היה אומר, גם ערבי נימול, וחגורות הנפץ אינן מענְיָן המילה, והיו ממשיכים בחיפושיהם. ובאמת באותו הזמן שהנחתי את גופי להם החלו נולדות חגורות נפץ על לבי, החלו תופחות ומסרבות להיות מנוטרלות, רועמות רועמות. אבל בגלל שלא היו עשויות פלדה או אבק שריפה הצליחו לחמוק מן הגלאים המוכשרים.

ובסוף כשהיו השוטרים עוזבים אותי לנפשי חופשי אך לא חף, הייתי ממשיך בדרכי והולך בדרך מַרְפּוּס היורדת לתיאטרון ירושלים מן הבניין היפה של הקונסוליה הבלגית והכיכר שעל רחוב ז'בוטינסקי. הייתי מחכה לראות שם איזה סרט אמריקאי מרובה אוסקרים, אבל פתאום לא היה שם תיאטרון בקצה הרחוב, ופתאום לא היה זה רחוב מרכוס, היה זה רחוב עם שם ערבי, והבתים היו שבים להיות ערבִּיים, גם הקונסוליה הבלגית, וגם האנשים בחצרות, משפחות משפחות, היו ערבּיים, לא רק גברים צעירים פועלי בניין, לא רק מנקי רחובות ועושי שיפוצים.

But all of a sudden my Ashkenazi friends weren't answering me at all, they wouldn't hear the plea of my ringing and only in the evening or the next day would they call me back, ask what I wanted and refuse to identify my voice. And I'd remain standing there facing the policemen all alone and start to call my friends whose parents were from Aleppo or Tripoli or Tunisia saying maybe their Hebrew is not perfect, it isn't so pure, but nevertheless it's better than mine. And they'd answer right away, not hesitating at the sound of the ringing, and suddenly they too had such a heavy Arab accent and they'd be listening to some meandering oud in the background or some persistent qanoun, and they'd greet me with "ahlan bik" and call me "ya habibi" and ask me "ashlonek" and take their leave of me with "salamatek" and what could the policemen do, how could they believe me, after all of my friends had abandoned me, that I was an Israelite and not an Ishmaelite. And then they'd check me slowly, rummaging in my clothes, going over my body with metal detectors, stripping me of words and thoughts in their thorough silence, searching deep in the layers of my skin for a grudge, seeking an explosive belt, an explosive belt in my heart, eager to defuse any suspicious object. And when the policemen presented themselves to me in pairs, the one would say to his companion a few minutes into their examination, look, he's circumcised, he really is a Jew, this Arab, and the other one would say, an Arab is also circumcised, and explosive belts don't care about circumcision, and they would continue their search. And really, during the time when I left my body to them explosive belts began to be born on my heart, swelling and refusing to be defused, thundering and thundering. But as they were not made of steel or gunpowder they succeeded in evading the mechanical detectors.

In the end, when the policemen had left me alone, I would continue on my way from the beautiful Belgian Consulate building and the circle at the top of Jabotinsky Street and walk down Marcus Street to the Jerusalem Theater. There I would wait to see some American film plentifully endowed with Oscars, but suddenly there was no theater at the end of the street, and suddenly it wasn't Marcus Street, it was a street with an Arabic name, and the house had gone back to being Arab, and so did the Belgian Consulate, and the people in the yards, family by family, were Arabs, not only construction workers, not only street cleaners and renovators.

2

והייתי מתחיל להתהלך ברחובות קַטָמוֹן וברחובות טַלְבְּיֶה וברחובות בַּקְעָה, ובמקום לראות את עשירי ירושלים שהתכנסו שם בבתים המרווחים, ובמקום לקרוא שם "כובשי קטמון" ו"יורדי הסירה" בשמות הרחובות, ראיתי פתאום שוב את עשירי פַלַסְטִין, והם היו שם כמו שהיו לפני מלחמת ארבעים ושמונה, כמו לא הייתה מלחמת ארבעים ושמונה. אני רואה אותם והם הולכים בחצרות בין עצי הפרי וקוטפים פירות כמו לא סיפרו להם העיתונים כי יקמלו העצים, כי הארץ תִימָלֵא פליטים. והיה כאילו הזמן הלך היסטוריה אחרת, שונה, וזכרתי ששאלתי את אמא למה אנחנו מרבים כל-כך לדבר היסטוריה, די עם ההיסטוריה, די לנו מהיסטוריה, כי ההיסטוריה הזאת כובלת אותי, כובלת אותךָ, לא משאירה בי דבר, לא משאירה גם לך.

ובאמת נעשינו קבועים כל-כך בהיסטוריה שלנו, גם כבויים, אבל הנה היא הלכה לרגע מהלך אחר. והייתי אני צועד ברחובות עשירי פלסטין, וחשבתי אולי ידברו אלי הם בכבוד, לא כמו השוטרים, קיוויתי אוכל לספר להם כמה קראתי על הסופר והמחנך חַ׳לִיל אל-סַכַּאכִּינִי, וכמה רציתי להתיידד עם נכדיו, והייתי הולך ביניהם, מתקרב לחצרות ואיני מצליח להתערות ביניהם, כי לרשותי עומדת רק העברית במבטאה הערבי, ואילו הערבית שלי, שלא באה לי מן הבית אלא מן הצבא, פתאום הערבית שלי אילמת, חנוקה מן הגרון, מקללת את עצמה בלי להוציא מילה, יְשֵׁנָה באוויר המחניק של מקלטי-נפשִׁי, מסתתרת מבני-המשפחה מאחורי תריסי העברית. וכל הזמן כאשר ניסיתי לדבר אליהם ערבית מן הקצת והעילג שידעתי, יצאה לי איזו עברית במבטא ערבי, עד שחשבו כמעט אני לועג עליהם, ואלמלא המבטא שהיה עיראקי כל-כך, אלמלא זה, היו הם בטוחים שאני לועג להם.

אבל ככה עם המבטא התבלבלו, חשבו אולי אני לועג לעיראקים, לסדאם חוסיינים, או אולי אני איזה עיראקי יָשָׁן, שנותר לו מבטאו אבל נשתכחה שפתו. ולא עשיתי שמה חברים למרות רצוני, ונזכרתי איך שמעתי פעם דוד אחד שלי אומר על הערבים הללו של השכונות העשירות של ירושלים, אלה אֶפֶנְדִים, אלה הולכים בחליפות מערב ותרבושים לראשם, ושמעתי אז את המילה אפנדי במין בוז כזה, למרות שעכשיו אני יכול להיזכר שהוא לא אמר אותה כך, שמעתי בה בוז כאילו היית איזה פלמ"חניק בסנדלים ומכנסיים קצרים שלועג לבעלי הקרקעות הערביים ומשבח את הסוציאליזם הקדוש שלו ושל כל הסַהְיוּנִים. אלה אפנדים, אמר לי הדוד, והתכוון לומר

2

And I would start to walk the streets of Katamon and the streets of Talbieh and the streets of Baqa and instead of seeing the wealthy Jerusalemites who had gathered there in the spacious homes, and instead of reading there on the street signs "Kovshei Katamon" and "Yordei Hasira," I'd once again see the wealthy Palestinians, and they were the way they had been before the 1948 war, as if there had never been a 1948 war. I see them and they are strolling in the yards among the fruit trees and picking fruit as though the newspapers had not told them that the trees would wither, that the land would be filled with refugees. And it was as though time had gone through another history, a different history, and I remembered that I had asked my mother why we talked history so much, enough history, we've had enough of history, because this history binds me, leaving nothing inside me, and also nothing inside you.

And really, we have become so fixed in our history, and extinguished, but here for a moment history has followed a different trajectory. And I would walk through the wealthy Palestinians' streets, and I thought that perhaps they would speak to me respectfully, not like the policemen. I hoped that I would be able to tell them how much I had read about the writer and educator Khalil al Sakakini, and how much I wanted to make friends with his grandchildren, and I would walk among them, approaching their yards and I do not succeed in mingling with them because all I have at my disposal is Hebrew with an Arabic accent and my Arabic, which doesn't come from my home but from the army, is suddenly mute, strangled from my throat, cursing itself without uttering a word, hanging in the suffocating air of the refuges of my soul, hiding from family members behind the shutters of Hebrew. And all the time, when I tried to speak to them in the small, halting vocabulary of the Arabic I knew, what came out was Hebrew with an Arabic accent, until they thought that I was ridiculing them, and had my accent not been so Iraqi, had it not been for that, they would have been certain that I was making fun of them.

But like that, with the accent, they were confused, they thought I was making fun of the Iraqis, the Saddam Husseins, or maybe some old Iraqi who had kept his accent but forgotten his language. And I didn't make friends there even though I wanted to, and I remembered how I had once heard an uncle of mine say of those Arabs of the wealthy neighborhoods of Jerusalem, they are effendis, they wear Western suits and tarboushes on their heads, and I heard the word effendi at that time with a kind of scorn, even though now I can remember that he hadn't said it that way and I had heard the scorn as though I were some Palmachnik in sandals and shorts who scorns the Arab landowners and praises his own holy socialism and that of all the Zionists. They are effendis, my uncle told me, and he meant it

כבוד אך נעלמה ממני שפתם והם לא ידעו את שפתי, ונשאר בינינו מרחק המשטרות והדורות.
ובדרכי חזרה הביתה רק נהגי האוטובוסים היו מקבלים היטב את מבטאי, יודעים כי אין לצפות מה מבטאו של נוסע אשר עולה לאוטובוס בירושלים. ולא ידע לבי כי שבתי אל לבי, לא ידע, ולא ידעו פחדי כי הם כולם שבו עלי, לא ידעו.

3

וכך התחלף קולי בקול סבי, ופתאום הרחובות האלו שהתרגלו כל-כך למותו והיעלמו והעדרו מהם, פתאום התחילו שוב לשמוע את קולו. ופתאום הקול הזה, היפה, שהיה כלוא בתוך עברי, פתאום הוא היה יוצא ממני ולא כמבקש נדבות ולא כמבקש זכות בפירורים, אלא ממש קול שלי קול שלי חזק ורם. ורחובות ירושלים שהתרגלו לשתיקתי, לשתיקתנו, התקשו מאוד מאוד מול הדיבור, והיו משקיטים את הקול, משקיטים אותו לאט לאט אומרים לו זהירות, אומרים לי זהירות, אומרים לו אתה זר, אומרים לי די לך בשתיקתך. ולמרות פחדי, ולמרות שגם לי היה הקול הזה זר ממרחק שני דורות של שכחה, השמעתי את כל מילותי במבטא ההוא, כי לא יכולתי להתמיד בשתיקה, כי היה בי דיבור רוצה לצאת, והמילים היו משתנות לי עת היו יוצאות מעומק הגרון. וזר שלא היה מכיר היה חושב אני נכד נאמן, ולא היה יודע כמה הרביתי אי-זיכרון על זיכרון לאורך השנים, ולא היה מנחש כמה זיכרוני היטשטש וכמה זמנים הרבה הרבה זמנים לא קשרתי את קשר סבי על שפתי.

וכששבתי הביתה מן ההליכה הראשונה ברחובות עם מבטאי החדש וחיפושי השוטרים על גופי, היתה זוגתי מתפלאת על קולי, ותוך כדי דיבורה אלי והמלצתה לי לחדול התחילה נדבקת משינויי ובשפתיה התקשרו בערבוביה המבטא התימני של ערבית אביה והמבטא האיסטמבולי של ספניולית אמה. ואחר כמה ימים החלה חוזרת הביתה מעבודתה מדווחת כמה חוששים במדורים, כבר מתפשטת מגיפה קטנה בין אנשים במשרדה, יוצאים המבטאים הישנים שמקווה היה כי נעלמו. וידיעה קטנה בשולי אחד העיתונים החשובים גילתה כי הממונים על הביטחון עוקבים מי נדבק ממי במבטאים האסורים ומקוננים איך מתהפך להם יובל שנים של חינוך מוצלח, והם כבר חוששים כי תימלא הארץ ערבים, הרבה הרבה ערבים, על כן החליטו לתגבר את הרדיו בקריינים בעלי עברית כה רהוטה כך

respectfully, but I had lost their language and they didn't know my language and between us remained the distance of the police forces and the generations.

On my way back home, only the bus drivers were accepting of my accent, knowing that it is impossible to expect what the accent of a passenger who boards a bus in Jerusalem might be. And my heart did not know I had returned to my heart, he didn't know, and my fears didn't know they had all returned to me, they did not know.

3

And thus my voice was replaced by my grandfather's voice, and suddenly those streets that had become so accustomed to his death and his disappearance and his absence from them began to hear his voice again. And suddenly that beautiful voice, which had been entirely in my past, started coming out of me and not as a beggar and not asking for crumbs, but truly my voice, my voice strong and clear. And the streets of Jerusalem that had grown accustomed to my silence, to our silence, had a very hard time with the speech, and would silence the voice, gradually telling it careful, telling me careful, telling me I am alien telling me my silences are enough. And despite my fear, and even though this voice was foreign from the distance of two generations of forgetting, I spoke all my words in that accent, because there was speech in me that wanted to come out and the words would change on me as they came out of the depths of my throat. And a stranger who didn't know me would have thought that I was a loyal grandson, and would not have known how much I had piled non-memory on memory over the years, and would not have guessed how much my memory had blurred and how many times, how many, many times, I had not made the connection to my grandfather on my lips.

And when I returned home from that first walk in the streets with my new accent and the policeman's searches of my body, my life's companion wondered about my voice, and as she spoke to me and advised me to stop she was infected by my transformation and her lips connected to a jumble of her father's Yemenite Arabic accent and her mother's Istambouli Ladino accent. And a few days later, she began coming home from work with reports that there was anxiety going around the different departments and a small plague was spreading among the people at her office and the old accents that were hoped to have vanished are coming out again. And a small item in the margins of one of the major newspapers revealed that the security authorities are keeping track of who has been infected by whom with the forbidden accents, and there is already concern that

שיובטח לנו כי נחוש זרים בדיבורנו. ועוד מעט, היתה מסבירה לי זוגתי דבורה רועץ, רגע מצפין אל מְצָרֵי הַבּוֹסְפּוֹרוֹס ורגע מדרים אל מפרץ עֵדֶן, הדיבוק הזה נוגע גם באשכנזים. אצלם תהא ההשתנות איטית יותר, התנבאה, כי השתכנעו ילדיהם שמבטא הוריהם והורי הוריהם היה במקורו אמריקאי, אצלם מועט יותר הזיכרון המוחש של דיבורם הישן. אבל עוד מעט יישמע כאן מחדש ברחובות המבטא הפולני וההונגרי והרומני והגרמני והאוקראיני, ומכך חוששים יותר מכל הממונים על ביטחון הציבור, חששם שאז לא יימצאו קריינים לשלוח אל צבאות הרדיו, לא יימצאו מורים להורות סוד מבטא נכון לילדינו.

ולמרות התנבאויותיה על גל גדול של השתנות, הורי עמדו עיקשים מולי ומול פני המגיפה, זוכרים בכמה שנים של מאמץ קנו להם את מבטאם הנקי, והחלו רומזים לי נחרצות לחדול, מזכירים לי את תוכניותי ללמוד. והיו מבקשים מאוד מה יכולתי לעשות, איך אוכל לכסות על געגועי וגעגועי פתאום בתוך הקול הזה שהוא כל-כך זר לי, ואני מצר ומצטער כי הוא יוצא ממני, אבל גם לא יכול ככה, ככה סתם ברגע אחד לעצור אותו כי אין בו מחסום מתוכו ואין בו מעצור. אם תמשיך את הדיבור הזה הנמשך ממך תרחק מן המלגות, אמר אבי וצדק מאוד מאוד, אם לא תשוב אל דיבורנו הפשוט מה יהיה עליך, אמרה אמי וצדקה מאוד מאוד, בכל ראיונותי היו כל הפרופסורים והפרופסוריות תמהים נורא על מבטאי, מבקשים למצוא בי דיבור אחר, אוניברסיטאי יותר, חרף שהיו המילים כמעט אותן מילים, אולי מעט יותר שבורות. איך תמשיך אם תדבר כך, אמרו ביקשו הורי מאוד, מה יכולתי לעשות, והם דואגים מאוד את עתידי, ולא שלווות לבי החרבה, ולא אבני לבי השבורות, ולא פינות לבי המחודדות, לא יכלו לעזור להעביר ממני את הגזירה. אבל אותם ימים של דאגתם לא היו אוזני פקוחות לשמע דיבורם, ונעשתה שפתי חירשת ונעשה לי מבטאם זר ומרוחק, ונהניתי איך חולפים כך וכך הירחים ונבואות זוגתי מתגשמות ומשתנים רחובות ירושלים, רק הורי נשארים לבד עם אי-השתנותם. וגיליתי את אוזני זוגתי, אמרתי לה התחלתי כותב את סיפורי באותיות הָעֲרָבִיּוֹת, שוב יזדעזעו במדורים החשובים. והיא אחרי מספר ימים חזרה הביתה לספר כי צחקו ראשי המדורים, אמרו, יכתוב כך, יכתוב סיפורים שרק הוא יוכל לקרוא, לא יקראו בו הורי או ילדיו, וגם ילדינו לא ייפלו בסכנה, ואנחנו נעניק לו, אם יבקש את כל פרסי ראש-הממשלה לספרות ערבית בלי שנקרא מילה מתוך ספריו.

the country will be filled with Arabs, many, many Arabs, and therefore they have decided to reinforce the radio with announcers whose Hebrew is so pure that we will feel alien in our speech. And shortly thereafter, my life's companion was explaining to me in an unsteady voice, one moment veering north to the Straits of the Bosporus and one minute veering south towards the Gulf of Aden, that this dybbuk was also haunting Ashkenazim. For them, the change would develop more slowly, she prophesized, because their children were convinced that their parents' accent and their grandparents' accent had originally been American, and they have less concrete memories of their old speech. But in a little while the Polish and the Hungarian and the Rumanian and the German and the Ukrainian accents will be heard again in the streets, and this is what is most feared by those who are responsible for public security, their fear being that they will no longer be able to find announcers to send to the armies of the radio and teachers will not be found to instruct our children in the secret of the correct accent.

And despite her prophecies of a huge wave of change, my parents stood staunchly against me and against the plague, remembering the years of effort they had invested to acquire their clean accent, and they began to hint strongly to me to cease and desist, reminding me of my plans to study. And they would ask me earnestly what could I do, how I could cover up my longings, my longings so suddenly in this voice that is so foreign to me, and I am so sorry and regretful that it is coming out of me, but I can't, I can't stop it just like that in a single moment, because there is no barrier inside me and no brakes. If you persist in this speech that keeps coming out of you, you will distance yourself from the scholarships, said my father, and he was very, very right, if you don't come back to our plain speech, what will become of you, said my mother, and she was very, very right. In all my interviews all the professors and the women professors were very surprised at my accent, trying to find a different speech in me, something more like university speech, more academic, even though the words were almost the same words, perhaps a bit more broken. How will you go on if you speak like this, they said plaintively, and they are very concerned about my future, and neither my heart's ruined tranquillity nor my heart's broken stones nor my heart's sharp corners could help lift the decree from me. But during those days of their worry my ears were not opened to hearing them, and my language became deaf and their accent became alien to me and distant, and I took pleasure as cycles of the moon went by and my life companion's prophesies were being fulfilled and the streets of Jerusalem were changing and my own parents were alone in their non-transformation. And I revealed to her ear that I had started to write my stories in Arabic letters, and soon the important departments would be shocked again. And some days later she came home to tell me that the department heads had laughed and said, let him write like that. Let him write stories that only he

וצדקו כמובן ראשי המדורים, וזוגתי החלה מתנבאת על המציאות בפתגמים ספָּנְיוֹלְיִים, אומרת לי פתגם זה בו אמי היתה משתמשת, אמנם איני זוכרת איך היתה אומרת בשפתה, אך את מבטאה אני זוכרת. זה הביקור האחרון של הבריאות לפני המוות, לחשה ואז החלה מבארת, אלו פרפורי גוסס ולא תחיית מתים, וכבר יודעים בגבוהים שבַּמדורים, החליטו כי אפשר להירגע, יַתְנו את המשרות בדיבור העברי הנכון, ויחשוב כל אחד למקורות פרנסתו וכלכלת ימיו ודוחק משפחתו ואז תשוב העברית הרגילה כמו לא היתה כאן מגיפה.

4

ולבי התחיל נותן בקולותי סימנים, אומר זה קולי וזה אינו קולי, זאת לָמֶ"ד יוצאת מפי וזאת קו"ף זרה היא ללבי. והייתי מאט את קצב מחשבותי, כדי לחשוב, לחשוב גם על מחשבותי ולא רק את מחשבותי, אבל עת לא היתה לי, והייתי זורה מילים לרוח כמו המלח של הים אשר ודאי איש לא זורה אותו אל תוך הים. והיה סבי מדבר אלי, שואל אותי בקולי האם יש סוף לסיפור הזה, ומה ההיסטוריה זו שלי מתערבת בשלךָ, איך באתי להפר חייךָ, אני דור מְדֻבָּר ואיך אתה קם לחדש אותי, אתה הדור חיכינו אותו שלא יהיה מבדיל בין עברו לעבר מוריו, כי כבר כאב מאוד עברנו, ונשארתי במדבר למאכל עופות דורסים בשבילךָ, כדי שלא תזכור אותי, שלא תהיה כואב כמונו, ואיך שיניך נוגסות שוב את מילותי, ואיפה, מחוזות ירושלים אחרים, אין בתי-תה, אין חידקל חוצה את העיר לרחמים, אבל אני לא מצאתי את מותי בירושלים, גם לא בעיר הולדתי, אני מת בַּמדבר שביניהן, הרבה מְדַבֵּר שתיקה. בְּנה אגפים בלבךָ, נכדי, היה אומר לי, עשה אותו מדורים מדורים, ושַכֵּן אותי באחד המדורים הנחבאים, ובשאר המדורים חייה. או עבור למדור השתיקה, כי השינוי אשר חיִשַבְתָ כי מתחולל פשוט מדי, ואם ידובר מבטא אחר מה ישתנה, האם אחיה שוב, האם תחיה אתה את חיי חדשים? די לךָ מן הרחובות, לךָ אל הוריךָ, אותם לא ישכנע מבטאי, הם מכירים אותו וכבר הניפו אלף מרידות. אולי שתיקה תשים בלבם פחד ההווה מן העבר והעתיד. ולמה לא תראה להם את סיפורךָ, אולי כך יתעוררו, אמר סבי כמעט משביע אותי מן המתים.

can read, his parents or his children will not read them and our children will not fall into the danger and, if he applies, we will give him all the government prizes for Arabic literature without having read a word in his books.

And of course the department heads were right, and my wife began to prophesize the future in Ladino proverbs, telling me this proverb my mother had used and though I don't remember how she said it in her language, I do remember the accent. This is the last visit of health before death, she would whisper and then begin to explain, these are death throes and not the resurrection and in the highest of the departments they already know, they've decided that it is possible to relax, they will assign job slots for correct Hebrew speech and everyone will think back to the source of his income, earning his living and his family's penury, and then regular Hebrew will return as if there had never been a plague.

4

And my heart began to give indications in my voices, saying this is my voice and this is not my voice, this is a lamed coming out of my mouth and this is an alien quf, alien to my heart. And I would slow down the pace of my thoughts, in order to think, to think about my thoughts and not only about my thoughts, but I had no time and I would scatter words to the wind like the sea salt that certainly no one is scattering into the sea. And my grandfather would speak to me, asking me in my voice whether there is any end to this story, and why is this history of mine mixed up with yours, how I have come to trouble your life, I am the generation of the desert and how have you arisen to renew me. You are the generation for which we waited so that there would be no difference between its past and the past of its teachers, because our past was already very painful and we remained in the desert for the birds of prey to eat us for your sake, so that you would not remember me, so that you would not be hurting like me and how is it that your teeth are again biting into my words and where, the districts of Jerusalem are different, there are no teahouses, there is no Tigris River flowing through the city for pity's sake, but I did not meet my death in Jerusalem, nor in the city of my birth, but rather in the desert between them, a great desert of silence. Build extensions in your heart, my grandson, he would say to me, make many departments, and lodge me in one of the hidden departments, and live in the rest of them. Or move into the silence department, because the change that you thought is occurring is too simple, and what is going to change if a different accent is spoken? Will I live again, will you live my new life? Enough of the streets for you, go to your parents, my accent will not convince them, they know it and have already raised the flags

והתחלתי מודד את שתיקותי, זאת שתיקת יום, זאת שתיקת שבוע, זאת שתיקת חודש ממוסגרת היטב בתוך קירות הבית, ואין פוצה פה, אין חלון פוצה, ואין אוויר נכנס, ואין תמונות החול מגיעות אבל אין גם קודש, ואין מחסיר, ואין מוסיף. והכול הקול שתיקותי, שתיקותי הרבה מילים הרבה מילים נשתקות, ואין אני הווה, ואין מתהווה, ואין גמר סוף הסיפור, ואין כבר טרם שהיה הסיפור, אין התחלה. ושתקתי עוד ועוד הרבה זמנים, עד שהוֹרַי היו אומרים דַּבֵּר, אם לא תדבר איך תקבל מלגה איך תמשיך בלימודיך ומה תעשה עם חייך, ואיה חיוכיך, לאן הלכו מקום מסתור, דבר, דבר בכל מבטא כי בא עלינו פחד השתיקה.

5

אין חידקל חוצה את ירושלים, והמיתו לא משתיקה את הגבולות הקמים עלינו, הגבולים המפרידים ביני לבין עצמי, אני לא שם לא כאן, לא מזרח לא מערב לא מזרח במערב לא מערב במזרח, לא קולי עכשיו ולא קולות עברי, ומה יהיה בסוף. אילם אני הולך ברחובות וגם מעט חירש, הפעם רק חזותי טורדת את השוטרים, רק זקני העבות, ועקשנותי לא להוציא מילה מפי, שוב חודש תמוז הולך גווע בתוכי, ולמרות החום אני מתעטף במעילים לכסות על חגורות הנפץ של לבי. וכך מתוך נאמנות השוטרים למשימתם אני מובא אל בית-המעצר והורי באים אחרי לראות את בנם ואנה הוא מובל.

אני שותק מול הורי, ואיך יגיבו, אני שותק מול הורי ומוסר להם את כל סיפורי שהסתרתי מהם, רומז הנה הנה כאן כתבתי עליך אמא, וכאן עליך אבא. הנה אני כותב שירי התנגדות לעברית בְּעברית, אני מרבה את רמזי, כי אין לי שפה אחרת לכתוב בה, מרוב בושה לא הורשתם לי דבר. והזמן הזה אוסר עלי שירה בזמן שהם מתגודדים עלי גדודים, מתגודדים גם עליכם, והשפה שהיתה לשפתי מצווה עלי להשתפך בה, להיות חליל ריק למשביה, עד שנפיק ביחד צליל, נהיה נאי צרוד יחדיו, נתחזה שפה אחרת, נעדרת. וזה באמת אותו סיפור שוב ושוב חוזר, כמה סיפורים יש לי, אמא אבא, כמה סיפורים יש לאדם, אותו סיפור הוא מנסה לספר כל פעם במילים מעט שונות, כל פעם מנסה לפתור מעט אחר את אותו סיפור

of many revolts. Perhaps silence will put the present's fear of the past and of the future into their hearts. And why don't you show them your story, perhaps that way they will wake up, said my grandfather from the dead, almost making me swear an oath.

And I started to measure my silences, this is a day's silence, this is a week's silence, this is a month's silence, well-framed inside the walls of my house, and no mouth opens and no window opens and the scenes of the profane do not come in, but there is nothing sacred either, and nothing is subtracted and nothing is added. And everything is the voice of my silences, my silences are many, many silenced words, and I am not being, and I am not becoming, and there is no end to the story and there is no before there was the story, there is no beginning. And I was silent for more and more time, until my parents would say speak, if you don't speak how will you get a scholarship, how will you continue your studies and what will you do with your life, and where are your smiles and where have they gone into hiding, speak, speak in any accent because the fear of silence has descended upon us.

5

There is no Tigris flowing through Jerusalem, and its murmur does not silence the borders that rise up against us, the borders that separate myself from myself. I am not here not there, not East not West, not my voice now and not the voices of my past, and what will happen in the end. I walk through the streets mute and also somewhat deaf. This time only my appearance worries the police, my thick beard and my stubbornness not to utter a word. Again the month of Tammuz is waning in me and despite the heat I wrap myself in coats to cover up the explosives belt of my heart. And thus out of the policemen's devotion to duty I am brought to the jail and my parents come after me, to see their son and where he is being taken.

I stay silent in front of my parents, and how they will respond, I stay silent in front of my parents and give them all my stories that I had concealed from them, hinting here I have written about you, Mother, and here about you, Father. Here I have written poems of opposition to Hebrew in Hebrew. I give them many more signs, because I have no other language to write in, out of so much shame you have not bequeathed me anything. And these times prohibit me poetry and force me to sing, and while they are crowding in on me, crowds and crowds, crowding in on you too, and the language that has become my language is commanding me to pour my soul in it, to be an empty flute for its gusts, until together we produce a sound, and together we would become nay – an arab flute, we would be disguised

בלתי-נפתר, והאם אין אתם מזהים כאן גם את סיפורכם, בכל זאת מעט סיפרה לי שתיקתכם. הנה עכשיו ניסיתי לכתוב את הסיפור במבטא הערבי, אך מה עלה מכך, תראו היכן אנחנו נפגשים. קחו, קראו את סיפורי, אמא אבא, קראו את כל סיפוּרַי שכך הסתרתי מכם שנים רבות, הרי גם אתם אותה גלות, אותה שתיקה אותה זרות בין לב לגוף ובין מחשבה לדיבור, אולי תדעו כיצד תיפתר העלילה.

והורי דיבור ראשון התכחשו, אמר אבא לא זה בננו ולא זה הזָקֵן אותו גידלנו, אמרה אמא ואיפה, לנו אין מבטא הזה, אמרו ביחד לפקידים לא היה לו מאין לרשת מבטא זה, לא מן המשפחה הפנימית, סבא שלו אָנְוַואר מת טרם לידתו, בן שלנו לא. דיבור שני רמזו, ואם לא תֵיטִיב שְׂאֵת נשוב הביתה ממתקן הכליאה מאוכזבי דורות, ואם תֵיטִיב שְׂאֵת ותעזוב את הסיפורים, את הסיפור הזה, את הדיבור הזה והשתיקה הזאת ותדבר עמנו בשפתנו, נשאר כאן עִמְּךָ עד שתהיה נידון לצאת לחופשי, עד שנהיה כולנו יחד נידונים.

ולא ידעו הורי כי שבתי אל לבם, לא ידעו, ולא ידעו כי פחדיהם כולם שבו עלי, לא ידעו.

אדר ב' ה'תשס"ה, ירושלים

as a different language, an absent language. And this really is the same story, recurring over and over again, how many stories do I have, Mother, Father, how many stories does a person have? Each time he tries to tell the story in different words, each time he tries to resolve the unsolved story a bit differently, and aren't you identifying your own story here, nevertheless your silence has told me a little. Look, now I've tried to write the story in the Arabic accent, but what has come of it. Look where we are meeting. Take them, read my story, Mother Father, read all my stories that I have hidden from you for many years, you too are the same exile, the same silence, the same alienation between heart and body and between thought and speech, perhaps you will know how the plot will be resolved.

And the first speech my parents uttered was a denial, Father said this is not our son and this is not the beard we have raised, said Mother, and where, we don't have this accent, they said in chorus to the officials, he had nowhere to inherit this accent from, not from the nuclear family, his grandfather Anwar died before he was born, our son wasn't there.

And the second speech they uttered was the implication that if thou doest not well we shall go home from the jail disappointed in the cycle of generations and if thou doest well and drop the stories, this story, this speech and this silence and speak to us in our language, we will stay here with you until you are judged fit to go free, until all of us together are judged.

And my parents did not know that I had returned to their heart, they did not know, and they did not know that all of their fears had returned to me, they did not know.

Adar Bet, 5765, Jerusalem

Yael Kenan
"The Same Words, Perhaps a Bit More Broken": Multiple Belongings in Almog Behar's "Ana Min al-Yahoud"

> At that time, my tongue twisted around and with the arrival of the month of Tammuz the Arabic accent got stuck in my mouth, deep down in my throat. Just like that, as I was walking down the street, the Arabic accent of grandfather Anwar of blessed memory came back to me and no matter how hard I tried to extricate it from myself and throw it away in one of the public trash cans I could not do it. (Behar 2005, 1)[1]

"Ana Min Al-Yahoud," written in Hebrew by the Jewish-Israeli writer Almog Behar, begins with a tongue twisting that disrupts the narrator's life by undermining his language. The story opens ("at that time") in the tone of a folktale, yet it remains grounded in a particular historical moment throughout. Similarly, the language is rife with echoes and layers of allusions and hints from various Jewish traditions, but it is clearly situated in contemporary Jerusalem. The story and its narrator oscillate between places, times, and languages, wrestling the accent "stuck in [his] mouth" and grappling with its origins and current state. Throughout the short story, language both constitutes and destabilizes subjecthood, enacting the fragility of identities in the historic-cultural space of Jerusalem. This space of contentious belongings serves to simultaneously perform identity and subvert it, complicating and constantly modifying what it might mean to belong and not to belong, and suggesting a space of in-between but not shying away from the danger and exigencies of such a volatile locus. In the following, I read Behar's short story as a space of multiple identities and belongings – personal, familial, ethnic, and national. These overlapping identities, and the fraught relationships between them, are enacted on various levels – on the body and in language, in the past and in the present – and generate a destabilized and indeterminate subject and language, and thus a reconsideration of the perimeters of the political.

---

[1] "בזמן ההוא התהפכה לשוני, ועם שהגיע ראש חודש תמוז נתקע לי בפה, עמוק עמוק בגרון, עמוק מן הגרון, המבטא הערבי. כך כשהייתי באמצע הליכת רחוב חזר אלי המבטא הערבי של סבא אנואר עליו השלום, וכמה שניסיתי להוציאו מתוכי ולהשליכו באחד הפחים הציבוריים ככה לא הצלחתי" (Behar 2008a, 55e).
The English translation is by Vivian Eden, with some modifications. The translation of the story can be found at: http://almogbehar.wordpress.com/english/, and references correspond to the relevant section of the story. The story was first published in the Israeli daily newspaper *Haaretz*, where it won first place in the short story competition in 2005. A year later it was translated into Arabic by Muhammad Abood and published in Egypt.

The narrator, whose name is never mentioned, tries to lose the accent which has infiltrated his physical and metaphoric tongue; his efforts are in vain, however, as every attempt to soften the hard letters and pronounce them "smoothly" – without an accent, that is, without the unacceptable accent but with the consensual, transparent one – founders. In both Hebrew and Arabic, the word for tongue refers both to the bodily organ and to language. Moreover, it is the same word in both – *lisaan* in Arabic (لسان), *lashon* in Hebrew (לשון). Thus, the crisis of identity is manifested in the body and demonstrates the significant link between body and language, as sites of marking and signification, as well as between the two languages. The Arabic accent renders the narrator a suspicious figure on the streets of Jerusalem, and policemen start "stopping me and inquiring as to my name and my identity." The narrator tries to defend himself and deploys language as an identity marker: "I would want to stop walking and pull out my identity card and point out the nationality line and tell them, as if I were revealing a secret that would absolve me of tremendous guilt: 'Ana min al yahoud, I'm a Jew'" (Behar 2005, 1).[2] Thus, the words which are supposed to clarify his identity end up blurring it even further – the words by which he states his Jewish identity are in Arabic, and they appear in the story in Hebrew characters. In trying to stabilize and prove his Jewish identity through words, the narrator loses control over language and is left with a seemingly paradoxical proclamation. This unstable marking, a kind of ironic *shibboleth*, displays an indeterminate identity and undermines the seemingly natural link between national identity and language.

The phrase *Ana min al-Yahoud* (and the story as a whole) is an act of defamiliarization (or estrangement), in Shklovsky's terms, for Hebrew and Arabic alike, as well as for the identities they seek to create. Proving his "Jewishness" translates, in the current Israeli context, to being a non-threat, and so language is perceived as a qualifier, in the identity-proclaiming phrase as well as in the search for the ID which contains the nationality clause, a potential exonerating and vindicating factor. This use of the ID is particularly ironic, as one of the few Arabic phrases many Israeli Jews know, resulting from military service in the occupied territories, is "*Jib al-huwiye*" [give me your ID]. Much as the Hebrew language escapes the narrator when he needs it most so does the other marker, the ID: "But when the policemen stopped in front of me I couldn't find any document at all that would tell them about my past and my future" (Behar 2005, 1).[3] These linguistic signs, which could have served to redeem the narrator, are revealed as

---

2 The phrase more accurately means: I'm one of the Jews, or of the Jews. In the Hebrew text, there is no translation; the Arabic words in Hebrew characters appear twice.

3 "אבל כשהשוטרים היו נעצרים מולי לא הייתה נמצאת לי ולו תעודה אחת שתספר להם על עברי ועתידי" (Behar 2008a, 56).

unstable and destabilizing; they are empty signifiers, with no stable signifieds, insisting on signifying but unable to do so.

But where does this Arabic come from? The tongue twisting in the story, the accent "stuck" in the narrator's mouth, derives from the past; the narrator's personal-familial past, namely, his grandfather Anwar (an Arab name juxtaposed with a Jewish-Hebrew honorific phrase for the dead, עליו השלום [*Alav Ha-shalom*; of blessed memory]), but also the cultural memory of the *Mizrahi* past. This is the cultural identity of Jews who lived in Arab countries (Iraq, in the case of the narrator's family, but also Morocco, Yemen, Syria, Tunisia, and others) before immigrating to Palestine (later Israel) and elsewhere. Their cultural heritage was considered incompatible with the new monolithic Jewish identity which Zionist leaders were seeking to establish, an identity based largely on their own European values and codes.[4] Likewise, as a measure for constructing the Arab as the ultimate "Other" for Jews in the Middle East, *Mizrahi* culture and much of the Arab-Jewish tradition were considered inferior.[5] As Lital Levy (2014, 27) puts it in her *Poetic Trespass: Writing Between Hebrew and Arabic in Israel/Palestine*: "Hebrew hegemony was realized through the persistent stigmatization and suppression of 'diasporic' languages." Thus, it is telling that asserting a Jewish identity in Arabic through the titular phrase "*ana min al-yahoud*" has an enigmatic and destabilizing effect, as only sixty years ago or so many Jews living in Arab countries – where Jews had lived for centuries – spoke Arabic and saw no contradiction between Arabic and their identity as Jews. Moreover, Judeo-Arabic was largely written in Hebrew letters, like the sentence in the story. The presentation of Jewish identity as inherently at odds with the Arabic language is a consequence of a historical-political process of defamiliarization, one needed perhaps especially because of the cultural and lingual proximity and affinity between Hebrew and Arabic. This process amounts to an active severing of close ties, thereby enforcing a chasm of un-belonging in order to generate a new, different belonging of Jews in Palestine.

In the story, the seemingly clear distinction between categories falls apart; language, always important in solidifying and defining the national subject through establishing an imagined historic and cultural link to the past, is here

---

4 In an effort to create a new Jewish identity, Zionism also denigrated certain Europe-based characteristics which were considered diasporic and exilic (*Galuti*) and therefore weak. The story addresses this point in suggesting that old *Ashkenazi* accents also start reemerging. However, European Jews were and still are the cultural and political elite, and therefore their situation is nonetheless different.
5 For more on this social category, see Sami Shalom Chetrit's *Intra-Jewish Conflict in Israel: White Jews, Black Jews* (2010) and Ella Shohat's "Dislocated Identities: Reflections of an Arab Jew" (1992).

responsible for unraveling the monolithic, Hebrew-speaking national subject.⁶ It does so precisely by disclosing a cultural and historic link to the past, but one deemed improper by the hegemonic strands of Zionism. In effect, language exposes the plurality of historical narratives where there was an effort – common in nation-building – to forge a homogeneous, monolingual, and single narrative. In this way, the category of the *Mizrahi*, the Arab-Jew, transgresses the binary opposition and functions as a complex identity, or, in Homi Bhabha's terms, an identity that is hybrid or unhomely.⁷ This in-between state subverts monolithic definitions of language and subject, as well as their products – personal and national identity. Calling this state "unhomely" also reveals its effect on belonging, as a complex identity can never feel quite at home in a monolithic place. Thus, both sides of the process become clearer: the solidification of the nation requires subjects who feel unquestionably at home, and therefore it excludes any indeterminate positions. Later, those same in-between identities return to reclaim their place, as the homogenous home never felt entirely whole to them, and thus its mythical status is exposed.

The use of Arabic within Hebrew creates a crevice in language's seemingly unified structure, similar to what Deleuze and Guattari term "minor literature," which they famously model on Franz Kafka. They define minor literature as "that which a minority constructs within a major language" (Deleuze and Guattari 1986, 16).⁸ While minor literature is "the problem of minorities," it is also a general issue of "how to tear a minor literature away from its own language, allowing it to challenge the language and making it follow a sober revolutionary path" (Deleuze and Guattari 1986, 19).⁹ Behar does this as a Jew writing in Hebrew, which is different from Arab writers (such as Anton Shammas, Sayed Kashua, and Salman Masalha) writing in Hebrew.¹⁰ The Arab Jew is a minority, especially in cultural terms, but a

---

6 Benedict Anderson (1983) emphasizes the role of language in the creation and solidification of national identity throughout his *Imagined Communities*, for example see pages 144–145.
7 The terms *Mizrahi* and Arab-Jew denote roughly the same social group; the differences between them indicate both generational shifts in discourse and often political preferences. For more on this, see Yehuda Shenhav's *The Arab Jews: A Postcolonial Reading of Nationalism, Religion and Ethnicity* (2006).
8 "Celle qu'une minorité fait dans une langue majeure" (Deleuze and Guattari 1989, 29).
9 "Problème des minorités [...] mais aussi pour nous tous: comment arracher à sa propre langue une littérature mineure, capable de creuser le langage, et de le faire filer suivant une ligne révolutionaire sobre?" (Deleuze and Guattari 1989, 35).
10 Shammas and Kashua are known in Israel primarily for writing in Hebrew; the former has published in both languages and is an important translator between the two, but is vastly known for his important Hebrew novel, *Arabesques*. The latter famously stated that his Arabic is not good enough to write literature. Masalha has written in both Arabic and Hebrew.

complex one – similar to Arabs, on some counts, but dissimilar on others. Minor literature is an unusual use of the central language; this use estranges it from within, as Deleuze and Guattari put it, "to be a sort of stranger *within* his own language" (Deleuze and Guattari 1986, 26).[11] This state of being an internal stranger already assumes a sense of belonging ("*within* his own language"), one which Behar's story does not abandon yet certainly complicates; the story underscores the fact that simultaneously being and not being a stranger results not only in creative uses of language, but in a veritable crisis. In that sense, while Deleuze and Guattari's term seems to channel the political and personal discomfort to artistic purposes, which perhaps reconcile the meaning and consequences of such an unhomeliness, Behar's story instead dwells upon and within this unstable space.

Spatial terms are especially significant here, as in Behar's story the narrator's dwelling place shifts as the twisting of the tongue unfolds. After the policemen release the narrator he wanders the streets of Jerusalem, "but suddenly there was no theater at the end of the street, and suddenly it wasn't Marcus Street, it was a street with an Arabic name, and the houses had gone back to being Arab" (Behar 2005, 1).[12] For Deleuze and Guattari, minor language destabilizes the seemingly natural link between language and space, rendering both unstable loci of identity construction. In Behar's story a similar deterritorialization ensues, through language. Thus, as the Arabic past peeks through the present-day Hebrew, David Marcus Street, at the heart of Jerusalem, can no longer be named for an Israeli general killed in the 1948 war; the street's old Arab name now resurfaces, as do the Arabs themselves:

> "And I would start to walk the streets of Katamon and the streets of Talbieh and the streets of Baqa and instead of seeing the wealthy Jerusalemites who had gathered there in the spacious homes, and instead of reading there on the street signs 'Kovshei Katamon' and 'Yordei Hasira,' I'd once again see the wealthy Palestinians, and they were the way they had been before the 1948 war, as if there had never been a 1948 war" (Behar 2005, 2).[13]

The narrator wanders through parts of Jerusalem where Arabs had lived before the establishment of Israel; since then, Jews have lived there, in houses known

---

11 "Être *dans* sa propre langue comme un étranger," (Deleuze and Guattari 1989, 48). Emphasis in the original.

12 "אבל פתאום לא היה שם תיאטרון בקצה הרחוב, ופתאום לא היה זה רחוב מרקוס, היה זה רחוב עם שם ערבי, והבתים היו שבים להיות ערביים" (Behar 2008a, 57).

13 "והייתי מתחיל להתהלך ברחובות קטמון וברחובות טלביה וברחובות בקעה, ובמקום לראות את עשירי ירושלים שהתכנסו שם בבתים המרווחים, ובמקום לקרוא שם את 'כובשי קטמון' ו'יורדי הסירה' בשמות הרחובות, ראיתי פתאום שוב את עשירי פלסטין, והם היו שם כמו שהיו לפני מלחמת ארבעים ושמונה, כמו לא הייתה מלחמת ארבעים ושמונה" (Behar 2008a, 56).

in Hebrew as "Arab houses," a term referring to their signature architecture – a contemporary status symbol – and not to their previous residents. Moreover, the current street names are not only Hebrew but specifically related to Zionist history, as naming and renaming is a common and effective national practice. Levy (2014, 49–50) notes that "this policy of renaming obscured the recent Palestinian Arab presence and its Arabic-encoded history, manufacturing an unbroken continuity between biblical antiquity and the Israeli present," a process she terms "a translational cartography" and which is reversed by the story's tongue twisting. If the street names and inhabitants of the present are Hebrew-Zionist, the neighborhoods – Katamon, Talbiya, and Baqa – are known to this day by their Arab names.[14] Thus, even within the homogeneous view of Jerusalem, Arab names persist, as indelible remnants or traces that cannot be entirely erased from the city. Destabilizing the territory metaphorically shakes the ground the narrator stands upon. However, the story demonstrates that this spatial transformation is not merely metaphoric but also has consequences in the actual world. Language shapes the world in a highly concrete way, and when the Arabic phrase marks and demarcates the Jewish subject, it undermines the exclusivity of the link between Hebrew and the Jewish-Zionist identity and presence in Jerusalem, a city revealed as more of an archeological barrow than a monolithic space. This stems from the presence of the past in the present space, turning it into a Bakhtinian chronotope of sorts.

The question of language is also a question of borders, as it is used to define and delimit identities and consequently to establish political facts. Renaming streets and neighborhoods is a clear example of this, still taking place in Jerusalem nowadays.[15] Arabic therefore undermines the borders of Hebrew and questions its ability not only to mark but also to constitute an exclusively Jewish subject in this territory. This is especially resonant in the mention of 1948, the year Israel was established and thereby sought to solidify such an exclusivity. The story is concerned with setting borders and crossing them (out?), and with borders as confinements, "that rise up against us, the borders that separate myself from myself" (Behar 2005, 5).[16] Minor language is itself a hybrid category: it belongs to both languages, and to neither. It is not exactly Hebrew, nor exactly

---

14 The neighborhoods have official Hebrew names – Gonen, Komemiyut, and Ge'ulim, respectively – but these are rarely used, and many Jerusalemites do not even know them.
15 So, for example, the Jerusalem tram system labels the station in Sheikh Jarrah as "Shim'on ha-Tzadik" [Simon the Just], in Hebrew, a reference to a Jewish gravesite related to two Second Temple figures and to a contemporary Jewish settlement, and not to the Palestinian village in east Jerusalem.
16 "הגבולות הקמים עלינו, הגבולים המפרידים ביני לבין עצמי" (Behar 2008a, 63).

Arabic; rather, it is foreign to both, analogous to the narrator's feeling that he does not comfortably belong in either region of Jerusalem. He is a stranger in his own language, in his identity, and in the space where he resides, much as Bhabha (1994, 3) explains that minorities are "estranged unto themselves." The narrator, himself a poet, addresses the impossibility and necessity of using this split language: "Here I have written poems of opposition to Hebrew in Hebrew. I give them many more signs, because I have no other language to write in" (Behar 2005, 5).[17] This is similar to what Deleuze and Guattari (1986, 16) attribute to Kafka: "the impossibility of not writing, the impossibility of writing in German, the impossibility of writing otherwise."[18] The important historical difference, of course, is that Kafka, as a Jew in Prague in the early twentieth century, was a national and ethnic minority. Behar's use of language is somewhat different, as he and his narrator occupy a different complex position, that of belonging to a minority group within the political Jewish majority in Israel.[19]

The tongue twisting does not remain confined to the narrator. As it begins to affect the city streets it also spreads to other people and other accents. First is the narrator's spouse, who "was infected by my transformation and her lips connected to a jumble of her father's Yemenite Arabic accent and her mother's Istambouli Ladino accent." The strangeness proliferates and affects others, until "a small plague was spreading [...] and the old accents that were hoped to have vanished are coming out again." The change has social and political consequences, demonstrating the collective aspect which Deleuze and Guattari see in minor literature. In the specific context of Zionism, the process amounts to "symbolically transforming native speakers back into immigrants (and thus reversing the Zionist narrative)" (Levy 2014, 269–270). In the contemporary Israeli landscape, this often translates into terms of security risks, as described at the beginning of the story, and so security authorities are worried: "there is already concern that the country will be filled with Arabs, many, many Arabs" (Behar

---

17 "הנה אני כותב שירי התנגדות לעברית בעברית, אני מרבה את רמזי, כי אין לי שפה אחרת לכתוב בה" (Behar 2008a, 63). One might think of this in terms of Adrienne Rich's well-known formulation: "this is the oppressor language / yet I need it to talk to you"; however, in this context the lines and affiliations between oppressed and oppressors are complex and murky.
18 "Impossibilité de ne pas écrire, impossibilité d'écrire en allemand, impossibilité d'écrire autrement" (Deleuze and Guattari 1989, 29).
19 Chana Kronfeld complicates Deleuze and Guattari's analysis of Kafka on this point, among others, noting their disregard of his complex relation to Yiddish and Hebrew. See Kronfeld's *On the Margins of Modernism: Decentering Literary Dynamics* (1996), pages 10–11.

2005, 3).[20] The central fear is that the change in language will generate political and demographic shifts, and effectuate a sort of linguistic right of return. This is the same fear Prime Minister Netanyahu sought to fan when he infamously declared, on the day of the 2015 Israeli election, that Arab voters were "moving toward the polls in droves." In Behar's story, the instability of language exposes the instability of identity, or, rather, the threat which the national establishment sees in "forbidden" identities reclaiming their sense of belonging to a place, their insisting that the place is more diverse and multifarious.

The spreading of accents and languages demonstrates not just the vicissitudes of identity but also the inherent tension – crucial to the concept of the political – between individual and collective. The Jewish identity the narrator wishes to solidify early in the story is both a personal and a national one, and so he proclaims: "*Ana min al-Yahoud*," I am one of the Jews, announcing not only the group but the "I" within it. Deleuze and Guattari (1986, 18) emphasize the collective and insist that there is no subject, arguing instead that Kafka rejects individual acts in favor of "a collective multiplicity": "there isn't a subject; *there are only collective assemblages of enunciation.*" In so doing, however, they neglect to acknowledge the individual aspect of the political. Indeed, they see the political as an exclusively collective endeavor, whereas in Behar's story the political exists at the interstices of the collective and the individual. Deleuze and Guattari's focus on language as a collective mechanism, and their consequent de-emphasis of the subject, is a reaction to romanticism, yet, because they discuss identity, this focus remains incomplete, for undecidable language constitutes an undecidable subject – split and in-between, a "minor" subject.

In Behar's story the narrator's problem is precisely that he is both part of a group – or, rather, multiple seemingly incongruent groups – and an individual subject. These identities are supposed to be compatible and mutually constituent, but are revealed to be at odds. It is therefore impossible to read the story without or outside of the subject, who, in Louis Althusser's terms, is a product of ideology. For Althusser (1971, 170), ideology and the subject are intertwined, and "there is no ideology except by the subject and for subjects.".[21] The subject

---

20 "תוך כדי דיבורה אלי והמלצתה לי לחדול התחילה נדבקת משינויי ובשפתיה התקשרו בערבוביה המבטא התימני של ערבית אביה והמבטא האיסטמבולי של ספניוליה אמה" (59–60) ,(Behar 2008a); "שכבר מתפשטת מגיפה קטנה [...] יוצאים המבטאים הישנים שמקווה היה כי נעלמו"; "כבר חוששים כי תימלא הארץ ערבים" (Behar 2008a, 60). For more on the security discourse in contemporary nationalism, see, among others, Judith Butler's *Precarious Life: The Powers of Mourning and Violence* (2004), pages 42–45, and Jasbir K. Puar's *Terrorist Assemblages: Homonationalism in Queer Times* (2007).
21 "Il n'est d'idéologie que par le sujet et pour des sujets" (Althusser 1976, 109). Like the significance of language for the national project, it likewise partakes in Althusser's ideology, as he

enables ideology and activates it; ideology is directed at the subject. This is the basic premise of Althusser's argument, along with ideology's transparency and the subject's being always already a subject. In Althusser (1971, 174), the paradigmatic interpellation occurs when the individual turns around when called (by the police, for example) and thereby becomes a subject, that is, when the individual acknowledges her or his own pre-existing subjectivity.[22] This is similar to when Behar's narrator is required to prove his identity before the policemen. In both cases, this interpellation is representative of other forms of interpellation, institutionalized and internalized alike. However, the interpellation described in the story is an ironic one: the narrator is eager to prove his identity, and so portrays the good subject adhering to the interpellation, yet he fails and cannot properly prove said identity.

The subject's failure stems, perhaps, from his belonging to multiple types of collectives – in this case, familial and national – and the relationship between them being problematic. The story as a whole is narrated in the first person, and the narrator functions as both an individual and a national subject. Moreover, one could say that the story draws attention to the subject's dual role as both an individual and a part of a nation, and problematizes this link. The rift in national identity is created by the familial one, a remnant of the personal past which was erased from the national past and present. With the spectral voice of the dead grandfather once again being heard in the streets of Jerusalem, the Israeli space is destabilized by the Arab past in the form of the personal past. That is, the no-longer-silenced voice is not only a manifestation of a political situation; it is also the return of the personal into the national. In other words, Behar's story complicates not just Deleuze and Guattari's emphasis on the collective but also Althusser's emphasis on the subject: in short, it demonstrates why these notions are interconnected and cannot be read independently. Subjects participate in collectives, and collectives are intermingled, complex and imbricated in one another. Against the will of the national ideology and its major language, the subject's belonging is never whole, simple, and homogeneous; instead, it is problematic, porous, and unstable, with multiple remnants leaving their mark on her or him. This minor subject therefore uses minor language in multifarious ways, in response to the crevices she or he identifies.

---

proclaims: "[the subject] must therefore *inscribe* his own ideas as a free subject in the actions of his material practice" (Althusser 1971, 168, my emphasis).

22 The question of the subject's gendering, and even state as human or figure (her/his vs. its) is important and vexing in philosophical discourse and in Marxism in particular, but it goes beyond the scope of this article.

This instability leads to a hybrid language and subject, which are at the heart of Behar's story and which render monolithic notions of identity insufficient and even obsolete. This explains the failure of the attempt to replace the Jewish-Hebrew identity with an Arab one. The narrator tries his luck among the Arabs of Jerusalem but there, too, he is deemed suspicious: "I do not succeed in mingling with them because all I have at my disposal is Hebrew with an Arabic accent and my Arabic, which doesn't come from my home but from the army, is suddenly mute, strangled from my throat" (Behar 2005, 2).[23] Mere replacement is impossible, because identity is, by definition, indeterminate. Levy (2014, 278) explains this in terms of language, noting that the narrator's "Hebrew is too Arabic, his Arabic is too mute," but surely this is true for identity as well. Another example of this in-between status is the fact that the Arabic accent sticks to the narrator's throat specifically at the beginning of the month of *Tammuz* – a word that was originally the name of a Sumerian god and which is used in both the Jewish and Arab calendars. The identities, which were made to seem irrevocably disparate, are in fact intermingled. The policemen, for instance, are surprised to discover that the narrator is "circumcised, he really is a Jew, this Arab, and the other one would say, an Arab is also circumcised, and explosive belts don't care about circumcision" (Behar 2005, 1).[24] The distinction between Jew and Arab unravels in the body as well, as both are circumcised. Moreover, in Hebrew the word for circumcision is the same as for "word," מילה [*mila*]; the double meaning is reminiscent of the function of *lashon/lisaan* as both a system of signs and a body part. The hegemonic European Zionism was perhaps well aware of this proximity and consequently created the distinction, to avoid the threat of similarity, as "the words were almost the same words, perhaps a bit more broken" (Behar 2005, 3).[25]

Thus, the indeterminacy creates not an absolute fracture but rather an ongoing and diffuse one, leading to an aporetic subject, lodged between identities, belonging to both and to neither. As seen, both language and the subject turn out to be unstable, though not completely dismantled; instead, they are liminal, or, as Bhabha (1994, 12) would label them, "border conditions." This term seems particularly apt, as both the story and the region Israel/Palestine are constantly preoccupied with borders, even as they refuse to set them.

---

23 "ואיני מצליח להתערות ביניהם, כי לרשותי עומדת רק העברית במבטאה הערבי, ואילו הערבית שלי, שלא באה לי מן הבית אלא מן הצבא, פתאום הערבית שלי אילמת" (Behar 2008a, 58).
Arabs living in contemporary Jerusalem, whom the narrator presumably encounters, are Palestinians living under Israeli occupation, adding yet another complex category to the mix.
24 "הוא נימול, הוא באמת יהודי הערבי הזה, ושני היה אומר, גם ערבי נימול, וחגורות הנפץ אינן מעניין המילה" (Behar 2008a, 57).
25 "היו המלים כמעט אותן מלים, אולי מעט יותר שבורות" (Behar 2008a, 61).

The story takes this instability a step further; despite the dependence of both the subject and the text itself on language, the story opts for silence, which functions as another in-between category. When the dead grandfather's voice begins seeping through the Hebrew it disrupts not only the hegemonic Hebrew but also silence: "And the streets of Jerusalem that had grown accustomed to my silence, to our silence, had a very hard time with the speech, and would silence the voice, gradually telling it careful, telling me careful, telling me I am alien telling me my silences are enough" (Behar 2005, 3).[26] The major language, or ideology, seeks to silence the other, minor voice which refuses to be a good subject and thereby exposes ideology as such. In a poem depicting a similar moment of interpellation, Behar notes that: "My Arabic is mute / Strangled in the throat / cursing itself / without uttering a word."[27] The Jewish-Arab voice, upon which silence was once imposed, now appropriates such silence and renders it into an instrument of struggle, thus changing its function. While silence may seem to be a somewhat passive form of resistance, its indeterminacy makes it a suitable expression of the hybrid identity. So, whereas Deleuze and Guattari (1986, 26) regard the revolution of minor literature in terms of loud expression ("To use syntax in order to cry, to give a syntax to the cry"[28]), Behar's story presents a more nuanced position, one perhaps more practical and functional.[29] Moreover, this struggle through silence may be linked to its origin – within the home and familial space. Thus, in the poem Arabic hides "Behind the shutters of Hebrew," "Running around between rooms / And the neighbors' porches," and then "she settles in the living room." As Levy explains, for many Arab-Jews the intimate language of home was often Arabic (264), and so it is in this poem. Arabic's struggle, originating in the space of home yet never allowed to be at home anywhere, is, for Behar, deeply personal and entirely political.

Choosing silence as a paradoxical means of communication in the story is a complex form both of a minor language and of constituting a subject. Furthermore, silence is concomitant with speech, and so heightens its impossibility and

---

26 "ורחובות ירושלים שהתרגלו לשתיקתי, לשתיקתנו, התקשו מאוד מאוד מול הדיבור, והיו משקיטים את הקול [...] אומרים לי די לך בשתיקתך" (Behar 2008a, 59).
27 "הערבית שלי אילמת \ חנוקה מן הגרון \ מקללת את עצמה \ בלי להוציא מילה" (Behar 2008b, 15).
28 "Se servir de la syntax pour crier, donner au cri une syntax" (Deleuze and Guattari 1989, 48). "Cry out" is perhaps a more accurate English rendering.
29 The opposed approaches here are demonstrated by both texts' use of the metaphor of the desert: "la langue dans le désert" for Deleuze and Guattari (1986, 48); "a great desert of silence" for Behar (2013, 4).

undecidability. Through silence, the story operates from within the impasse rather than trying to surpass it. In an impossible (and therefore silent) conversation, the dead grandfather suggests to the narrator that "Perhaps silence will put the present's fear of the past and of the future into their hearts," but he immediately adds: "And why don't you show them your story" (Behar 2005, 4).[30] The grandfather offers a path of both silence and words, another impossibility and aporia. The narrator thus begins to measure his silences and arrives at "many silenced words." His muteness is perceived as a threat (as were his previous "improper" words) and he is arrested. While in custody he uses his grandfather's paradoxical method: "I stay silent in front of my parents and give them all my stories that I had concealed from them" (Behar 2005, 5).[31] He is silent yet at the same time tells the story, a silent story, and so silence becomes a sort of minor language which opens impossible and inevitable cracks of otherness within language. In other words, silence constitutes a profoundly split subject, one that oscillates not only between words and the lack thereof, but also between belonging to a language and un-belonging.[32]

The story ends without offering any resolution or deliverance, as language and subject remain aporetic. The narrator's parents continue to misunderstand him and offer only two, detrimental choices: either letting go of the past and leaving the actual prison while remaining in a prison of identity, or freeing language but remaining in the actual prison. This suggests that there are no clear-cut solutions, no unambiguous denouement. However, this does not result in a paralyzing impasse; rather, it points to the necessity of rethinking language and identity from within silence, through those formerly silenced, in a way that affords space for hybrid subjects and languages. To modify Bhabha's formulation, this could be a way not only to bring about "a more transnational and translational sense of hybridity of imagined communities" (Bhabha 1994, 5), but also to make language itself transnational and translational through silence. In this way, the fragmentary structure of subjectivity and of language may become an instrument of freedom rather than of imprisonment.

In certain later poems, Behar points to a few such possibilities, which neither gloss over nor resolve the previous silence and history, but instead offer potential political and lingual steps. If "my Arabic" has been "mute" or muted, then in

---

30 "אולי שתיקה תשים בליבם פחד ההווה מן העבר והעתיד"; "ולמה לא תראה להם את סיפורך" (Behar 2008a, 62).
31 "אני שותק מול הורי ומוסר להם את כל סיפורי שהסתרתי מהם" (Behar 2008a, 63).
32 Levy here evokes Derrida's formulation in *Monolingualism of the Other*, according to which "deprived of *all* language" one becomes both monolingual and aphasic, and thus "thrown into absolute translation" (quoted in Levy 2014, 278). Derrida, I think, still operates from within language, though to say that Behar is not is, of course, once again, a paradox.

a poem entitled "Our History" he suggests that nothing will change "until we might put an end / to the family's silence, until we teach our children to speak / Arabic" (Behar 2008, 56–57).[33] Silence, ambiguous as it is, may be a positive starting point of reclaiming, but it cannot be the end of a struggle. A parallel move is to employ the affinity between Hebrew and Arabic and to re-introduce language as plural; not to ignore the existing tensions by imagining a utopia, but rather to stay grounded within a place, using two languages at once. In a poem in his most recent book, *Poems for Prisoners* (2016), Behar laments the forgetting of his language, and does so through mixing Hebrew and Arabic. Each line is written half in Arabic and half in Hebrew, with the sounds and meanings echoing each other and mingling to create a bilingual poem: "نسيت لساني, אל הנשיה הטלתיה \ ولا أعرف איך נערפה ממני" (nasiytu lisaani, el ha-neshiya hitaltiha \ walaa aʕref eich ne'ʕerfa mimeni). This roughly translates to: "I forgot my tongue, threw it to oblivion / and I don't know how it was severed from me." The poem not only takes advantage of the similarities between Hebrew and Arabic and plays with them; it enacts an old-new dialogue between them, as it is impossible to read the poem without knowing both. Arabic and Hebrew are shown to be mutually and inextricably bound, tied to each other, translating each other, disrupting each other but also constituting one another in tandem.[34] Behar operates within the vicissitudes of language, of languages, dwelling in the doubleness, the space of belonging and un-belonging, rather than pushing it aside. Thus, the tongue twisting imagined in "Ana Min al-Yahoud" comes to fruition in this poem, evoking the familial ties between languages of the past and the present, of personal and public spaces, to generate a personal politics in which our children and our poems speak both Hebrew and Arabic.

References

Althusser, Louis. "Ideology and Ideological State Apparatuses." *Lenin and Philosophy, and Other Essays*. Transl. Ben Brewster. New York and London: Monthly Review Press, 1971. 127–188.
Althusser, Louis. "Idéologie et appareils idéologiques d'Etat." *Positions*. Paris: Éditions Sociales, 1976. 67–126.

---

33 My translation.
34 Complementing this in a way, Behar is part of a group instituting a new academic program at Ben-Gurion University in the Negev and Tel-Aviv University, which will be devoted to Arab-Jewish culture.

Anderson, Benedict. *Imagined Communities: Reflections on the Origins and Spread of Nationalism*. London: Verso, 1983.
Behar, Almog. "Ana Min al-Yahoud – I'm One of the Jews." Transl. Vivian Eden. 2005. *Kore ve-Kotev* [*Reading and Writing*] – *Almog Behar's blog*. http://almogbehar.wordpress.com/english/. (December 4, 2013).
Behar, Almog. "Ana Min al-Yahoud." *Ana Min al-Yahoud*. Tel-Aviv: Bavel Publishing, 2008a. 55–64.
Behar, Almog. "My Arabic Is Mute." *Tsima'on Be'erot* [Wells' Thirst]. Tel-Aviv: Am-Oved, 2008b. 15–16.
Behar, Almog. "My Arabic Is Mute." Transl. Dimi Reider. *Kore ve-Kotev* [*Reading and Writing*] – *Almog Behar's blog*. http://almogbehar.wordpress.com/english/. (December 4, 2013).
Behar, Almog. "Our History." *Khut moshekh min ha-lashon* [A Thread Drawing from the Tongue]. Tel-Aviv: Am Oved, 2009. 56–57.
Behar, Almog. (Untitled). *Shirim le-asirey batei ha-sohar*. Indibook (online self-publication), 2016. 54–55.
Bhabha, Homi K. "Introduction." *The Location of Culture*. London and New York: Routledge, 1994. 1–19.
Butler, Judith. *Precarious Life: The Powers of Mourning and Violence*. New York: Verso, 2004.
Chetrit, Sami Shalom. *Intra-Jewish Conflict in Israel: White Jews, Black Jews*. London: Routledge, 2010.
Deleuze, Gilles, and Félix Guattari. *Kafka: Toward a Minor Literature*. Transl. Dana Polan. Minneapolis: University of Minnesota Press, 1986.
Deleuze, Gilles, and Félix Guattari. *Kafka: Pour une littérature mineure*. Paris: Les Éditions de Minuit, 1989 (1975).
Kronfeld, Chana. *On the Margins of Modernism: Decentering Literary Dynamics*. Berkeley: University of California Press, 1996.
Levy, Lital. *Poetic Trespass: Writing Between Hebrew and Arabic in Israel Palestine*. Princeton: Princeton UP, 2014.
Puar, Jasbir K. *Terrorist Assemblages: Homonationalism in Queer Times*. Durham: Duke UP, 2007.
Shenhav, Yehuda. *The Arab Jews: A Postcolonial Reading of Nationalism, Religion and Ethnicity*. Stanford: Stanford UP, 2006.
Shohat, Ella. "Dislocated Identities: Reflections of an Arab Jew." *Movement Research: Performance Journal* 5 (1992): 8.

Part II

Ruth Ginsburg
French Scholem, or: Scholem's Purloined Letter

Mother-tongue father-tongue: opposite directions

In a note entitled *Sprache* [Language], written around 1970, Gershom Scholem writes:

> In 1923 I went to Palestine, then called by us, in translation of the Hebrew term, The Land of Israel. Till about 1930 I kept in touch with my mother tongue. In 1933, I lost contact with it and did not experience the period of the German language that was initiated by Hitler. So am I, when here and there I wrote German again, an old-fashioned author, still writing the German of my youth and then suddenly struck dumb when it transpires that words, images, and associations that had meaning, dignity, and connectedness have become *taboo*, and cannot be used anymore, because they were ridden to death by the 3 Riders, at least for this generation whom this word fits.
>
> But I had the same experience in Hebrew, only in the opposite direction. The language that we have developed in Israel is no longer the language that we attempted to learn from the old books 50 years ago, when a strange tempting gleam (I would almost say, the gleam of revelation) came toward us from there. What has happened in the meantime? What constitutes the process of the re-birth of Hebrew? It is constituted of the wandering of the old language – the language burdened with the heaviest load of religious associations in world history – from the book into the language of blubbering children [*die Sprache lallender Kinder*].[1]

Like most of Scholem's personal notes, diary entries, and letters, this melancholy note was composed in German. Instead of *Sprache*, it could well be entitled "A Lamentation on the Loss of Language." It is also a valediction to childhood and to the exciting yet innocent illusions of youth. Mourning their loss and evaporation, the writer uses language to bemoan his deprivation of them. Both languages that Scholem believed to be his – one (German) by right of birth and education, the other (Hebrew) by appropriation and mythic-historical ties – failed him due

---

[1] National Library, Jerusalem, Gershom Scholem Archive, Arc 4, 1599/277-I/56. On the same page Scholem refers to S. Y. Agnon's *A Guest for the Night*, which "has recently appeared" (in translation?), a reference that helps date the note to around that year (1970). In an article in the literary supplement of the daily *Ha'aretz* (31 July 2015), "I laugh when I think of the progress of our language and cry when I think of the price we paid for it" [in Hebrew], David Ohana dates the note to 1964. Unless otherwise noted, all translations from German, French, and Hebrew into English are mine.

to historical processes beyond his control. To gauge the full meaning of this late expression of the writer-scholar's despair vis-à-vis history and the collapse of his linguistic dream(s), this note deserves closer scrutiny in the language in which it was written.

The text bears the title *Sprache* [Language] – language in general and in the singular – yet it speaks of two particular, discrete languages, devoting a paragraph to each. The only place in the text where the two languages intersect is its first sentence. There, the territory which is the cause of the inner turmoil is named by a translated pronoun that slips between languages: Palästina – The Land of Israel. From the perspective of 1970 Israel, *das Land Israel* is presented as a translation of the Hebrew term of a time past [*damals*, then]. Strikingly, when referring to the Hebrew term for the Land, Scholem uses the word *Terminus* [*in Übersetzung des hebräischen Terminus*], a conspicuously non-Germanic word, most often used in the combination *Terminus technicus*, and thus voids the name of its affective, historical load. It is a neutral geographical-cartographical designation[2] and is rendered in a double translation: the German translating the Hebrew translating the German. German and Hebrew meet and intermingle in a name that no longer functionally exists.[3]

But the text opens with a date, 1923, a date that marks the writer's migration from Germany to Palestine and tells the story of his relations with both *his* languages. He had "contact" with his mother tongue till the early 1930s and then, following the language's appropriation by the Nazis, he lost touch with it – or so he claims.[4] After the war, upon resuming contact with his mother tongue, he discovered that it was no longer one which he could use naturally or un-self-consciously. Although he did not personally experience the language's years of abuse (there is a definite tone of apology here), he and German had become estranged. Contaminated by Hitlerism, the old words that had carried meaning for him could no longer be used; their purity gone, they were now taboo. This contamination of the language has been lamented by many, in particular by those who, like Scholem, continued to write in German during and after World War II.[5] And yet

---

2 It also refers back to the mandatory official name of the territory, in Hebrew: פלשתינה (א"י)
3 After 1967, it has of course been re-introduced into politico-religious discourse, first by the settlers of the Occupied Territories, and since then has gradually infiltrated all political Hebrew discourse. So, too, has the term "Palestine," as the target-land of the Palestinian Arabs.
4 This is of course not quite correct, as he had continued writing in German throughout that period.
5 Because of Scholem's special relationship with Hannah Arendt, her interview of 1964 entitled "Was bleibt? Es bleibt die Muttersprache" [What Remains? It is the mother tongue] should be mentioned in this context.

the formulations he uses to apologize for writing the kind of German he *does* write merit attention. Scholem presents himself as the "old-fashioned" gentleman who has been caught unawares [*plötzlich betroffen*] by the younger generation's prohibitions on language use, prohibitions which had somehow escaped him.

His two languages are the "same" [*dasselbe*] but "opposite" [*entgegengesetzt*]. If the story of his German is the story of his moving away, geographically and temporally, from his mother (tongue), the story of his Hebrew, which proceeds in the opposite direction [*entgegengesetzten Richtung*], is the story of the old language straying away from him and from itself. It is the move out of The Book and into the streets, into the language of mumbling children [*die Wanderung der alten Sprache [...] aus dem Buch in die Sprache lallender Kinder*]. In what sense is this an opposite direction? After all, here too there is a new fallen language, one emptied of old meanings that has betrayed its speaker and itself. Yet new German is fighting the profanation, whereas the New Hebrew is celebrating it. In whichever direction he looks the bereft Scholem is left with no language that is properly *his*.

Yet probably the most interesting formulation regarding the state of the two languages concerns their characterization: old German has become *taboo* – a term semantically associated with the sacred – whereas old Hebrew has become infantile, or drunken babble, something associated with the most secularly profane; that which must not be spoken, in German, is opposed to that which is uttered uncontrollably, in Hebrew.

The verb *lallen*, which Scholem chooses to describe Modern Hebrew speech, means to babble, or to mumble (when referring to drunkards). As its onomatopoeic sound (*la-la-la*) reveals, it is used to describe baby talk, referring both to pre-linguistic mother-infant communication and to the impure pronunciation of inebriation. Interestingly yet unsurprisingly, *lallen* has a history in German-Jewish language relations. Like the notorious *mauscheln*, *lallen* was used to refer to Yiddish and to the peculiar, ludicrous pronunciation thought typical of Jews when speaking German.[6] It was associated with the impurity of a language considered to be the mother tongue [*mamme-losh'n*] of the Jews. In short, Hebrew had deteriorated into a mother tongue.

Tabu and *lallen*: both terms belong to the semantic field of pure/impure, yet originate from different perspectives, or "directions." Taboo stems from the untouchable sacred; *lallen* stems from the lowest, not-yet-civilized or already-not civilized, the indiscriminately touched. Both are the deed of the young. Yet one is effected by a young generation determined to obliterate a hideous, human linguistic past, whereas the other is done thoughtlessly, by strong-headed

---

6 For further details see Yildiz (2012, 51).

infants ignorant of a glorious language of past Revelation. The first seeks to save its mother tongue and thereby restore its earlier cultural value and dignity. The second, inadvertently, is creating an ignoble one. Although the riders of the apocalypse rode certain German words to death [*Worte* [...] *in der Sprache der 3 Reiter zu Tode geritten worden sind*], the new generation is reviving it by rendering them taboo. The young Hebrew generation is riding towards disaster precisely by riding the old words, divesting them of their sacredness. Children thus rob fathers of their tongue. Orphaned of language, the old Scholem is left with none he could claim his own. No mother tongue, but no Word of the Fathers, either.

But was the old Hebrew of the Fathers, that book-mediated language that fifty years earlier Scholem had worked so hard to appropriate from the "old books" [... *die Sprache, die wir vor 50 Jahren aus den alten Büchern zu lernen unternahmen*], as benign as memory would have it? In a defiant gesture of revolt against the old of those days, Scholem, as one of a young generation [*wir*] whose fathers had betrayed the language of *their* fathers, immersed himself in the study of the language that had carried the promise of Revelation. Yet he seems to sense that there may have been something deceptive about it, something beckoning him with a strangely seductive glitter [*merkwürdig verführerischer Glanz*]. The terms describing the attraction that Hebrew exerted on the young are taken from the field of seduction; it is reminiscent of children's fairy tales about a witch's hut in a dark forest. The light emanating from language came invitingly towards them, promising accommodation; the German *entgegenkam* that the text uses to describe the encounter does not simply mean "coming towards" but includes the gesture of invitation. Into what house was the Hebrew language inviting them? The light, so the mournful note implies, has failed to provide a home. Hebrew has become un-homely [*unheimlich*]. Or, rather, Scholem has become linguistically homeless.

Long before this lamentation of 1970, the young Scholem was already distressed and wary because of the process Hebrew was undergoing. Yet it was not so much the *lallen* that was now bothering him; rather, it was the blind violation of a taboo of the sacred that frightened him. His *Bekenntnis über unsere Sprache* testifies to this anxiety and concern.

Ambivalent robbery/stealing

Gershom Scholem was twice robbed of his languages: first by history, then by translation. The first robbery he lamented bitterly; the second he may have approved, if asked. The first section of this essay has focused on the historical robbery, the following primarily addresses the second, translational one. Indeed, the latter robbery involves the pillage, by one language, of certain possessions of another, specifically the robbing of semantic property through the agency of translation. This should not be considered an ordinary crime, however, but rather a beneficent act achieved via a wrongful deed, a kind of "redemption through sin" [מצווה הבאה בעבירה]'. "Redemption" can be taken quite literally, since translation concerns redeeming from oblivion, or at least, an act of resuscitation.

The redeemed text of my discussion is Scholem's *Bekenntnis*, which he wrote, in German, in Palestine in 1926; it was included in a "Gift" [*Gabe*] presented to Franz Rosenzweig on his fortieth birthday. In this text Scholem expresses his doubts and fears about the looming, disastrous consequences of an inevitable but thoughtless secularization of Hebrew, which he considered a necessary outcome of the Zionist enterprise. Written in a quasi-biblical, often quite antiquated German abounding in vivid metaphors, its manifesto-like formulations convey the acutely troubled state of mind of someone in crisis. Apprehension, warning, and hesitant hope are often expressed in ambiguous, ambivalent wording. Though written in 1926, it has reached its present fame and influence due to translation. Yet it seems that it was not merely translation that brought it fame; in fact, it was a particular kind of translation, one that has led to a specific reading and interpretation that made possible its unusual ubiquity *at a particular historical moment*, which is *now*. Translations spread a veil between the original text and its translation, through which a slightly distorted image is reflected; it is precisely this distortion that helps lead the work into its age of fame, which is ripe to receive it. This is because translations are the children of that ripe age. Fitting into the atmosphere of *now*, translation of the *Bekenntnis* has impressed one kind of reading, and suppressed possible alternative readings which would have afforded greater attentions to the original German and its connotations and associations. Many readers and critics of the document have discussed Scholem's text as if it were written in Hebrew, yet it was not. Reading the essay in *German as German* should have enabled a more balanced reading, one allowing rays of hope to filter through the text's looming apocalyptic darkness.

Scholem's text has become a celebrity of sorts in German-Jewish and Hebrew literature and history studies. Indeed, Elad Lapidot (2013, 284) has written that it "has not only become canonical, but poses a kind of *Urtext* of the critique of the resurrected Hebrew, which Jacques Derrida named a 'prophecy.'" Prophetic, canonical Urtext – no less. At the same time, this document of ancestral authority has been celebrated as a text returned from the dead. Thus, Gil Anijar (2002, 191) introduces his own translation of the *Bekenntnis* in the following uncanny Derridean eulogy:

> This letter has no testamentary character, though it was found after Scholem's death, in his papers, in 1985. Here it is, nonetheless, arriving and returning to us, speaking to us *after* the death of its signatory, and something in it henceforth resonates like the voice of a ghost [*fantôme*]. [...] One has at times the impression that a *revenant* proclaims to us the terrifying return of a ghost.

Hallowed in mystique, Scholem as ghost and prophet has become a focus of critical buzz, with his text serving as ur-proof in current Zionist/Post-Zionist controversy, where its political import is paramount. An *unheimliche* ghostly apparition, the letter, which is not quite a letter, which was indeed found though never really lost, finds us as a belated, agitated audience of attentive addressees. Yet, we, the majority of us to whom this missive has returned, have never truly read *it*. We have come to know it primarily through translation. The acclaim that has greeted its renderings in Hebrew, French, and English (which now boasts five translations) seems to confirm Walter Benjamin's observation about the role of translation in the *Fortleben* [afterlife] of texts:

> Translations that are more than transmissions of subject matter come into being when in the course of its survival a work has reached its age of fame. [...] The life of the original attains its ever-renewed latest and most abundant flowering. (Benjamin 1997 [1916], 153–154)

We seem, indeed, to be "the age of fame" of Scholem's *Bekenntnis*.[7]

In modern translation studies it has become cliché to stress that translations are never innocent, that is, that translators have agendas, conscious or unconscious. This is by no means an ethical judgment; rather, it highlights the reality that translational decisions are not always purely linguistic, but can instead involve cultural-political considerations, conventional and/or personal. And since translation inevitably involves renunciation, or decisions that cannot help but relinquish double-meanings and ambiguities of the original, the *untranslated* meaning, *the left-out*, is at least as important as the meaning selected for translation. The two Hebrew translations of Scholem's title offer a case in point. "Bekenntnis" means both "confession" and "declaration of faith" (credo). English and French echo the same ambiguity; Hebrew has no parallel term, and thus the translators had to choose. The two Hebrew translators made their respective opposing decisions, each suppressing – necessarily – one aspect of the original ambiguity: the first, Broide (1985), translated it as *Vidu'i* [confession]; the second,

---

[7] On the reception of Scholem's *Bekenntnis* in present-day Israel see my forthcoming essay "A Text and Its Vicissitudes: Gershom Scholem between Confession and Credo" (in Hebrew, forthcoming 2018).

Huss (1989), rendered it *Hats'harat Emunim* [declaration of faith, allegiance]. The starkly dissimilar titles indicate only too clearly that translation means choosing on the basis of interpretation and, although not explicitly stated, or perhaps even unintended, on the basis of an agenda. While disambiguating the text, translation simultaneously forges new ambiguities. Just as the first title omits the more optimistic mustering of faith, so too does *Emunim* attached to "our language" in 1989 accrue an echo absent from the original; the reader has no way of knowing this, unless she is informed explicitly via a translator's preface or footnote.

The two Hebrew translations have been recently re-published in a collection of Hebrew essays entitled *A Weak Messianic Power: Political Theology, Religion and Secularism in Hebrew Literature* (2014); the volume's editor, Hanna Soker Schwager, referring to the problematic nature of the Hebrew translations of Scholem's text, rightly notes that

> It is surprising that although not little has been written about Scholem's famous letter to Rosenzweig, critics have not paid attention to the momentous implications of the translational decisions implied in the two titles given to the letter in two different translations into Hebrew – ideological decisions that reveal the double meaning of the letter and its double function in Israeli discourse. (Soker Schwager 2014, 8)

"Double meaning" and "double function": translational decisions are clearly ideologically dependent.

What does it mean then when we use Scholem's name, as the ghostly proprietor-signatory of the *Bekenntnis*, when we attach it to a translation?

A wandering text

Like that of a ghostly wandering Jew, the history of Scholem's document is one of roving, of crossing geographical, linguistic, and generic boundaries, and of a rising from the dead. Although quite well known, let me repeat its main stations. The text was part of a collection presented to the severely ill Rosenzweig on his fortieth birthday, in 1926. Forty-six contributors, from myriad different walks of life, accepted Martin Buber's application, and presented – each from his or her own viewpoint, in German, Hebrew, Russian, and French – a written gift. Indeed, the collection was named *Gabe* [gift], and contained essays, notes of congratulation and well-wishing, letters, poetry of differing lengths, and even a piece of drama and a drawing, all handwritten. Presented to Rosenzweig, it was never published in his lifetime, and was kept in his private library. After his death (1929), his wife decided in the early 1930s to immigrate to Palestine, and it was sent, together with his other belongings, on a cargo ship, which was captured off the shores of Tunisia; all the cargo was confiscated and kept in Tunis till after the war. Lengthy negotiations were followed by a transfer of the Rosenzweig archive to the Leo Baeck Institute in New York, where it has since been kept. In 1986, the Institute decided to celebrate the centenary of Rosenzweig's birth by producing a bibliophile facsimile reproduction of the collection, and an English translation. The limited edition of 300 copies was offered for sale, for $500 each.

Around the same time, in the years 1985–1986, some sixty years after it was written, parallel efforts were made to bring the text to public attention – in translation. French, Hebrew, and English translations appeared almost simultaneously. One had limited success (300 very lucrative copies); the others were highly successful, initiating critical buzz that has remained until today. Yet there is a twist to this story, for, unlike the French and Hebrew translations, the English translation was undoubtedly made from the original *Gabe* document.

The document translated into French and Hebrew is indeed an original handwritten text by Scholem; however, it is *not* the one incorporated into the collection presented to Rosenzweig and kept in New York. Instead, the French and Hebrew translations are based on a handwritten copy Scholem must have made (as was his habit with regard to documents he considered important), which he kept among his papers that were eventually transferred to the Jerusalem National Library by his widow.[8] This is notable, not only for the light it throws on the question of originals and ownership, but also for the differences that are thereby revealed between these so-called original texts, known to us as Scholem's *Bekenntnis*. These differences may seem slight – a word or a phrase missing here and there (an oversight, perhaps), and emphatic underlinings glaringly missing from the text submitted at the time. We have no way of knowing whether what is missing was considered unfitting for Rosenzweig's ears and added later; as tempting as it may be to assess them as such, it would be mere speculation. Nevertheless, these differences may explain some (certainly not all) of the decisions made by the French and Hebrew translators that would otherwise remain enigmatic.

But the visits to the two archives, the one in New York, the other in Jerusalem, provide the visiting scholar with additional interesting experiences. Upon entering the Franz Rosenzweig Portfolio at the Leo Baeck Institute (on the web), the reader is confronted with a plethora of texts pertaining to the *Gabe*: the original handwritten texts, the typed transcriptions (done by secretaries?), the galleys of the translations with proofreading corrections, and the finished, bibliophile product. Needless to say, there are differences, mostly minor but one or two major,

---

8 The Scholem archive in the National Library in Jerusalem is *Arc 4, 1599/277-I/56*.

between the handwritten and the typed versions. What strikes the visitor in particular is the diversity of both contributors and contributions, the latter ranging from theoretical, essayistic meditation to personal, touchingly emotional note.

The visit to the Jerusalem archive, the leafing through the quite thin portfolio of Scholem's notes on language, is rewarding from a different aspect. Apart from the *Bekenntnis*, it contains another handwritten text by Scholem, dated 1925 and entitled *Sprachbekenntnis*; at the bottom he added: "worked over: to Franz Rosenzweig on his fortieth birthday." The document can be read as a kind of *nachträgliche* [retroactive] draft for the later contribution. It is a shorter, simpler, much less blazing text than the reworked one. It sounds less ambivalent and less apocalyptic. It does not contain the much quoted "apocalyptic thorn" of the *Bekenntnis*; likewise, it contains no *abyss*. In this version of the text, the Hebrew language is said to be pregnant with content, not with impending disaster (*inhaltschwer* – not *unheilschwer*). Thus, the language of the text is less urgent, its aura less holy, its critique of Zionism muted, and the semantic choice more compassionate. Unlike its famous descendant, it refers explicitly to the impossibility of secularization of *all* language, not of Hebrew alone.[9] Given that this note, too, is written in German, it is an interesting difference, with far-reaching implications beyond the scope of this essay.[10] Another interesting difference concerns its reference to the Arab question being a major problem, not subsumed under the language question as in the later text.[11] Less cabbalistic in tone, this text also alludes quite openly to the new Hebrew of the pioneers, using, inadvertently perhaps, some of its slogans.

Again, we have no way of knowing why Scholem reworked his text as he did. Some changes were most probably introduced for syntactic and stylistic reasons. However, this is insufficient to explain the completely different tones of the two documents. Was this due to the time that had elapsed between the writing of each and the disappointments this entailed? Was it due to the bitter controversy with the renovators of the language, especially with the national poet, H. N. Bialik?[12] Or was it indeed the new addressee, Rosenzweig, who called for the bitterly provocative tone of the *Bekenntnis* as we know it? Regardless of the exact reason, it is clear that Scholem's preoccupation with the language problem predates the 1926 text, independent of a

---

9 "*Die Säkularisierung der Sprache, jeder Sprache, ist eine bloße façon de parler*" is Scholem's formulation [The secularization of language, every language, is a mere *façon de parler*].
10 Let me just hint that this declaration compels us to seriously consider the *holiness* of the language of the text, its Lutheran connotations and other German religious associations.
11 "*Man spricht von Araberfrage werden die beiden Völker zueinanderfinden*" [The Arab question is being discussed, will the two nations ever find a way to each other] is the early formulation.
12 On this see my forthcoming essay "A Text and Its Vicissitudes" (2018).

confession or an apology to Rosenzweig, to whom it was finally presented. Likewise, it is the later text that became historically important – in translation.

The *Bekenntnis* between German, Hebrew, and French

Although written in German, two languages vie for dominance in the *Bekenntnis*, Hebrew and German. There is no doubt that a particular kind of Hebrew filters through the German of the text, pointing in two directions: Cabbalistic phraseology and H. N. Bialik's polemical essays regarding the renaissance of Hebrew, his *Revealment and Concealment* (1915) in particular.[13] And, indeed, so prominent is the echo of Hebrew that a Hebrew reader of the text may sometimes forget its original language. Yet it is a German text, its linguistic connotations and associations often pointing in an "opposite direction" [*entgegengesetzt*]. In reading it one should keep in mind Scholem's painful acknowledgement (1925) of the immortality of one's own "old languages" that inhabit a person, and should be conscious of "the difficulty associated with it of finding a place in evanescent existence [*Dasein*]."[14] A translator is therefore hard put when trying to do justice to all three languages – the original German, the underlying Hebrew, and the target language – even when the target itself is Hebrew.

Although both the Hebrew and the French translations appeared around the same time, the impact of the latter and its reverberations in the academic world were greater. I shall therefore concentrate on this translation. There is another reason for doing so: if there is a translation that is, in Benjamin's formulation, "more than the transmission of subject matter," exposing the complexity of the proprietorship of translation, it is Stéphane Mosès's French translation of Scholem's German text. An impassioned, beautiful text in its own right, it has played a major role in the critical discourse surrounding the *Bekenntnis*, particularly via its influence on Derrida's *The Eyes of Language* (2002), arguably the most influential discussion of Scholem's text thus far. The translation renders

---

13 Many have written on the complex relation of the document to Bialik's essay, including Ginsburg (forthcoming), Shahar (2008), and Tsamir (2014).
14 *Problem einer des eigenen "alten Sprachen" innenwohnenden Unsterblichkeit und der damit verbundenen Schwierigkeit, einen Ort im vergänglichen Dasein zu finden* [The problem of the inherent immortality of one's own "old languages" and the difficulty associated with it of finding a place for evanescent existence] . This is taken from a note entitled: "Januar 1925: Dasselbe wie stets" ["January 1925: The same as always/ever] and quoted in Weigel (2000, 39).

the French *Bekenntnis* a doubly personal text: behind Scholem's outcry, one can sense the translator's identification with it, perhaps his own distress and crisis.

Stéphane Mosès discovered the text (so to speak) and brought it to the attention of the academic community, not in its original German but in his French translation, first in *Arch. Soc. des Rel.* (1985), and later incorporated into his *L'Ange de l'Histoire* (1992). In his groundbreaking discussion of the text Mosès states:

> That which is striking here [in Scholem's text] is the passion with which Scholem, historian of Jewish mysticism, takes upon himself the themes that he studies and identifies with them. An identification, which, without any doubt, casts/sheds a new light on the relations between Scholem the scholar and Scholem the man, between the specialist committed to objectivity and the individual engaged in a history. In this sense, the text of 1926 illustrates perfectly the complexity of the correlation, in Scholem, between the writing of history and the historicity of the historian. (Mosès 1992, 345, my literal translation).

Reading Mosès's translation of Scholem's text may illustrate another aspect of this complex correlation and identification – that between translator and *translatee*. It seems that Mosès, the Scholem scholar, fervently identifies with the object of his research, in particular with the sense of personal crisis that he reads within the document and which he seems to feel a part of. Mosès, whose spiritual biography was one of *wandering* between lands and languages, whose engagement with Zionism was not unlike Scholem's, and whose struggles and disappointments with Jewish history within and without Israel became ever more bitter and painful in his last years, seems to speak his own sense of catastrophe through Scholem's voice; or vice versa. The two voices blend in a rather subjective translation. Deliberately or not, Mosès uses, quite systematically, a translational strategy that leads away from the *Credo*-possibility of the *Bekenntnis* and to the confessional one, away from hesitant faith and towards disastrous retribution for sin. It also leads away from the original German, as far as it is possible to go. To substantiate this claim requires a close reading of the translation.

From the beginning of the document, from its very title, the reader is given the impression that she is reading a confessional letter from Scholem to Rosenzweig. The first publication in French, in the *Archives*, introduces the document as UNE LETTRE INEDITE DE GERSHOM SCHOLEM A FRANZ ROSENZWEIG, thus establishing its private, personal genre for the next generation of readers. The title is rendered as *A PROPOS DE NOTRE LANGUE. UNE CONFESSION*,[15] whereas

---

[15] All citations in French are from Mosés (2006, 341–344). The book presents the text as follows:
A propos de notre langue. Une confession.
Pour Franz Rosenzweig
A l'occasion du 26 décembre 1926 (341)

the original is a four-word phrase in the opposite order: *Bekenntnis über unsere Sprache*. By placing the confession separately and at the end, the French title draws attention to it, indicates a genre, and dramatizes the address-situation of confessor-culprit. It lends a tone of "mea/nostra culpa" right from the start. Like the German *Bekenntnis*, the French *confession* denotes both an acknowledgement of guilt and a confession of faith. Highlighting the confessional aspect therefore not only directs the reader's attention to a sin or a crime, but also accentuates the fact that the word "Bekenntnis" is, for Mosès, the linguistic core of the address.

Misleadingly straightforward, the original title is all but unequivocal. True, there is something personal about it, and not just because of the proper noun. The writer includes himself in the addressing situation by using the first-person plural *unsere* [our], though it is not quite clear whom this pronoun includes or excludes. Likewise, it is uncertain which language "our language" is, given that the text is in German. The French, of course, has the same "our" [*notre*], but it is preceded by an "*a propos*" (for the German *über* ["on," "about"]; this is certainly a legitimate choice, albeit one that adds a slight hue of intimacy, of continuing an interrupted debate, thereby enclosing the text within a *tête à tête* conversation.

An analysis of the first sentences, in German and in French, will clarify the translator's strategy: having underscored *confession*, the translation consistently leads away from the *Credo*-meaning of *Bekenntnis* and towards the confessional-juridical one, from faith and towards disastrous retribution for sin. The German opens with: "*Dies Land ist ein Vulkan. Es beherbergt die Sprache*" (literally: "This land is a volcano. It houses/lodges language").[16] The volcanic land is a site of imminent dangerous eruption, yet at the same time the benign, German *beherbergt* attributes an opposite characteristic. A *Herberge* is a mountain cabin or lodge, a term implying provision of shelter to the wandering, perhaps exhausted, mountaineer. Echoing the German *verbergen*, it also connotes concealment. In other words, the opening metaphor of the volcano is immediately modified, if not subverted; as is proper for all intimacy, it is ambivalently *unheimlich*. Ambiguous or *unheimlich*, an intimate tie is created, right at the beginning, between land and language, and the double meaning *beherbergt* is central to our understanding of this tragic tie. The French, as we shall see, disambiguates the tie: "*Ce pays est pareil à un volcan où bouillonnerait le langage*" [This land resembles a volcano where language has been boiling] (Mosès 192, 341).

Combining the two simple sentences, the French translation not only makes "language" the subject of the relative clause (as opposed to its object function in

---

[16] The literal translations are mine, based on amendments to the various extant English translations.

the original); it also critically denies the land its sheltering function. It attributes to language a boiling that is never mentioned in the original. In the translation, language is turned into lava in a state of constant boil, the tense of the French verb (present conditional) implying an unexpressed threatening *if*.[17] The text is on fire right from the beginning, a fire by which Derrida will later be scorched. If the original language leaves room for a ray of hope, ever so dim, the translation leaves no doubt as to the future destructive eruption of the volcano. The atmosphere of impending, unavoidable doom, hinted in the first sentence, is augmented by the strategic choice of translating many of the following active verbal structures into passive ones, thereby implanting a growing sense that what is about to happen is, necessarily, in the Hands of Heavenly Doom/Fate, definite and unavoidable. We are led, in French, whereas the original German leaves at least some of the future developments in our own hands. Thus, strangely, when the German text speaks of the danger that the Zionist enterprise has unavoidably evoked (*heraufbeschwören* connotes the taking of an oath, (swearing, *schwören*)), the French translation reads simply: "*une conséquance nécessaire de l'enterprise sioniste*" ["a necessary consequence of the Zionist enterprise"]. This is a peculiar decision, since it forgoes the *Unheimlichkeit* implied in the German verb, and dramatically gives up a host of biblical associations, alluding to the connection between the Seer and the conjuring up from the dead (*I Samuel*, 28). The biblical chapter which backgrounds the German text announces the catastrophe about to befall Saul and, at the same time, promises the rise of the House of David. This eschewing of the French *conjurer*, which would have carried the same implications as the German (including the swearing *jurer*), undermines the possibility of an allusion to a confession of faith and the association of a catastrophe to a promise. It also suppresses the allusion to the problematic tension between prophet and state, which is the kernel of the Saul-Samuel story. It brackets other facets of *Bekenntnis*.[18]

---

[17] Interestingly, the French uses *langage* (language in general), and not *la langue*, and oscillates throughout between the two, *langage* and *langue*, whereas the German uses *Sprache* throughout, using here the definite article (*die*) to particularize the language.

[18] In "A Text and Its Vicissitudes," I discuss in great detail the connection between Scholem's document and Luther's translation of the *Samuel* chapter. To give the reader an idea of the latter, here are a few verses: Saul hat die Geister*beschwörer* [...] vertrieben. ...Sucht mir eine Frau die Tote *beschwören* kann, [...] Siehe, in En Dor ist eine Frau die kann Tote *beschwören*. [...] weil du Geister *beschwören* kannst [...] wie er die Geister*beschwörer* ausgerottet hat [...] Saul aber *schwor* [...]. (Emphasis mine.)[And Saul had ousted the necromancers (who conjure the spirits of the dead). [...] Seek me a woman who can conjure spirits, [...] Behold, there is a woman who conjures spirits at En-dor[...] . because you can conjure the spirits of the dead ... as he wiped out those who conjure up spirits] ... But Saul swore [...].] (Literal translation mine)

Interestingly, the exchange of passive structures for the original active ones is installed in the translation at strategic junctions where the fore/seeing of the impending danger is at stake ("*la vue nous sera rendue*" [literally: "sight is given back to us"] "*Car s'ils avaient été doués de clairvoyance*" [literally: "For, if they had been endowed/granted with clear-sightedness/perceptiveness"]). In French, the possibility of seeing properly is not in the hands of the (non)seer; instead, he must be granted sight.

There are many dramatic moments in the text; there are more in the translation. Particularly striking is the rendering of "*schwer vergessliche Minuten*" ["moments that can hardly be forgotten"] as "*tels instants qui nous stigmatisent, que nous ne pourrons jamais plus oublier*" [literally: "those moments that stigmatize us, which we shall never be able to forget"]. The inflation of the three-word phrase into a complex sentence, whose main clause is not in the original, heightens the feverish tone of a much more restrained text, one that prefers *schwer vergesslich* to the potentially stronger *unvergesslich* [unforgettable]. And *stigmata* calls attention to itself, the body bearing witness to the linguistic trauma, associated with religious frenzy, the added *jamais* [never] emphasizing irrevocability. Inscribed Fate, never to be erased from our bodies, attunes with the tone of the translation's ending: in the final sentence the restrained German "may" [*möge*] is rendered "*Fasse le ciel que ...*" [May heaven].

For the sake of intellectual and academic integrity and precision, this last paragraph must be rewritten. The text Mosès translated includes "stigmatized"; the text in Rosenzweig's *Gabe* does not. Whether a later addition or an oversight is involved is impossible to say; nonetheless, the very use of the term, with its non-Jewish connotations, is notable.

Apart from the intentional or unintentional desire to increase the pressing tension of the drama and toll the bells of doom, there is another streak in the translation, probably less conscious or intended. It concerns the relation to the German language in which the text is written. It seems that the translator not only attempts to render the text in "good" French (as would any translator), but also seeks to actively shun its original language, or at least keep as wide a distance as possible from it. Why should a word like *senken* ["sink," here in the meaning of "invest"] be rendered *nourrir* [nourish], the German *Schöpfer* become a French *initiateur* (instead of "creator"), or a *neue Sprachbewegung* become a *movement de renaissance* (and not a "new language movement")? Yet most crucial is the explicit example, already considered, where for no particular reason the translation avoids any simple French parallel (synonym) for the original German (*beschwören/conjurer*). This is all the more striking since this German verb does not let go of the text and becomes an increasingly violent act that cannot but grow on the reader of the original. It is unquestionably one of the text's *leitmotifs*. In a passage overshadowed by such words as *Macht*, *Potenz*, *Gewalt*, and *Kraft* [power/might, potency, violence, and force, respectively], distributed evenly between the power enclosed in the holy language and the violence needed to raise it from the dead, the translation again prefers to use *invoquer*, for both the German *beschwören* and *wachrufen* [arouse], the second being the consequence of the first (in the original). And again it is the small detail that adds fuel to the flames: where the original is satisfied with *grosser Gewalt* [great violence], the French has *une violence terrible*. So strong is the hold of the demonic *Schwur* [oath] over the text that it is sounded from above in its closing sentences, where Judgment is *beschworen* over us (judgment conjured upon us), and is completely avoided in the French translation (*Jugement auquel ils nous soumettent*).

The German passage overwhelmed by the shunned verb is the one which opens with: "Language is name" [*Sprache ist Namen*], and it is with the "name" that Mosès performs the translation's strangest convolution. In a way, the original text is doubly signed. It is signed by the "German" *Gerhard* Scholem, followed by the Hebrew date in transliteration (Jerusalem, Teveth 7, 5687). The French text, however, is signed by the "Hebrew" *Gershom* Scholem. Is this an act of tearing Scholem away from his German language and origins? Whose Confession, then, is this *Bekenntnis*?

Contagious translation

Jacques Derrida was a major agent of dissemination of the *Bekenntnis*. He was deeply touched by Scholem's text and by Stéphane Mosès's treatment of it. Not unlike Mosès's emotional involvement, Derrida's empathetic reading also verges on identification. His personal biography, his wandering between languages, and his ambivalent attitude towards Zionism may have much to do with it. A long footnote devoted to Scholem and Mosès in his semi-autobiographical *Le monolinguisme de l'autre* (1996) and his *Les yeux de la langue* (1987),[19] which is wholly dedicated to the text, are evidence for this. There is hardly any critic of the *Bekenntnis*, in any language, who does not quote Derrida. With him, and with Mosès, critics continue repeating the same phrases and expressions from the translated Scholem text. Since, as already hinted, the text has become a favorite support in the "Zionist" controversy, Derrida's reading-translating of it is therefore not only of theoretical interest but of political import. This is particularly so in view of the

---

[19] Translated into English, by Gil Anijar, as "The Eyes of Language" (2002).

fact that most people read Derrida's text only in English translation, and thus when it is presented in Gil Anijar's translation readers are given to understand that Derrida states unequivocally that Scholem "cannot but recognize in Zionism an *evil*, an inner evil that is anything but accidental" (Anijar 2002, 194). That is, *Zionism incorporates evil*, as Derrida appears to declare in the name of Scholem. This view of Zionism offers a prime example of the manipulative appropriations of translation, innocent or tendentious. Between all possible alternatives, Anijar elects to translate Derrida's "*mal (un mal qui n'a rien d'accidentel)*" with the English "evil," which, unlike Derrida, he italicizes. He could have chosen "trouble," "difficulty," "pain," or, closer to the harsher, original meaning, "disease." To be sure, "evil" is a legitimate translation for the French "mal," but there is no corresponding evil in Scholem's text. There is stupidity, blindness, arrogance, and disease, but no evil. Via translation, villainy is attributed to Zionism, with the word "evil" being repeated six times in the single paragraph from which the previous quote is taken. The sense of wickedness is hammered in. Derrida's *mal* is detrimental enough, there being no explicit *malness* in Scholem's text (the only allusion being "*unheilschwer*," which Anijar rightly translates as "pregnant with catastrophes"), yet Anijar's "evil" is worse. It is a downright politically slanted translation.

Let me draw attention to the way Derrida uses the French translation, augmenting Mosès's feverish reading, using a fiery rhetoric that naturally relies on the French language, and although attentive to Scholem's ambivalent position, pulling the text, as a confessional letter (very *confessional* and very much *letter*), in the direction of inevitable catastrophe. The text that reaches the reader via Derrida is a stinging text ablaze. The state of boiling hinted in the first sentence of the French translation, which Derrida quotes, turns into an open fire via his inflammatory rhetoric. In the Scholem text there is no mention of fire; the ambivalent volcano is mentioned only once, as Derrida himself admits. Yet for him "[L]anguage is overheated, words burn, one can hardly touch them" (Derrida 2002, 195). Not letting the conflagration abate, his rhetoric keeps stoking the fire:

> The staging that blends the passion of language with the elements [...] privileges *fire*. [...], language will speak through *fire*,[...] return through this *fire*hole: [...], and mouth of *fire*,a jealous and revengeful God who is a God of *fire* ([...] Spinoza's fright before this God of *fire*). [...] a *burning* bush. (Derrida 2002, 196, my emphases)

Who is the inflamed stage director of the scene? Engulfed by threatening divine fire, the reader forgets that "this fire hole" the volcano, may also have a shielding role, that it "*beherbergt*" [shelters] language. (Confined to translation, the reader was probably not made aware of it in the first place.) Derrida's exhilarating performative rhetoric absorbs the French translation, augmenting its fiery underlying interpretation by the elementary device of alliterative repetition and repeated repetition. *Fire* accumulates; no escape from it is provided.

Repetition is indeed a major device, yet it is French-based. Thus Derrida develops an enthusiastic argument entirely dependent upon the peculiarities of the French, on the prefix *re-*, and on the hypnotic chant of its *repetition*:

> The "neue Sprachbewegung" – which Stéphane Mosès was right to translate "mouvement de renaissance de l'hébreu" – is indeed a movement for the re-turn, the re-birth, the resurrection even, the re-turn, one more time, one more turn [*volte*], revolution, not to mention the revenant whose sign is marked by the return of the word *gespenstisch* (spectral, ghostly) on two occasions in the confession. This semantic chain of *re-* (return, repetition, reawakening, resurrection, revolt, revolution, revenance) crosses the essential question of *re-* in the language, *as* language insofar as it inaugurates the possibility of vengeance as revenge, punishment, or retaliation. (Derrida 2002, 208–209, italics in the original, underlining mine).

A reader cannot remain indifferent to the brilliantly insistent beat of the "semantic chain," even in the English translation, but do retribution and revenge speak the same language in German "*as* language"? The German for the French/English prefix *re-* is *wieder-*. Some of the nouns in the semantic chain open with *wieder-*, others do not, some have no prefix: "return" – *zurück* or *wiederkommen*; "rebirth" – *Wiedergeburt*; "resurrection" – *Wiederbelebung, Auferstehung*; "repetition" – *Wiederholung*; "reawakening" – *Wiedererwachen*; "revolt" – *Aufstand*; "revolution" – *Revolution*; "revenge" – *Rache*; "retaliation" – *Vergeltung*. Revenge, punishment [*Strafe*], and retaliation are not inaugurated by the "essential question of *re-*" in the German that speaks of them. One cannot but succumb to Derrida's charm, yet his French weaves a linguistic net which links revenge and retaliation to Hebrew Renaissance, in a relational chain exclusive of other possibilities.

Derrida's influence cannot be overrated. Nevertheless, his collaboration with Mosès, the combination of translation with a translation-based reading that has re-introduced the *Bekenntnis* into present-day discourse, is an act of stealth. Yet, this act fulfills Benjamin's dictum about successful translations that both are culturally productive and also save texts from oblivion at the right historical moment – by being mistranslations of a kind. They are indeed "redemption through sin," מצווה הבאה בעבירה, without which we would be so much the poorer.

A very personal note

I have been working on this essay in Jerusalem during the abominable summer months of the war of 2015. Despite the rays of hope I have tried to find shimmering through Scholem's original German text, I cannot but add my prayers to his: "May the thoughtlessness that has led us on this apocalyptic path not lead us to our ruin."

References

The document and its translations

Scholem, Gerhard. "*Bekenntnis über unsere Sprache.*" http://www.archive.org/stream/franzrosenzweig_01_reel01#page/n200/mode/1up. (30 July 2015.)
Scholem, Gerhard. "*Bekenntnis über unsere Sprache.*" National Library, Jerusalem, Gershom Scholem Archive, Arc 4, 1599/277-I/56.

French
Mosès, Stéphane. "A Propos de notre langue. Une confession." *Arch. Soc. des Rel.*, 60/61 (1985): 83–84.

Hebrew
Broide, Ephraim. "Vidu'I al leshoneinu." *Molad* 9.42 (1985): 118–119.
Huss, Avraham. "Hatsharat emunim lasafa shelanu." Gershom Scholem *Sof Davar*, Tel Aviv: Am Oved, 1989. 58–59.

English
Cutter, William. "Ghostly Hebrew, Ghastly Speech: Scholem to Rosenzweig, 1926." *Prooftexts* 10.3 (1990 [1985]): 413–433.
Scholem, Gershom. "Confession on the Subject of Our Language: A Letter to Franz Rosenzweig, December 26, 1926." *Acts of Religion*. Ed. Gil Anijar. New York and London: Routledge, 2002. 188–190.
Wiskind, Ora. "On Our Language: A Confession." *History and Memory*, 2.2 (1990): 97–99.

Secondary Literature

Benjamin, Walter. "The Translator's Task." Trans. Steven Rendall. *TTR: traduction, terminologie, réduction* 10.2 (1997): 151–165. http://id.erudit.org/iderudit/037302ar. (30 July 2015.)
Derrida, Jacques. *Acts of Religion*. Ed. Gil Anijar. New York and London: Routledge, 2002 [1987].
Ginsburg, Ruth. "A Text and Its Vicissitudes. Gershom Scholem between Confession and Credo," (in Hebrew, *Mikan, Journal for Hebrew and Israeli Literature and Culture Studies*, forthcoming 2018).
Lapidot, Elad. "Fragwürdige Sprache: Zur modernen Phänomenologie der heiligen Zunge, Sprache und Zunge." *Jahrbuch des Simon-Dubnow-Institut (JBDI)*, XII, Göttingen: Vanderhoek & Co. KC, 2013, 271–298.
Mosès, Stéphane. *L'Ange de l'Histoire*. Paris: Editions Gallimard, 2006 [1992].
Scholem, Gershom. National Library, Jerusalem, Gershom Scholem Archive, Arc 4, 1599/277-I/56.

Shahar, Galili. "The Sacred and the Unfamiliar." *The German Review: Literature, Culture, Theory* 83.4 (2008): 299–320.

Soker-Schwager, Hanna. Preface to *A Weak Messianic Power: Political Theology, Religion and Secularism in Hebrew Literature. Mikan, Journal for Hebrew and Israeli Literature and Culture Studies* 14 (2014): 5–12.

Tsamir, Hamutal. "Blindness and the Abyss: Political Theology and the Secularization of Hebrew in Scholem and Bialik." *Mikan, Journal for Hebrew and Israeli Literature and Culture Studies* 14 (2014): 82–119.

Weigel, Sigrid. "Scholems Gedichte und seine Dichtungstheorie: Klage, Adressierung, Gabe und das Problem einer biblischen Sprache in unserer Zeit." *Gershom Scholem – Literatur und Rhetorik*. Eds. Stéphane Mosès and Sigrid Weigel. Cologne: Böhlau, 2000, 16–47.

Yildiz, Yasemin. *Beyond the Mother Tongue: The Postmonolingual Condition*. New York: Fordham University Press, 2012.

Shlomith Rimmon-Kenan
Belonging Destabilized: Anton Shammas's *Arabesques*

Underlying Anton Shammas's novel *Arabesques* (first published in 1986) is a radical political vision which challenges the ethnic-religious identity of Israel as a Jewish state, and aspires to replace it with a civic-linguistic identity whereby anyone in this country who speaks/writes in Hebrew is Israeli, Arabs included. In light of this inspiring yet somewhat utopian ideal, which Anna Bernard later termed "civic belonging" (2013, 136–159), Shammas both constructs and deconstructs Israeli/Jewish culture from the point of view of a minority, supporting, in this sense, Homi Bhabha's contention that "Increasingly, 'national' cultures are being produced from the perspective of disenfranchised minorities" (1995, 6).

However, *Arabesques* goes beyond this: not only does it destabilize two opposed narratives; it also attempts to bridge them in a vision which, though not yet realized in the political world, can nonetheless be imagined in literature. It is precisely this product of literary imagination that will be the focus of my paper, in which I will analyze Shammas's view of belonging and the poetics that it generates, as well as the divergent techniques by which he simultaneously subverts the categories of author-language-text yet also anchors them in an uncanny co-existence.

Anton Shammas

Anton Shammas was born in Fassuta, a village in the north of Israel, in 1950 – two years after the 1948 War of Independence and the Palestinian *Nakba* (catastrophe). He now lives in the United States and is a professor of Comparative Literature at the University of Michigan. In Israel, he is a minority within a minority within a minority: first, as an Arab within the predominantly Jewish population of Israel; second, as a Christian within the predominantly Muslim Arab population of Israel; and third, as an Israeli within the surrounding Arab countries (Hever 2002, 285). From this position of a three-fold minority, Shammas has written a novel that playfully, but also painfully, crosses the boundaries between literary genres, national and religious identities, majority and minority, self and other, fiction and reality, related languages and literatures. Furthermore, the novel was written in Hebrew, thus crossing over from Shammas's mother tongue, Arabic, to the language of the hegemony, a language associated with the rise of the Zionist movement. My discussion here relies on Vivian Eden's English translation, which, of course, also poses the question of belonging: does a translated text belong to the source language or to the language into which it is translated? (Bassnett 1993, 45). This specific translation declares accessibility – i.e. reading like an English-language novel – as its main intent, while inevitably sacrificing the original text's otherness (as Hebrew literature written by an Arab citizen).

Another Place

Through the depiction of place, *Arabesques* interrogates its relation to belonging, both in the "tale" sections and in those of "the teller".[1] The tale unfolds the history of the Shammas family and its many branches, beginning in the early nineteenth century, when the family's father left the area known today as Syria and moved to the Galilee. The story continues in Palestine under the British Mandate, in the period preceding the establishment of the state of Israel, and describes everyday life under Israeli military government between 1948 and 1967. It concludes in the 1980's, noting almost twenty years of Israeli occupation of the West Bank and Gaza. From this family history, it becomes clear that in earlier periods there was greater flexibility concerning geopolitical belonging, and that changes of residence – from Syria to the Galilee, from Haifa to Beirut or to the villages of Rmeish and Bint Jbeil in Lebanon – were not uncommon. Even emigration was not rare, as indicated in the story of Uncle Jiryes, who spent ten years in Argentina and eventually died there, though his decision to emigrate had encountered emotional objection from many, including Jiryes's wife, who refused to join him. The Israeli War of Independence in 1948 caused population displacement, described in the novel as "fleeing Arabs who would come to be known as Palestinian refugees in the course of time and their wanderings" (187). One individual case is the deflection of the course of Laylah Khoury's life "to [an] eternal exile within her own homeland" (35), an oxymoronic formulation conveying radical destabilization of belonging and of the concept of home.

Whereas "the tale" represents a place that is not *one* but many, "the teller" focusses on a place that is *not* one, i.e. not quite a place.[2] En route from Israel to

---

[1] "Tale" and "the teller" are Shammas's denominations. I have refrained from translating them into narratological terms.
[2] I have taken the liberty of playing with Irigaray's title *This Sex which Is Not One* (1985) to foreground the double meaning of "not *one*" and "*not* one". I used this pun in an earlier essay, published in *Narrative* (2009, 220–234), about Michal Govrin's *Snapshots*.

the International Writing Workshop in Iowa City, the narrator-protagonist, whose name is identical to that of the author, spends a day in Paris. The day reaches its peak with a visit to Père Lachaise Cemetery, which is both "the most beautiful place in Paris", as a Lebanese relative puts it, and a commemoration, a celebration, of death. In Foucault's terms, it is a heterotopia (Foucault 1984), a dwelling place whose only inhabitants are the dead.[3]

Other visitors to Père Lachaise are Amira, an Egyptian writer of Jewish descent who is also on her way to the International Writing Workshop, and her photographer-lover, who insists on placing her between him and the tombstones he photographs. "Have you noticed", she asks him, "that you always bring me back to the dead?" (87). The Parisian cemetery revives memories of Amira's father and his resting place in Alexandria. She recalls that she used to write to him in Arabic and he would answer in French, and that she was surprised to see Hebrew letters on his tombstone, because he lived his life in Arabic. She then muses: "Come to think of it, maybe that's why Hebrew is the language of death for me" (94). For Amira, Hebrew is directly, concretely, related to death, through letters engraved on her father's tombstone.

In Père Lachaise, the protagonist notices an uncanny proximity between two tombstones: that of Mahmoud Al-Hamshari, a PLO representative, engraved with a verse from the Koran "promising eternal life in the world to come to those who died for their country" (135), and that of Marcel Proust, who died fifty years earlier. The narrator comments: "It must have been the French sense of humor that granted both of them, the man of the lost country and the man of the lost time,[4] nearly identical graves […] and under the black marble lay the two lost men, each of them in the blackness of his own tomb, a Jew of Time and an Arab of Place" (136).

Great is the temptation to apply "a Jew of Time and an Arab of Place" beyond the graves and onto the Israeli-Arab conflict represented in the novel, so as to show how Shammas both poses and subverts this opposition. The preceding discussion of the tale's representation of the family's history in the Palestinian-Israeli space – "a place that is not *one*" – has provided a glimpse of the complexity with which this tension is treated in the novel; I now wish to address the entanglement between Jew and Arab on two other black stones in a different place that is *not* one:

---

[3] And see Ezrahi 2018, 85–97.
[4] I have taken the liberty of slightly changing the quotation, which originally makes explicit what is implicit in the Hebrew. The original translation reads: "[…] granted both of them, the man of the lost country and the man of the *temps perdu*, nearly identical graves".

> There are two great black stones in the world, the late Abu Mas'ood used to say, the black stone in the Ka'bah in Macca, which was quarried by almighty Allah himself, and the black stone on Herzl's tomb, which was quarried by the mortal Abu Mas'ood himself, and both of them are sites of pilgrimage. Allah, however, does not have an official document from the Technion to prove that he quarried His stone (39).

This humorous comparison between one of the most sacred places of Islam and Herzl's Tomb points to the latter's secular form of sacredness, which is created and attributed by Zionist ideology. The comparison is one of many examples of how Shammas undermines such forms of sacredness.

Another Language, Other Texts

The Israeli equivalent of Père Lachaise is Mount Herzl in Jerusalem, the burial place of Israeli leaders, and the adjacent military cemetery, where a public commemoration service is held each year on the Memorial Day which precedes Independence Day. The canonical Israeli poet Yehuda Amichai, who was born in Germany, wrote an elegy in which he criticizes these official ceremonies that commemorate dead soldiers. Three verses from this poem, entitled "Memorial Day for the War Dead", became the motto of the second part of *Arabesques*:

> Dresses of beautiful women, in blue and white.
> And everything in three languages:
> Hebrew, Arabic and Death. (Amichai 2003 [1974], 110)

This quotation,[5] one of the many which alludes to Hebrew literature throughout the novel, establishes a direct link between death and the two languages of the conflict, foreshadowing Amira's statement at Père Lachaise, as well as the tragic end of the forbidden love affair between Anton, the protagonist, and his married Israeli-Jewish beloved, Shlomit. After a scandal that follows Shlomit's husband's discovery of Anton's letters, "the world reverted to its former state of 'Hebrew, Arabic and Death'" (95). Here – and even more so in Amichai's poem – "death" is syntactically equivalent to "Hebrew" and "Arabic". In what sense, then, is death a language? As mentioned above, Amichai's poem relates to a mourning procession, a ceremony commemorating death. As a system of signs, symbols, and rituals, the representation of death is similar to a language, one which is unfortunately not less common in this area than Hebrew or Arabic. Interestingly,

---

5 The English rendering here is from Vivian Eden's translation of *Arabesques*.

Shammas's quotation omits the first verse of the stanza: "A flag loses touch with reality and flies" (my translation). This Israeli flag flies high enough to render its national characteristics indiscernible, thus loosening the sense of national belonging implied by the flag's "blue and white".

Sharply opposed to the notion of a language of death is the view that Hebrew is in fact the language of Grace. This view is imported from yet another language and text, Dante's *De Vulgare Eloquentia* (1302, book 1, Ch.6, verse 6). "The exiled Florentine" suggests that Hebrew remained the language of Grace (*lingua di gratie*), uncontaminated by the confusion of tongues during the collapse of the Tower of Babel, so as to enable Jesus to use a pure language. This suggestion is repeated in Shammas's text by the fictional Israeli writer Yosh Bar-On[6]: "An Arab who speaks the language of Grace, as Dante once called it. Hebrew as the language of Grace, as opposed to the language of Confusion that swept over the world when the Tower of Babel collapsed. My Arab will build his tower of confusion on my plot. In the language of Grace. That's his only possible redemption" (92). While this may be perceived as a patronizing thought on the part of an unpleasant character, the biographical Shammas later endorsed this view of Hebrew, at a (non-fictional) conference about Literature in Exile:

> I'm fond of using this quotation [from Dante] whenever I need to explain the awkward position I'm trapped in – that of an Arab who writes in Hebrew. I use this quote as a pretext and a justification, adding that the language I use to go home [...] is the language of Grace, and that this language of Grace – Hebrew – is the perfect language to describe my Palestinian confusion. (1990, 85–86)[7]

Note the difference between Hebrew as the language Shammas uses "to go home", and Laylah Khoury's being an "eternal exile within her own homeland".

There are many other intertextual relations between *Arabesques* and Hebrew literature, but for the purpose of this essay I'll mention only two more. In an interior monologue by Yosh Bar-On, he quotes a question put to him by an ex-Israeli painter in a café in Paris: "What do Arabs dream about? [...] What do they dream about? The twins Aziz and Khaleel after they appear in Hannah Gonen's nightmare in *My Michael*[?]" (84).[8] In this novel, by the late eminent Israeli writer Amos Oz,

---

[6] The fictional writer Yosh Bar-On is an allusion to A. B. Yehoshua, whose novel *The Lover* was translated into Arabic by Shammas. Yehoshua, a prominent representative of Israeli left-wing intellectuals, took part in a vitriolic exchange with Shammas in an Israeli newspaper before the publication of *Arabesques*.

[7] For an ironic interpretation of "the language of Grace", see Ginsburg 2014, 239–263.

[8] The explicit reference to Oz's novel *My Michael* was added by the translator, who took upon herself the function of a cultural mediator.

the Arab twins are stereotypically characterized as both sensuous (thereby contrasted to Hannah's husband, Michael) and violent. Bar-On, Shammas's fictional narrator, does not reply, but it seems quite clear that both he and Shammas are vexed by the hostile, stereotypical description on the part of a great writer who is also active in the Israeli political left.

A more subversive quotation appears in the narration of what could be referred to as the violation of the lake. Here, the international group of writers assembled in Iowa City visits their hosts' somewhat wild farm, where a lake is concealed. The description of the lake is full of allusions to Haim Nachman Bialik's poem "The Pond". Although Bialik himself is mentioned only in the English translation of *Arabesques* (in yet another mediating explanation), the language used in this scene is saturated with that of the poem. Shattering the intense stillness of the lake, Paco, the Palestinian writer, throws a beer can into the water. Even though the aggressive act is an obvious violation of both elementary politeness and ecological ethics, Bar-On's reaction of extreme rage is nonetheless excessive. The narrator remarks: "It seemed as if he could forgive Paco his support of Palestinian terror as a last resort, or at least understand it; but there was no way he could forgive the throwing of the beer can" (254). Why is that so? The Israeli postcolonial literary critic Michael Gluzman has written extensively about the incident (2003, 327–347), and I wish to put forward his compelling insight as to the pond's symbolic status. "The Pond", argues Gluzman, is an *ars poetical* poem, in which Israel's national poet transforms the lake into a major site of Hebrew literature. In *Arabesques*, it is Shammas's desire that a Palestinian should inhabit this site, but it is also what Bar-On, a left-wing Zionist Israeli writer, experiences as an intolerable appropriation of his language.

In this context, I would like to elaborate on Shammas's very decision to write in Hebrew. Shammas has chosen to write not only in the language of the Israeli majority; it is also a language whose renaissance has a strong affinity with the Zionist movement as well as with the Israeli occupation, which has demonstrated its linguistic possession over the land by changing the names of Arab villages into Hebrew ones (Deir-Al-Kassi has become Moshav Elkosh, El Bassa – Moshav Betzet, etc. – all narratively anticipated by the technique of prolepsis). Indeed, Shammas writes what Gilles Deleuze and Félix Guattari call "a minor literature": literature written by a minority in the language of the majority. According to Deleuze and Guattari, this may be carried out either through the enrichment and over-determination of language, "swell[ing] it up through all the resources of symbolism, [...] of esoteric sense, of a hidden signifier", or with its under-determination, rendering it minimal, "sober" and poor (1975, 18).[9]

---

[9] For Deleuze and Guattari, Joyce is an example of the first path, Beckett of the second.

Shammas chooses the first path, most likely without being familiar with the distinction proposed by the French thinkers. His Hebrew is particularly rich, replete with idioms from various periods in the development of the language, inflated by symbols and esoteric meanings. These do not always come across in Eden's translation, but two examples of an integration of very well-known Biblical idioms will suffice to illustrate Shammas's ironic "swelling up" of his style. At one point in the novel, the narrator, Anton, tells of his father's insistent courting of Elaine Bitar, the woman who would become his mother. Again and again the father asked for Elaine's hand, but was consistently refused by her older brother, Elias. However, after a long period during which Elias hardened his heart (a Biblical expression said of Pharaoh, King of Egypt), he "finally agreed that she should go forth, leaving her father's house and her kin whom she loved and her city, and link her fate with the fate of this stubborn barber-cobbler [...]" (27). This is an obvious allusion to God's commandment to Abram: "Get thee out of thy country, and from thy kindred, and from thy father's house, unto a land that I will shew thee" (*Genesis* 12:1). The Bible, and this well-known verse in particular, has been often used by the Zionist movement as a semi-legal document, certifying that the land of Israel belongs to the Jews. The analogy invoked by Shammas, between the Lebanese Elaine leaving Beirut to get married and live in an Arab village in the Galilee, and Abram's leaving Haran to own this same land bestowed to him by god, challenges the relationship of belonging between the land and its residents. Moreover, as my earlier discussion has shown, *Arabesques* as a whole can be seen as a "Lech-Lecha" ("לך לך", "Get thee out", *Genesis* 12:1) narrative, with its characters perpetually on the move from one place to another. Shammas's biographical story is also one of emigration, regrettably not to but from Israel, the country in whose language he had wanted to write and live.

Abram's descendants continue to condense Shammas's language with Biblical echoes. In a scene from Anton's childhood, his brother lowers him into the cistern he has been told to clean: "With some last words of warning and encouragement, and promising that he will not sell me to the Ishmaelites, my brother pays out the rope bit by bit" (50). Here, the Biblical story of Joseph and his brothers (*Genesis* 37) is subjected to an ironic twist, since it is Arabs who Jews consider to be Ishmaelites. To what ethnicity does Anton belong, that he needs to be reassured by his brother that he will not be sold to Ishmaelites?

Following the suggestion that Anton has usurped Joseph's place in a story of sibling jealousy, one might wonder if Shammas has respectively usurped and appropriated the Hebrew language. As aforementioned, I wish to argue contrarily: Shammas's use of Hebrew seems to challenge the Israeli/Jewish notion of identity between nation, ethnicity, and language (Hever 2007, 284).

Can we Israeli Jews claim to own Hebrew? And are we its exclusive owners? Or, taking a more deconstructive perspective, does *anyone* own language? In the spirit of Bhabha's view of mimicry, one can construe Shammas's writing in Hebrew both as an internalization of the colonizer, "as a text written in a language of the conquerors" (Hever 2002, 176), and as a subversion of colonization by a parodic imitation (Bhabha 1983, 18–36). Thus, Shammas's choice to write in Hebrew may be viewed as a way of emphasizing his sense of being a stranger in his homeland. This problematization of the relation between language and belonging is also evident in the novel's epigraph, from Shaw's *Pygmalion*: "You told me, you know, that when a child is brought to a foreign country, it picks up the language in a few weeks, and forgets its own. Well, I am a child in your country" (Shammas 1986, 2). Nonetheless, Shammas, the "child", has mastered the dominant language, to an amazing degree and without forgetting his own; he speaks (or, in the spirit of deconstruction, is spoken by) two or three languages, manifesting a rupture between different fields of belonging.

Another Self

In Shammas's novel, this rupture is most concretely dramatized by the *doppelgänger* motif. There are various partial doublings, related to writing, in *Arabesques*: Anton and Yosh Bar-On write about each other, causing the Dutch author to wonder who is the ventriloquist of whom (145); Anton and Amira, who are both in love with someone already married, are said to have written together one version of the section titled "Père Lachaise" (167); Anton and Paco are two objects of Bar-On's potential novel. The novel also puts forward a fully developed double figure, that of the two Anton Shammases. The details of this double narrative are quite complex, hedged with doubt, and consist of at least two versions. The protagonist-narrator of *Arabesques* is named Anton, after his cousin (the son of Uncle Jiryes and Almaza), who was said to have died of typhoid fever before he was a year old. The infant was hurriedly buried, without his mother having a chance to see the body; all she could ask of the hospital was the pillow on which he had slept. Many years later, it transpires that this other Anton did not die but was secretly adopted by the wealthy Abyad family in Beirut and re-named Michel. Anton hears this secret twice: once from Surayyah Said (formerly Laylah Khoury) and once from Michel-Michael Abyad, whom he meets at a friends' house in Iowa City. The two versions are not identical, thereby giving rise to questions about their reliability (for instance, whether Laylah or Almaza, the bereaved mother, was a servant for the Abyad family). More imperative is the information regarding Michael's adult life. According to Laylah/Surayyah, when Michael was twenty, a staff member at the hospital came to the Abyad's home, demanding money in return for continuing to conceal Michael's true origins; or, according to Michael's version, it was a woman in black who had come to the house, claiming to be his mother and demanding the return of her son. In order to circumvent the threat, Michel was sent to the United States, where he became "Michael", and later "Dr. Michael Abyad". In 1978 he returned to Beirut, working periodically for the Palestinian Research Center. Later, in the United States, he meets Anton Shammas and tells him his story. According to this version, Almaza's Anton died as a baby, whereas he himself had indeed been adopted by the Abyad family, where Almaza had been like a mother to him. From Almaza he heard often about little Anton, and slept on his pillow and came to identify with him: "sometimes I used to imagine that I was he" (258). When he heard about the living Anton, named after the dead infant, he "decided to write my autobiography in your name and to be present in it as the little boy who died" (258).

Whether Michael Abyad is indeed the infant believed to have died, or an adopted child who came to identify with the dead Anton, the meeting between him and Anton the narrator in the United States presents, at least figuratively, two Antons, who are one and not one: doubles. In their meeting in Iowa City, the duplicity is heightened as it becomes clear that both are also writers. Michael gives Anton his autobiography, saying: "Take this file and see what you can do with it. Translate it, adapt it, add or subtract. But leave me in" (259). Could it be that the text we are reading, or at least the sections of "the tale", including the Abyad-Shammas story as told by Laylah Khoury, is part of Michael's fictional autobiography? If so, what becomes of Anton Shammas's authority as a narrator? This momentary destabilization of authority/authorship is immediately corrected by Shammas's comment:

> If Michael were the teller, he would have ended it like this: "He opened a drawer and took out a pencil and wrote on the file: My Tale. He frowned at this a moment, then he used an eraser, leaving only the single word Tale. That seemed to satisfy him". (259)

The play on "My tale" and "Tale" recalls Willa Cather's *My Antonia* and belongs to Anton's world, not Michael's: not only is his own name encrypted within "Antonia", but, by his own evidence, this was the first novel he read in Arabic translation. Furthermore, Michael's words and actions are the complete opposite, a mirror image, of those of Jim Burden when the latter addresses the female narrator of *My Antonia*. Jim, who tells the narrator that he has been sporadically writing his childhood memories of Antonia, calls at her apartment one stormy afternoon, carrying a leather portfolio and saying:

"Here is the thing about Antonia. Do you still want to read it? I finished it last night. I didn't take time to arrange it; I simply wrote down pretty much all that her name recalls to me. I suppose it hasn't any form. It hasn't any title, either". He went into the next room, sat down at my desk and wrote across the face of the portfolio the word "Antonia". He frowned at this a moment, then prefixed another word, making it "My Antonia". That seemed to satisfy him. (Cather 1954 [1918], unpaginated Introduction)

While Burden prefixes "my", Shammas omits this possessive pronoun, explicitly pointing to the interrogation of belonging.[10] How can a story be labelled "my" when there are two Antons, who may in fact be one? To whom does this "my" refer? The conundrum is further intensified by the chapter's last sentence: "But maybe, out of polite arrogance, he might have finished with a paraphrase of Borges: 'Which of the two of us has written this book I do not know'" (259). Thus, the *doppelgänger* motif not only undermines unified subjectivity, introduces otherness into sameness, raises the question of translatability, and crosses the boundaries between reality and fiction; it also destabilizes the very origin of writing.

Structural Intricacy

Other bounded or traditionally restricted frameworks, such as continuity and linearity, are also ruptured in *Arabesques*. The novel alternates between chapters entitled "The Tale" and "The Teller". Enhancing the sense of fragmentation, the first "Père Lachaise" section consists of twenty-one interior monologues by different characters. As mentioned, "The Tale" depicts the history of the Shammas family and its many branches. It is narrated in non-chronological fashion, full of analepses, prolepses, digressions, skipping from one generation to another, mentioning characters in an associative way, as if assuming the reader is already acquainted with them. This mixture of periods, nations, and even religions seems to me to imply a political doubt as to the importance of the endless debate regarding precedency over the country and what right (if any) is conferred by it. "The Teller", on the other hand, is the novel's narrative present, located mainly at the International Writing Workshop in Iowa City. It is narrated much more chronologically. Whereas "The Tale" is told in particularly rich, even inflated Hebrew, and often with semi-mythical overtones, "The Teller" is, on the whole, naturalistic and colloquial.

---

[10] For a more detailed and inspiring analysis of the relation between the two novels see Ginsburg 2014, 239–263 [Hebrew].

The interlacing of chapters of "The Tale" with those of "The Teller" replaces the linear and causal Western structure of plot with that of the arabesque, a classical Muslim pattern that is static, symmetrical, and spatial. The text often uses the metaphor of the arabesque to characterize both its own structure and the characters' manners of telling. For instance, the narrator says that Uncle Yusef's stories, which are an important basis for his own, "[...] were plaited into one another, embracing and parting, twisting and twining in the infinite arabesque of memory" (226). He adds: "Now that my life has followed the course of this winding arabesque, I find myself once more at the place where I started" (226).

Most critics of *Arabesques* have discussed this structural pattern, which imparts to the novel its title.[11] Nonetheless, I know of no critic who has claimed that this pattern co-exists with a time-bound, "Western" principle. The novel terms this second principle "a capricious thread", one which introduces an unexpected element that generates change and development: "All at once a story that had apparently come to its end is exposed to a capricious thread, which will draw it into unexpected regions in an adventure whose outcome we cannot foresee" (36). This statement occurs when Anton is on his way to a meeting with Surayyah Said, during which he adds: "From a tale that was apparently drawing to an end, a new unruly thread shoots out and turns the tale in a startling direction" (54). This meeting, as we might recall, reveals what is perhaps the most unruly thread in the novel: the existence of two Anton Shammases. Interestingly, the narration of this conversation with Suryyah is constantly interrupted by Anton's memories of the childhood scene in which he was lowered by his brother into a cistern in order to clean it, and was forced to accept assistance from a neighbor's daughter, to whom he found himself attracted. Many analogies, which I cannot analyze here in detail, are established between the two scenes in the fashion of a symmetrical arabesque. The two principles, the "Arabesque" and the "capricious thread", thus co-exist throughout the novel, just as two nations, two languages, and three religions could possibly inhabit together a utopian vision of our conflicted region.

In spite of the novel's destabilization of belonging, which takes place on so many levels, it seems to me that *Arabesques* has come to belong to the Hebrew/Israeli literary canon both because of its political agenda – more acceptable today than at the time of its publication – and because of its intrinsic literary excellence. Moreover, Shammas has paved the road for other Israeli-Arab novelists and poets who write in Hebrew, such as Salman Masalha, Sayed Kashua, and Ayman Sicseck. He has also inspired Israeli-Jewish writers who integrate Arabic into their Hebrew, such as Almog Behar, one of whose stories paradoxically announces, in

---

11 For a post-modern interpretation of the title, see Feldman 1999, 377–378.

Arabic but in Hebrew letters, that "I am One of the Jews" ("Ana min al Yahoud"). Behar has also written an untitled poem which combines Hebrew and Arabic within almost every word.

Are these literary relations intimations of a double belonging, or is it only wishful thinking on my part? I admit, it is to co-existence that I long to belong.

References

Amichai, Yehuda. *Poems by Yehuda Amichai*. Jerusalem and Tel-Aviv: Schocken Publishing House, 2003 [1974] [Hebrew].
Bassnett, Susan. *Comparative Literature: A Critical Introduction*. Oxford: Blackwell, 1993.
Bhabha, Homi K. "The Other Question". *The Politics of Theory*. Ed. Francis Baker. Colchester: Essex University Press, 1983. 18–36.
Bhabha, Homi K. *The Location of Culture*. London and New York: Routledge, 1995.
Cather, Willa. *My Antonia*. Boston: Houghton Mifflin Company, 1954 [1918].
Dante Alighieri. *De Vulgare Eloquentia*. 1302.
Deleuze, Gilles and Felix Guattari. *Kafka: Pour une littérature mineure*. Paris: Les Editions de Minuit, 1975.
Ezrahi, Sidra. "Not Israel, Not Palestine: Other Spaces in *Arabesques*". *A Sort of Solution to Silence – Modern Arab Literature in Hebrew*. Eds., Omri Grinberg, Hannan Hever and Yiftach Ashkenazy. Tel Aviv: New World Press, 2018. 85–97. [Hebrew].
Feldman, Y. S. "Postcolonial Memory, Postmodern Intertextuality: Anton Shammas's *Arabesques* Revisited". *PMLA: Publications of the Modern Language Association of America* 114.3 (1999): 373–389.
Ginsburg, Shai. "The Bookcase and the Language of Grace". *Mikan* 14 (2014): 239–263 [Hebrew].
Gluzman, Michael. "Throwing a Beer Can into Bialik's 'Pond': Postcolonial Intertextuality in Anton Shammas's *Arabesques*". *Jerusalem Studies in Hebrew Literature* 19 (2003): 327–347 [Hebrew].
Foucault, Michel. *Des espaces autres*. Paris: Editions Gallimard, 1984.
Hever, Hannan. *Producing the Modern Canon: Nation Building and Minority Discourses*. New York and London: New York University Press, 2002.
Hever, Hannan. *The Narrative and the Nation: Critical Readings in the Canon of Hebrew Literature*. Tel-Aviv: Resling, 2007 [Hebrew].
Irigaray, Luce. *This Sex which is Not One*. Transl. Catherine Porter with Carolyn Burke Ithaca: Cornell University Press, 1985.
Rimmon-Kenan, Shlomith. "Place, Space, and Michal Govrin's *Snapshots*". *Narrative* 17.2 (2009): 220–234.
Shammas, Anton. "Exile from a Democracy". *Literature in Exile*. Ed. John Glad. Durham: Duke University Press, 1990. 85–86.
Shammas, Anton. *Arabesques*. Transl. Vivian Eden. Berkeley: University of California Press, 2001.

Vivian Liska
Derrida's Appurtenances: A Footnote on Language and Belonging

> Appurtenance: something subordinate to another, more important thing; adjunct; accessory. Origin: 1350–1400; Middle English < Anglo-French, equivalent to *ap-* ap-1+ *-purtenance* a belonging.[1]

> I do not define myself on the basis of elementary forms of kinship. But it also means, more figuratively, that I am not part of any group, that I do not identify myself with a linguistic community, a national community, a political party, or with any group or clique whatsoever, with any philosophical or literary school. "I am not one of the family" means: do not consider me "one of you," "don't count me in," I want to keep my freedom, always: this, for me, is the condition not only for being singular and other, but also for entering into relation with the singularity and alterity of others. When someone is one of the family, not only does he lose himself in the herd, but he loses the others as well; the others become simply places, family functions, or places or functions in the organic totality that constitutes a group, school, nation or community of subjects speaking the same language. (Derrida and Ferraris 2001, 27)

Language is generally counted among the markers of a collectivity, such as ethnicity, nationhood, territory, or religion. But linking language to belonging is a contentious issue. Suspended between the consensual and the singular, language never reaches either pole. Although it is shared with others, the meanings it generates among its users never fully coincide. However far poets bend words towards the radically singular, the ineffable, or the as yet unsaid, language inevitably retains the traces of its origin as a tool for common usage. This makes of language both a coveted and an ultimately unattainably currency for consolidating a collectivity: it reinforces bonds and the illusion of belonging, yet at the same time can reveal the limitations of both communal togetherness and its opposite, the desire to stand apart, to be "singular and other."

Jews, arguably more than any other group, borrowed, absorbed, and appropriated the languages spoken in the multiple dwelling places they traversed during their diasporic wanderings. At the same time, they also retained through the millennia a sacred language believed to be divinely bestowed. Neither the multilingualism resulting from Jewish history nor the belief in the divine origin of the Hebrew language is conducive to an association of language with

---

[1] "Appurtenance." *Dictionary.com Unabridged*. Random House, Inc. http://www.dictionary.com/browse/appurtenance (10 March 2017).

https://doi.org/10.1515/9783110525519-012

belonging. On one hand, the historical experience of linguistic plurality is too mobile, decentered, and diffused to ensure belonging. On the other, what is sacred can neither be owned nor fully adhered to. This unresolved duality between the plural and the singular centrally informs reflections on language and belonging in the Jewish tradition from Biblical times until modernity. The truth to which the Tower of Babel points – that any willfully constructed unity must fall apart – has its reverse: that language is a collective endeavor and so any attempt at linguistic singularity, at standing apart, cannot succeed. Something will eventually betray both the drive to cohesion and the drive to uniqueness. The question remains how these forces are weighted and how they interact with and against each other.

Enacting Oscillation

"I only have one language; it is not mine" (Derrida 1998, 1): this paradoxical, or rather aporetic, remark opens Jacques Derrida's essay *Monolingualism of the Other; or, The Prosthesis of Origin*,[2] a complex reflection on language and belonging situated in the interstices between the French, the Algerian, and the Jewish. The sentence captures Derrida's uneasy relation to his "only language," French, which, he hastens to add, cannot fully belong to someone such as himself, a Jew of colonial Algeria. Like these opening remarks, Derrida's essay as a whole intersperses subtle autobiographical references with conceptual arguments about the possibility of "having a language" that neither falls together with a particular national identity nor amounts to a universally accessible and transparent means of communication. Weaving together the experiential and theoretical strands of his argument, he explains that his childhood experience in Algiers led him to envision a radical philosophical and political language of non-belonging. His community spoke the French of the colonies, which "will always remain incoherent" (Derrida 1998, 2). Cut off from Arabic and Berber, and from hybrid Jewish languages such as Yiddish and Ladino, there was no "idiom internal to the Jewish community," no protection of a "home-of-one's own" (Derrida 1998, 54) – "*chez-soi*," in the original – against the language of the surrounding culture. As a result, he remained "outside" and turned this non-place into the locus where any grounding, and any belonging, becomes undone.

Shifting between conceptual and narrative modes, Derrida's essay is not propositional but performative. It enacts the unsettling of the fixations involved

---

[2] Originally published in French as *Le monolinguisme de l'autre, ou La prothèse d'origine* (1996).

in discourses of identity or belonging, without obliterating them into a defense of universalism. If Derrida is fundamentally suspicious of identitarian allegiances, he is also skeptical of the idea that they are arbitrary constructions or could be invented from nothing. Reflecting explicitly on his own – and, more generally, on Jewish – belonging, he performs a voyage that prefigures the vertiginous *mise en abîme* at the core of his reflections on what he calls "national exemplarism." He turns this discourse – a symptom of an affirmative approach to identifying with a collectivity – into a dizzying and undecidable oscillation. He achieves this effect through his performative style of writing. Creatively pursuing such paradoxical thinking to its ultimate logical impasse, Derrida declares:

> If the self-identity of the Jew or of Judaism were to consist of this exemplarity, that is, in a certain non–self-identity ... the more one dislodges self-identity, the more one says "my own identity consists in not being identical to myself, in being foreign, non-coincident with myself," etc. the more one is Jewish! And at that moment, the word, the attribute "Jewish" ... the logical proposition "I am Jewish" thus loses all assurance, is swept up in an ambition, a claim, an outbidding without end![3] (Hollander 2008, 134)

Derrida regards this figure of thought itself as Jewish, an attribute that, in turn, is put into question by that very groundlessness, and so on, *ad infinitum*. Derrida sees in this very structure of infinite regress an opening toward an ethical stance no longer grounded in or aiming for either a stable identity or a fixed belonging, but, on the contrary, emerging from and oriented toward this vertiginous dynamic itself.

Critics have repeatedly charged Derrida with an excessively abstract, playful, or metaphorical approach to Jewish identity.[4] Yet concrete historical experience and cultural traditions are far from absent in his reflections on issues of identity. Derrida confronts the concepts of identity with his own situation and writing. The "absolute habitat" (Derrida 1998, 1) of his "only language" has no clear-cut borders; it dwells "on the shores of the French language ... on the unplaceable line of its coast" (Derrida 1998, 2), as does his literary style. In *Monolingualism of the Other*, his general reflections on the illusion and futility of "owning" a language or "belonging" to a group based on a common language are closely related to his own "traumatic memory of a 'degradation'" (Derrida 1998, 16), the loss of French citizenship under the Vichy regime, the insecurities of an Algerian Jewish boy who discovers French literature as "the experience of a world without

---

3 This quotation is from Derrida's essay "Zeugnis, Gabe," in *Jüdisches Denken in Frankreich* (1994, 65). Cited in English in Dana Hollander's *Exemplarity and Chosenness. Rosenzweig and Derrida on the Nation of Philosophy* (2008).
4 See Jonathan Boyarin's *Thinking in Jewish* (1996).

any tangible continuity with the one in which we lived, with almost nothing in common with our natural or social landscapes" (Derrida 1998, 45), and – paradoxically – with his longing for a "pure," accent-free French: "I cannot bear or admire anything other than pure French" (Derrida 1998, 46). Derrida is neither a historian who hews to the particular nor a traditional philosopher who aims at universal abstractions. Circumventing both conceptual fixation and factual description, he introduces historical concreteness in a performative mode of writing that bears far-reaching consequences. Derrida's writings between philosophical conceptualization and personal narration open a perspective beyond both universalism and particularism and thematize passages and ruptures that occur when particular experiences, situations, and linguistic forms become general possibilities. Derrida enacts this perspective in accordance with his view that the most universalist approach to questions of belonging is necessarily articulated in a specific narrative mode, a particular idiom, and from within a specific historical, cultural, and existential situation. The multivarious and literary style of *Monolingualism of the Other* renders the origin of his own idiom explicit without acceding to the "national exemplarism" he rejects, thus remaining true to his desire to "keep [his] freedom" and to stay at a distance from any linguistic or ethnic community.

Footnote 9

In Chapter 7 of his essay, Derrida interrupts his cogitations about his "standing apart" from any group with a striking fifteen-page footnote. In this note, Derrida confronts his personal approach to language and belonging, yet also contrasts his own linguistic situation with that of Ashkenazi, mainly German-speaking Jews, particularly Franz Rosenzweig, Gershom Scholem, Hannah Arendt, Emmanuel Levinas, Paul Celan, and Franz Kafka. In these authors he finds an echo of his own views on the aporia of having a language without owning it, but also emphasizes significant differences to his own vision of language. Although – or maybe precisely because – the footnote is less explicitly autobiographical than the main text, and mainly appeals to a quasi-objective argumentation, the specter of Derrida's own belonging reemerges.

As marginalia, the peculiar footnote opens a mere sideline, an appendix to the problem of language and belonging discussed in the main text. However, in the note itself Derrida points to the revealing significance of such "interrupting" remarks: "Why are such serious things [matters of belonging] often spoken about on the occasion of public conversations," he asks, in reference to an interview Levinas gave on his relation to the French language, "as if the speakers were caught off guard and spoke in a kind of improvisation?" (Derrida 1998, 91). A footnote, like an interview, allows extemporaneous digression, a writing off-guard on "serious things." But seriousness does not necessarily imply familiarity. Indeed, Derrida announces that he will explore in the footnote a territory far less familiar to him than his Algerian experience. He presents the footnote as a preliminary to a "general study to come," to be titled "*The Monolingualism of the Host: Jews of the Twentieth Century, the Mother Tongue, and the Language of the Other, on Both Sides of the Mediterranean*" (Derrida 1998, 78, italics in original). The study was never written as such, though many of Derrida's later texts such as *Of Hospitality* (2000), *The Eyes of Language* (2002), and others can be traced to this footnote. This addendum – a supplement, in Derrida's parlance – acts as a seemingly subordinate appurtenance that both conceals and reveals a "serious thing": an *appartenance*, a French term that means belonging.

In the footnote itself, Derrida outlines the "emergence of a taxonomy or a general typology" (Derrida 1998, 78) of approaches to a language of one's own, classifying them according to their views of origin and belonging. His reflections on the Ashkenazi thinkers and authors are driven by a set of implicit questions: Do the authors' approaches to the question of language and belonging preclude the idea that language could *belong* or that one can *belong to* it? How do they relate to the radical aporia Derrida aims at? Are there remnants of a longing for origins? And what is it that underlies their nostalgia for foundations, for a language of belonging?

Derrida distinguishes between the philosophers – Rosenzweig, Arendt, and Levinas – and the literary authors – Celan and Kafka. He contends that the latter are closer to his own views on language. The footnote's taxonomic form (in contrast to the elliptical and suggestive interweaving of argument and autobiographical narration in the main text) makes Derrida's identification with the literary authors particularly striking. This discrepancy can partly be explained by Derrida's characterization of the footnote as "modest reflections" and "hypotheses" (Derrida 1998, 78), based on "taking in the view of the other shore of Judaism, on *another* coastline of the Mediterranean, in places that, in another way, are even more alien to me than Christian France" (Derrida 1998, 79, italics in original). The footnote's typological categorization perhaps betrays the desire to make a grasp of, to "take in," the territory of the other. Yet this mode of writing inevitably affects the meaning, scope, and ultimately the alterity itself – the claim to his own and the other's singularity – that Derrida aims at in his book, an attitude expounded in the quote that introduces this essay.

Jewish Experience, Origin, and Language: A Taxonomy

> *Une voix vient de l'autre rive. Une voix interrompt le dire du déja dit* [A voice comes from the other shore and interrupts the continuous saying of what has already been said]. (Levinas 1990, 230)

When Derrida turns to "the other shore of the Mediterranean," his style shifts from the performative, dense, and literary writing of the main text of *Monolingualism* to what he calls a "typo-taxonomy." Here, Derrida's enacted oscillation grinds to a halt. The "ordering" gesture of Derrida's footnote, along with its polemical argumentation, implicitly presupposes a foundation, a grounding, a proper position, a "place" of his own. In his footnote, Derrida departs from narration and turns instead to ranking the thinkers he discusses in terms of their proximity to his own views. The footnote raises a dual question: how does Derrida listen to these voices from "the other shore," and what does this mode of listening reveal about his own speaking?

Rosenzweig's Attenuation

Derrida begins his discussion of Ashkenazi thinkers with Franz Rosenzweig's thoughts on language in *The Star of Redemption* (1921). Derrida initially insists on the affinities between Rosenzweig's views and his own, but ends up pointing to the limits of this similarity. Derrida extensively expounds upon Rosenzweig's ideas about the Jews' de-propriation of language, which he regards as close to his own stance: the Jewish people live in foreign lands and speak languages that are not their own. They do not even possess their own language, for their sacred language, like their holy land, belongs to God and cannot be owned by people. Having no idiom of their own, Jews speak languages borrowed from their hosts and use languages of immigrants, such as Ladino and Yiddish. Derrida briefly remarks that Rosenzweig's identification of people, blood, and language edges dangerously close to anti-Semitic notions. Yet his main reservation towards the German-Jewish thinker is only seemingly conceptional. It arises from a more personal incompatibility and thereby points to Derrida's own grounding in an experience and an origin different than those of Rosenzweig. Derrida lists three ways in which Rosenzweig "*attenuates*" the de-propriation of a language available to German-Jews but inaccessible "to the 'French-Jew-from-Algeria' who speaks, and of whom I am speaking, here" (Derrida 1998, 82, italics in original). When he invokes the French-Jew-from-Algeria, he does not speak only *of* this figure. This hyphenated Jew is, as Derrida writes, the one "who speaks ... here" – it is Derrida himself. But why this strange, distancing syntax that both circumscribes and circumvents the speaker's identity – his belonging?

Derrida begins his enumeration of the ways Rosenzweig weakens and limits his insights into linguistic dispossession with a reprimand of his *"unreserved"* attachment to the German language (Derrida 1998, 82, italics in original): Rosenzweig, in short, loves it as his own; he even translated the Hebrew Bible into German, which he could consider "the language of his country" (Derrida 1998, 82). Rosenzweig's lack of reservation about the German language, his unrestrained loyalty to it, contrasts with Derrida's ambivalent, oscillating relationship to French.

Rosenzweig's attachment to German differs even more strongly from Derrida's own *experience*: "The Algerian Jew," Derrida writes, had only "a French *of the colonized*" (Derrida 1998, 84, italics in original) at his disposal, the language of the colonizer which he could not affirm. Furthermore, neither Judeo-Spanish nor Hebrew, Rosenzweig's second and third potential ways out of the monolingual prison, offered viable alternatives for the Algerian Jew; neither of these languages was spoken or taught in Franco-Maghrebian Jewish communities. Derrida concludes that Rosenzweig, who loves German, who can relate to Yiddish, and who calls Hebrew "a language *proper* to the Jewish people when they practice, read and understand it – at least in liturgy" (Derrida 1998, 84), fails to account for the radical aporia of having a language which is not "one's own." Derrida seems to conduct his critique of Rosenzweig on purely objective, historical, and sociological grounds; the conceptual argumentation leaves his personal stakes unexpressed. The mode of writing he deploys in the footnote appears designed to ward off any direct recourse to his own situation which could belie his idea of language as signifier of non-belonging.

Arendt's Mother Tongue

Derrida next turns to the linguistic ethics of Hannah Arendt. He fiercely criticizes her "ineradicable attachment to a unique mother tongue" (Derrida 1998, 84) and her "unfailing fidelity to [the German] language" (Derrida 1998, 85). Derrida has hardly anything positive to say of Arendt's approach to language and belonging. His only praise comes in his remark that she is not as misguided as Adorno, who returned to Germany after the war – and went even further than Arendt in admiring the German language for its metaphysical qualities. Derrida accuses her of linguistic essentialism and of misleading convictions about origins, a sovereign subject who is the master of language and ultimately her own rootedness in – and belonging to – her own provenance. He refers to Arendt's famous interview with the German journalist Gunther Gauss in 1964. Replying to a question about her relation to the German language after the catastrophe, Arendt says: "I was telling myself: What is to be done?" When asked about her feelings towards the contamination of German by Nazism, Arendt famously replies: "It is not really the German language, after all, that has gone mad. And in the second place, nothing can replace the mother tongue."[5] Analyzing these two statements, Derrida calls attention to the grammatical structure of "not really... after all." He concludes that Arendt "is visibly seeking to reassure herself" (Derrida 1998, 86) when she insists on the sanity of the German language despite its having been the means of expression of Nazism. Unlike in the case of Rosenzweig (and later of Levinas), Derrida suspects Arendt of unconscious motivations and massive repression of the unsettling insights behind her statements. Could there be an (unconscious) gender bias in Derrida's assessment of the motivations behind the views stated by "the German Jewish woman named Hannah Arendt" (Derrida 1998, 84)? And/ or could this bias be related to Arendt's invocation of her *mother* tongue and its rationality?

According to Derrida, the mother, like language, can become a place of political and existential madness: "In both cases, what becomes mad is something like the law or the origin of meaning (the father, the king, the queen, the mother)" (Derrida 1998, 88). Similar, or rather concurrent, to language, the very place of origin, the mother of language, Derrida claims, *can* go mad: this madness resides in what is absolutely unique (and thus remains unclassifiable and outside of any norm and "normality"). At the same time, it is also absolutely replaceable: "It could be demonstrated," Derrida argues in characteristically counterintuitive fashion, "that absolute uniqueness renders one as crazy as absolute replaceability" (Derrida 1998, 89). For Derrida, the origin is thus not *one*, as language is neither absolutely opaque nor absolutely transparent, but simultaneously both. Because of her need to leave both mother and origin intact, the "German Jewish woman named Arendt" fails to see this aporia.

Derrida finds just one line of Arendt's interview worthy of consideration. Asked about the possibility of forgetting one's mother tongue, she mentions the traumatic rupture that the discovery of Auschwitz represented for German Jewish immigrants. The reference to Auschwitz, Derrida claims, shows that language lies beyond the grip of fully conscious subjects. In this moment, Arendt conveys, in his eyes, a "proper" de-propriation of language. But Derrida's momentary

---

5 "Was bleibt? Es bleibt die Muttersprache": Hannah Arendt in conversation with Günter Gaus, ZDF, broadcast 28 October 1964.

endorsement returns, a page later, to sharp disapproval: Arendt's notion of language, says Derrida, "remains the ultimate essence of the soil, the foundation of meaning, the inalienable property that one carries within oneself" (Derrida 1998, 91). Why does Derrida so quickly dismiss Arendt's admission of the shock that temporarily suspended the bond with the mother tongue? This admission renders Arendt's renewed attachment to the German language neither "essential" nor organically "necessary," but rather a matter of choice.[6] The renewed attachment, or what Arendt would call "a new beginning," implies neither the subject's mastery over language nor its deterministic subjection to it. It implies, rather, the possibility of what none other than Derrida prizes as an open future – a "future still without a name" (Derrida 1998, 93). Perhaps this "German-Jewish woman" comes too close to what Derrida believes belongs to him alone.

Levinas's Paternal Law

For its third example, the footnote takes up Levinas's views on language and belonging. Derrida begins by praising Levinas's multilingualism: he "wrote, taught, and lived almost all his life in the French language, whereas Russian, Lithuanian, German and Hebrew remained his other familiar languages" (Derrida 1998, 90–91). Moreover, Derrida does not find in him a solemn reference to a mother tongue, nor does Levinas succumb to "Arendtian radicalism, namely, the attachment to a certain *sacrality* of the *root*" (Derrida 1998, 91, italics in original). Although Levinas might not speak of roots, he does have another equivocal grounding in mind. Derrida refers to an interview in which Levinas uses the term "soil of language," in referring to the French soil (Derrida 1998, 91). To Levinas's credit, Derrida considers his French as "an adopted or elected language," an acquired familiarity instead of a maternal figure of origin. For Levinas, language is thus more an expression than a maternal idiom, and "perhaps not the place of the first meaning of beings" (Derrida 1998, 92), as Derrida quotes from Levinas's *Ethique et infini* (1992, 15). Even Levinas's affection for "the classical French of the Enlightenment" (Derrida 1998, 91) and his embrace of Greek as the language of philosophy are not appropriated; they are merely affirmed as a language of the other. But Levinas, too, seems to transgress the boundaries set so firmly by Derrida who is critical of Levinas's attempt to replace Rosenzweig's sacrality and

---

[6] For an illuminating article about Derrida's critique of Arendt's fidelity to her mother tongue, see Jennifer Gaffney's "Can a Language Go Mad? Arendt, Derrida, and the Political Significance of the Mother Tongue" (2015).

Arendt's repressed "maternal madness" – which Derrida considers remnants of pagan idolatry – with "the paternal holy law" (Derrida 1998, 92).

This runs counter to Derrida's notion of an aporetic relation of language and belonging. How legitimate is it, however, to call for a rejection of any foundation – territorial, maternal, or paternal – in the context of such polemics? In the name of what? Such a call cannot but turn into a law, a self-imposed one but nevertheless one which, in this case, is declared by none other than the French-Jewish-Algerian who claims to belong to nothing and no one, yet who seems, in this footnote, to be firmly and unwaveringly rooted on his own side of the shore.

Kafka, Celan, and a Literary Scene

At the end of his lengthy footnote, Derrida turns to Kafka and Celan, "some great writers whom I will not hasten to inscribe in the outline of this little taxonomy" (Derrida 1998, 92). Derrida admits that their achievements – what they "have made happen to the German language" – cannot fit within a footnote. He hesitates to assign a category to "these non-Germans (different in that way from Rosenzweig, Scholem, Benjamin, Adorno, Arendt) who wrote especially in German" (Derrida 1998, 92). The rationale that allows Kafka and Celan to escape Derrida's grid is, however, conceived entirely in terms of his own "origins." In a convoluted syntax that once again circumvents the agency of a subject, Derrida writes: "Let it suffice to mark this diacritic value, in a way, between destinies; for Kafka and Celan who were not Germans, German was nevertheless neither a language of adoption nor one of election." More importantly, German, in the polyglot cities of Prague during the Habsburg Empire and of Czernowitz before the Second World War, was, "unlike French for the Jews of Algeria, [neither] a 'colonial language,' nor a 'language of the master'" (Derrida 1998, 92).

At this point, Derrida abruptly quotes from a letter Kafka wrote to Max Brod: "What the majority of those who began to write in German wanted was to quit Judaism, generally with the vague approval of the fathers (it was this vagueness that was revolting); they wanted it, but their hind legs still stuck to the Judaism of the father, and their forelegs could not find any new terrain. The despair that followed constituted their inspiration" (Derrida 1998, 92–93). Kafka's view that language acts as a vehicle to move away from origins without reaching and settling new terrain, that language is an in-between space, undoubtedly resembles Derrida's own vision of possible and impossible linguistic belonging. Only after quoting this famous passage, in which Kafka reveals his own, literally abysmal, relationship to German, Jews, and fathers, does Derrida leave behind the categories of his taxonomy and his comparison of cultures and identities. In an imaginary scene that returns him to the literary bravado of his book's main text, he invites the reader to join him in "following Kafka to the cinema" and to "pause briefly over an image" of his own making:

> We are in central Europe, let us wonder what the plot is – what matchmaker, what marriage of convenience, could have linked the German of a mother tongue which would not by any means have "gone mad," the German of Hannah Arendt, with the German of Kafka, as those "who began to write in German' and to quit Judaism, generally with the vague approval of the fathers." Kafka and Arendt: neither an endogamy nor an exogamy of language. Reason or madness? (Derrida 1998, 93)

On the face of it, Derrida merely asks what Arendt's mother tongue – a German language of belonging, of moving towards roots and heritage – has in common with the German of Kafka, a signature of non-belonging, of overcoming family and tradition. But there is also another Derrida: the litterateur and choreographer who becomes a matchmaker. This Derrida marries the language of mad mothers (Arendt) and legal fathers (Levinas), German history and Jewish tradition, literature and philosophy. While the outcome is as uncertain as it is questionable, both non-belonging and belonging are invited to the wedding of these languages – a marriage neither endogamous nor exogamous.

In the footnote's final paragraph, Derrida gives birth to a child of this marriage. He briefly and somewhat abruptly expresses admiration for the Algerian-born French Jewish writer Hélène Cixous. Derrida considers her work an "intersection" of Ashkenazi and Sephardi experiences, "weaving *all* these filiations, regenerating them towards a future still without a name" (Derrida 1998, 93). Yet, rather than quote from Cixous's *work*, Derrida tellingly traces her (mixed) *parentage*: her Sephardi father spoke French, her Ashkenazi mother German. It is perhaps significant that the other "poetics of language" (Derrida 1998, 93) Derrida has in mind, his aim of a radical aporetic relation of language and belonging, becomes, at the end of his examination, a question of genealogy and, ultimately, a matter of parental lineage.

What Derrida achieves in this footnote may be more radical than what he does in the main text. His footnote, in which an occasional literary flourish merely punctuates a text that is otherwise suffused with traces of belonging, belies his posture of being free from such attachments to roots and origins. However, it also reveals that attachment to origins, to roots, and to belonging does not let itself be effaced easily, if at all. One might argue that Footnote 9, this appurtenance to *Monolingualism of the Other*, calls into question Derrida's postulated freedom from family, group and nation – from what he rather arrogantly labels the "herd" – thereby undoing the very paradox he seeks. And yet, one can conjecture that if the repressed moment of one's *appartenance* must reassert itself somewhere, there is maybe no better place than in the appurtenance of a footnote.

Bibliography

Arendt, Hannah. "Zur Person." "Was bleibt? Es bleibt die Muttersprache": Hannah Arendt in conversation with Günter Gaus, ZDF, broadcast 28 October 1964. http://www.rbb-online.de/zurperson/interview_archiv/arendt_hannah.html (23 March 2017).

Boyarin, Jonathan. *Thinking in Jewish*. Chicago: University of Chicago Press, 1996.

Derrida, Jacques. "Zeugnis, Gabe." *Jüdisches Denken in Frankreich*. Ed. and transl. Elisabeth Weber, Frankfurt am Main: Jüdischer Verlag, 1994. 63–90.

Derrida, Jacques. *Le monolinguisme de l'autre, ou La prothèse d'origine*. Paris: Éditions Galilée, 1996.

Derrida, Jacques. *Monolingualism of the Other; or, The Prosthesis of Origin*. Transl. Patrick Mensah. Stanford: Stanford University Press, 1998.

Derrida, Jacques, and Maurizio Ferraris. *A Taste for the Secret*. Transl. Giacomo Donis. Cambridge: Polity, 2001.

Gaffney, Jennifer. "Can a Language Go Mad? Arendt, Derrida, and the Political Significance of the Mother Tongue." *Philosophy Today* 59.3 (2015): 523–539.

Hollander, Dana. *Exemplarity and Chosenness. Rosenzweig and Derrida on the Nation of Philosophy*. Stanford: Stanford University Press, 2008.

Levinas, Emmanuel. *Autrement qu'être ou au delà de l'essence*. Paris: Biblio Livre de Poche, 1990.

Levinas, Emmanuel. *Ethique et infini*. Paris: Fayard, 1992.

Susanne Zepp
De-essentialized Belonging: Poetics of the Self in Joyce Mansour and Clarice Lispector

This paper traces the relevance of belonging in the literary experiments of the Ukrainian-born Brazilian writer Clarice Lispector (1920–1977) and the Franco-Egyptian poet Joyce Mansour (1928–1986). Polylingual and multicultural in their everyday lives, both authors developed poetics of belonging that resist the concept of a single, consistent identity. Both writers explored (in the 1950s, 1960s and 1970s) how textual selves can reflect diversity in language – Lispector through experiments with narrative voice, Mansour through transformations of the poetic self and the lyrical subject.

Significant research has already been conducted on the writings of the two respective authors. Often, they have been studied as highly individual, isolated, if not idiosyncratic phenomena of their respective linguistic communities. Joyce Mansour was a female second-generation surrealist who decided to write in French, which was not her first language. In both her prose and her poetry as well as in her visual art, Mansour vehemently challenged all current conceptions of what was appropriate for women to write.[1] Her texts broke sexual taboos, and she explored libidinal themes in her writing and in her art in manifold varieties. Clarice Lispector also wrote in a language other than the one her family had spoken when she was a child, and her writings were likewise perceived as "shocking", albeit for different reasons than Mansour's texts. One could mention other outstanding female writers of the era in question who "shocked" (and continue to shock) readers and who were fluent in more than one language (and culture): in the Spanish-speaking context, one might consider Alejandra Pizarnik

---

[1] In this context, Victoria Carruthers's important study of Mansour's poetry has to be mentioned ("Excessive Bodies, Shifting Subjects and Voice in the Poetry of Joyce Mansour", in: *Dada/Surrealism* 19 (2013), n. pag. Carruthers argues that it is Mansour's "very insistence on 'deconstructing' and fragmenting the body that creates a disembodied voice, one that layers disparate images together so compactly and lists parts of the body and bodily functions in such a repetitive mantra that they no longer imply a consistent whole, imaginative or otherwise", resulting in a resistance to "developing a 'voice' that espouses a single, consistent identity". Carruther's paper and its argument were not only crucial for encouraging my interest in Mansour's poetry; they also resonate with arguments in my readings of Mansour's poems – however, the question of Jewish belonging is not a focus of Carruthers's paper, which instead focuses on the female voice.

https://doi.org/10.1515/9783110525519-013

(1936–1972), whose writings are discussed in another contribution to this volume; in France, one might think of Natalie Sarraute.[2]

A comparative analysis of these polylingual female authors, who contributed immensely to the post-war literary landscape, is still a lacuna in literary studies, and one that cannot be filled by a short essay. Therefore, the modest ambition of this paper is to present a joint reading of Lispector and Mansour and to discuss how their endeavors coincide in their effort to transform transboundary and polylingual historical experience into literary representations of more than one linguistic and cultural belonging.

On the basis of previously existing biographies by Nadia Batela Gotlib,[3] Teresa Cristina Montero Ferreira[4] and Claire Varin,[5] as well as the autobiographic novel *No Exílio* by Elisa Lispector (Clarice Lispector's sister), Benjamin Moser had published in 2009 another biography tracing Clarice Lispector's life. In her review of the Brazilian edition of Moser's endeavor, Berta Waldman underlined that no biography will ever be able to decipher the relation between the complexity of Lispector's texts and her biographical experiences.[6] This paper will not attempt to do so. The following brief biographical remarks shall merely

---

[2] Sarrautes's 1939 "Tropismes" had featured kaleidoscopic experiments with narrative. In a brilliant essay, Cristina Zanoaga-Rastoll has recently demonstrated how Russian cultural heritage operates in the writings of Nathalie Sarraute. Zanoaga-Rastoll scrutinizes how the narrative entities in Sarraute's texts explore the subjectivity of what Sarraute calls "the human being in general", creating a "narrative space that makes possible the contact between several potentialities of the ego, but also between different languages and cultures".Cristina Zanoaga-Rastoll, "Les langues des tropismes chez Nathalie Sarraute", *Carnets* 7 (2016), n. pag., e-journal : https://carnets.revues.org/1062

[3] See: Nádia Battella Gotlib, *Uma vida que se conta*, São Paulo 1995, the augmented Spanish edition *Una vida que se cuenta*, Buenos Aires 2007 and the revised and augmented edition published in São Paulo 2009. See also Nádia Gotlib's essay "Viajar, dissimular, pulsar: para uma biografia de Clarice Lispector", *Revista de Letras* 5 (2010), 179–189.

[4] Teresa Cristina Montero Ferreira, *Eu sou uma pergunta. Uma biografia de Clarice Lispector*, Rio de Janeiro 1999,

[5] Claire Varin, *Clarice Lispector: Rencontres brésiliennes*, Montréal 2007 (1987).

[6] "Por mais que informe, por mais bem escrito que seja, por mais que acerte em muitos planos, a obra falha, a meu ver, no desafio de decifrar o enigma da esfinge. Ainda assim, suas qualidades são muitas e não podem ser minimizadas. Como a literatura de Lispector tende a assombrar cada vez mais os leitores de outros países e continentes, o trabalho deste jovem pesquisador norte-americano auxiliará, com certeza, a informá-los a respeito dessa escritora ímpar da literatura brasileira." Berta Waldman, "Decifra-me! Uma biografia de Clarice Lispector". In: *WebMosaica* 2,1 (2010), 135-138.

serve as a point of reference and are based on Nelson Viera's entry[7] on the Jewish Women's Archive website: Clarice Lispector was born on December 10, 1920 in Tchetchelnik, Ukraine, to Marieta (1889–1930) and Pedro (Pinkhas) Lispector (1885–1940), who were fleeing from the pogroms with their two daughters Elisa and Tânia. Traveling by ship, they arrived in the northeast of Brazil in 1921. In 1925, the family moved to the major northeastern coastal city of Recife. After the death of Marietta Lispector in 1933, Pedro and his three daughters moved to Rio de Janeiro. Clarice Lispector began writing stories as a young teenager. Her first novel, *Perto do Coração Selvagem*, was published in 1943, the year she married Maury Gurgel Valente, who became a Brazilian diplomat in 1944. During that same year, the couple left Brazil for a series of international posts until 1959. Viera continues:

> As a result of her burgeoning career, problems in the marriage led Lispector to return to Rio with her two sons in 1959 and this move resulted in the couple's legal separation in 1968. [...] Except for a number of short trips and a return visit to her childhood city in the Northeast a year before she died, Lispector made Rio de Janeiro her home until her death of cancer on December 9, 1977.[8]

Joyce Mansour was born Joyce Patricia Adès in Bowden, England on July 25, 1928. R. Victoria Arana's entry in the *Companion to World Poetry* continues as follows: "When the baby was just a month old, her parents returned with her to Cairo, where the poet grew up [...]." With her second husband Samir Mansour, the poet took residence in Paris in 1954, where she began to work with several surrealist artists. Her first anthology of poems, *Cris*, had been published by éditions Seghers in 1953 and had been reviewed in a surrealist journal. She cooperated with André Breton and was an active participant in Parisian cultural life. Joyce Mansour died of cancer in 1986. In 1991, *Actes Sud* published her complete works. An installation on display between November 2014 and February 2015 in the *musée du Quai Branly* in Paris honored her life and work. In his introduction to the English translation of Mansour's poems, Serge Gavronsky underlines Mansour's strict religious upbringing as a Sephardic Jew as well as her sense of belonging to Egyptian culture.[9]

---

[7] Nelson H. Vieira, "Clarice Lispector." *Jewish Women: A Comprehensive Historical Encyclopedia*. 1 March 2009. Jewish Women's Archive. (Viewed on March 25, 2018) <https://jwa.org/encyclopedia/article/lispector-clarice>.
[8] Vieira 2009.
[9] Serge Gavronsky, "Introduction", in: *Screams. Joyce Mansour*. Translated by Serge Gavronsky, Sausalito 1995, 1–11.

Joyce Mansour and Clarice Lispector are two writers who incorporated different aspects of "belonging" – whether their own or that of others – into complex aesthetic forms that, in their many variations and transformations, challenge the concept of the natural possession of a given language and, by extension, the concept of identity. Moreover, in playing with the structure of language itself and in displaying a high degree of conceptual self-reflection, their literary projects may be said to converge. The represented self of their texts – the narrator in Lispector's prose; the "I" in Mansour's poems – is the locus of these experiments. Their mode is that of conceptual self-reflection.

In the writings of both authors, belonging is reflected in literary form in a manner that overcomes the idea of one fixed identity. In her seminal essay on women writers and the avant-garde movement in France, Susan Rubin Suleiman introduced the trope of a "double margin":

> If, as this trope suggests, culture is like a space to be mapped or a printed page, then the place of women, and of avant-garde movements, has traditionally been situated away from the center, on the fringe, in the margins. One difference is that avant-garde movements have willfully chosen their marginal position-the better to launch attacks at the center-whereas women have more often than not been relegated to that position: far from the altar as from the marketplace, those centers where cultural subjects invent and enact their symbolic and material rites.[10]

Maryann de Julio has very productively discussed the notion of the double margin in her analysis of Joyce Mansour's feminist interpretations of Egyptian mythology.[11] If we extend Suleiman's notion from the French context to a more global level, it becomes apparent that the writings of Joyce Mansour and Clarice Lispector are framed by a triple margin. First, they are on the margins by virtue of their avant-gardism; secondly, they are marginal to the avant-garde as female writers; and thirdly, they are marginal (in terms of the evocation of ethnicity by Mansour; in terms of language by Lispector) on the canonic map of modernist Jewish literatures with regard to Europe, the Americas, and the Middle East. However, a reflection of this triple marginality can be extremely productive for a discussion of the poetic and critical methods of contemporary Jewish literary studies.

---

10 Susan Rubin Suleiman, "Double Margin: Reflections on Women Writers and the Avant-Garde in France", in: *Yale French Studies* 75, 1988, 148–172.
11 Maryann De Julio, "Joyce Mansour and Egyptian Mythology", in: Mary Ann Caws, Rudolf E. Kuenzli & Gwen Raaberg, *Surrealism and Women*, Cambridge 1991, 114–122.

When Walter Benjamin proposed in the prologue to *Ursprung des deutschen Trauerspiels* (1928) that ideas are to objects as constellations are to stars, he suggested that ideas could help us to perceive relations between objects. Ian Buchanan remarks in this context on Benjamin:

> It also means ideas are not the same as concepts, nor can they be construed as the laws of concepts. Ideas do not give rise to knowledge about phenomena and phenomena cannot be used to measure their validity. This is not to say the constellation is purely subjective or all in our heads. The stars in the night sky are where they are regardless of how we look at them and there is something in how they are positioned above us that suggests the image we construct of them. But having said that, the names we use for constellations are embedded in history, tradition and myth. So the constellation is simultaneously subjective and objective in nature. [...] Theodor Adorno adopts and adapts the term constellation in his account of negative dialectics, transforming it into a model. The notion of constellation allows for a depiction of the relation between ideas that gives individual ideas their autonomy but does not thereby plunge them into a state of isolated anomie.[12]

It is by means of a similar conceptual move that, within the writings of Lispector and Mansour, belonging becomes not only a mode of reflecting individual and collective historical experience, but of transforming the relation between various languages and origins into a non-essentialist poetics. Concepts of belonging are depicted as being related to one another, but it is of fundamental importance that the relationships amongst these concepts (as well as the relationships between these concepts and the various textual voices expressing them) is imaginative and therefore fundamentally open and unresolved. For the two authors, language is not to be thought of as an expression of the identity of sign and matter, but rather as a confrontation with the non-identical and with the ineluctable reality of language itself.

« La face triangulaire »: Joyce Mansour's poetic selves

In 1965, Yves Bonnefoy published his influential essay on the principle of identity in French poetry, a complex meditation on the relation between language, poetic

---

[12] S. v. "Constellation" in: Ian Buchanan, *A Dictionary of Critical Theory*, Oxford 2010, and F. Jameson *Late Marxism: Adorno, or, The Persistence of the Dialectic* (1990).

tradition, the self and the other.¹³ Bonnefoy attributed to the French language not only a longing to express essence, but also an ability to do so – features that unite French poets from Villon and Chrétien de Troyes down to the present:

> Je crois que la poésie d'une langue d'essences comme le français a pour tâche toujours urgente de constituer, ou de retrouver, l'ordre profond, infra-conceptuel, au sein duquel le poète pourra se vivre comme présence, ayant vérifié les analogies, ayant défait les aspects opaques, ayant rouvert la voie qui mène vers l'intérieur.¹⁴

Bonnefoy understood Poetry as a mode of expression of the desire for a suspension of the separation of subject and object, for an experience of oneness, of wholeness – in other words: identity.

At the same time, Joyce Mansour developed a poetic universe that expressed substantially different modes of exploring the self. While Bonnefoy's conception of poetry understood French as a language of linguistic 'densification' directed towards an inner center, Mansour's poems strove to open, simultaneously bringing different processes of becoming into language. Through code shifting and code mixing, the integration of verses and citations from classical French poetry into her own lyrical texts, the infusion of her works with neologisms and other liberties taken with syntax, lexicon and orthography, Mansour's poetry subverts the standards of the French language and of traditional poetry. Mansour takes the practices of surrealist poetics further, notably by expanding Breton's notion of automatic writing, when her texts explore the self, its languages and ethnicity as a constellation of coincidences. Belonging is evoked in Mansour's texts according to a causal logic similar to what the surrealists called *hasard objectif* (objective chance), a visible and sometimes surprising link between one dimension in our lives and another that is brought about by chance, but also by some sort of interior necessity.

This can be illustrated by means of numerous poems from different periods of Mansour's oeuvre. The two texts discussed here are therefore exemplary for a poetic oeuvre waiting to be discovered in its full significance as an important chapter not only in the history of surrealism, but also in the history of Jewish literatures.

---

[13] "La poésie française et le principe d'identité" (1965), in: Yves Bonnefoy, *L'Improbable et autres essais*, Paris : Gallimard, 1983, 245–273.

[14] Bonnefoy 1983, 286–287: "I believe that the poetry of a language of essences such as French always has the task of constituting, or recovering, the profound, infra-conceptual order in which the poet can live as a presence, having verified the analogies, having undone the opaque aspects, having reopened the path that leads inwards" (my translation).

The following poem was published in the volume *Carré blanc* from 1965, thus in the same year as Bonnefoy's essay on identity in French poetry. The title of the poem is a play on words suggesting an endless repetition of the sentence "personne n'écoute" [Nobody listens], evoking the surrealist technique of the palindrome poem:

Sonne n'ecoute personne n'écoute per[15]

Fulgurants sauvages chevaux d'Europe	Dazzling wild horses in Europe
Chaos de membres brisés	Chaos of broken limbs
Murs mouvants	Shifting walls
Soleils	Suns
5 Pavés sanguinolents lancés par des mains aveugles	Bloody cobblestones thrown by blind hands
Dans la mayonnaise	In mayonnaise
Dans la boue	In the mud
Dans l'égout familièrement béant	In the familiar gaping sewer
Dans tout ce qui se nomme et qui n'ose se montrer	In all that is named and doesn't dare to show itself
10 L'Arabe en moi grelotte sur chaque marche de chair	The Arab woman in me is shivering flesh on each step
Soumise	Submissive
Capable d'attendre longtemps la triste mâture promise	Capable to wait long for the sad promised maturity
Saluez ô mes amis la mort ses fuites ses fusions	Greet death, my friends, his leaks, his fusions
Pour elle seule il n'est guère de zone interdite	In itself it is hardly a prohibited area
15 Dans le brasier de l'amour passion	In the blaze of love's passion
Puis	Then
Une fois la nuit venue	After nightfall
La nuit la nuit l'orage	The night the night the storm
Je reviens vers ma jeunesse	I return to my youth
20 Le phosphore effréné	The frantic phosphorus
La chaleur bestiale	The beastly heat
Les vagues de la vengeance permise	The waves of permitted revenge
Le sable	The sand
Le bâillement de la nuit fragile	The yawning of the fragile night
25 L'éther	The ether

---

15 Quoted from Les oeuvres complètes de Joyce Mansour, Paris : Éditions Michel de Maule, 2014, 445–446 (my working translation).

A l'heure où Paris s'allume	At the time when Paris switches on her lights
L'animal libre court encore sous nos phares	The free animal still runs under our beacons
L'âme exquise	The exquisite soul
Là-bas sur la route sexe subtil du désert	Out there on the subtle sex road of the desert
30 La belle pomme voilée ne vomit plus son ver	The beautifully veiled apple no longer vomits her worm
Clair de lune	Moonlight
Je suis juive il est vrai	I am indeed a Jewish woman
Capable d'apprendre la liberté dans la rue	Capable of learning freedom in the street
Où l'infamie fait étalage	Where infamy is flaunted
35 Je maudis en moi la femme qui accepte	I curse the woman in me who accepts
La face triangulaire du cadenas	The triangular face of the padlock
Silence	Silence
Je crache sur ceux qui écoutent	I spit on those who listen
Derrière leurs prunelles limpides	Behind their limpid eyes
40 Leurs braguettes piétinées par trop de cerveaux fêlés	Their codpieces trampled by too many cracked brains
Leur portes salement closes	Their badly closed doors
Nomenclature du cauchemar	Nomenclature of a nightmare
Une seule goutte d'urine sur le trottoir	A single drop of urine on the sidewalk
Tous les museaux s'allongent	All snouts grow longer

In its intermingling of elements of the unconscious with fragments of distant realities, Mansour's poem can be situated at the core of the poetics of the surrealists. Indeed, the poem refers to substantial components of surrealist poetics, for example André Breton's demand for the omnipresence of the dream in art (line 42: "Nomenclature du cauchemar") or the exposure of the complex inner worlds of sexuality and desire (verses 29–30: "Là-bas sur la route sexe subtil du désert / La belle pomme voilée ne vomit plus son ver", but also verse 15: "Dans le brasier de l'amour passion").

But at the same time, the poem displays striking expansions of "classical" surrealist poetry. It establishes the lyrical speaker as a diverse but distinct female self (line 10: "L'Arabe en moi grelotte sur chaque marche de chair" and line 32: "Je suis juive il est vrai"). However, in these terms of belonging, the poem unfolds the core of Mansour's polylingual aesthetics: The text scrutinizes established concepts of belonging by removing them from their established patterns and rearranging them. The terms "Arab" and "Jewish" evoke the complicated dynamics of inclusion and exclusion with regards to French citizenship.¹⁶ This is by no means accidental in a text published three years after the end of France's last colonial war in Algeria. The lyrical speaker is depicted in French as Arab and Jewish, at the same time a performative statement that undermines its own presuppositions. This "triangle" (line 26) evokes the ideological heritage of French colonialism in the poetic language itself. French language policies in the colonized areas were rooted in a long history of associating the French language with notions of unity and homogeneity. Since Morocco and Algeria regained independence from France in 1956 and 1962, respectively, both countries have worked towards reinstating Arabic as the official, national language; that is, both Modern Standard Arabic and Classical Arabic. Though rarely spoken in informal daily settings, these represent (from the perspective of this policy) the universal language of the Arab World, as well as the language of Quran. However, both the French linguistic policy and the policies of postcolonial states in North Africa are based on hierarchical conceptions of language, and Mansour's poem can be read as a reaction against this kind of linguistic hegemony. Rather than conceptualizing the linguistic situation in North Africa and in France as a dualistic conflict between two tongues, two cultures and two worlds, the poem proposes linguistic and ethnic multiplicity. This resonates with a passage from Hélène Cixous's autobiographical text "Reveries of the wild woman" : "Dès qu'il y avait Français j'étais exultation arme où il avait Arabes j'étais espoir et plaie. Moi, pensais-je je suis *inséparabe*. C'est une relation invivable avec soi-même."¹⁷ [The minute there was French I was exultation arms where there were Arabs I was hope and wound. Me, I thought I am *inseparab*. This is an unlivable relationship with oneself.] With the neologism "inséparabe", Cixous created a thought-provoking term out of the adjective "inseparable" and the noun "Arab", evoking a complexity of belonging similar to that displayed by Mansour's poem. In Mansour's text, "Europe" (line 1) and the "shifting walls" (line 3) are designations or "call[ings]" (line 7) of a space in which "The Arab woman in me" appears as "shivering flesh on each step". The poem expresses not merely the body but flesh, never entirely one's own; also blood and spit and urine; and the kinetic body of a woman in that space. The grammar is crucial here – "the Arab woman in me is shivering"; "I am indeed a Jewish woman"; "I curse the woman in me who accepts the triangular face of the padlock" – three modes of inhabitation in that space, including inhabitation by and as the other, and all gendered in the feminine. The poem's focus on the

---

16 See: Edwige Liliane Lefebvre, "Republicanism and Universalism: Factors of Inclusion or Exclusion in the French Concept of Citizenship", in: *Citizenship Studies* 7.1 (2003), 15–36.
17 Hélène Cixous, *Les rêveries de la femme sauvage. Scènes primitives*, Paris 2000, 45.

sensual, physical and material dimensions of language does not equate to the biographical experiences of the author. Rather, it is committed to the encounters between different historical, cultural and linguistic realities and poetic creation. The poem becomes the embodiment of different ethnicities and religions. Nevertheless, not one element is sufficient on its own or identical with itself. What characterizes Mansour's literary texts is the merging of different elements into a poetic voice that is simultaneously subjective and objective in nature – just as the cut-up technique in the title ("sonne" as cut from "personne") establishes sound as the space of both poetic personhood and its negation. Through these techniques, Mansour forms a language for the shifting embodiments and ways of feeling and thinking of her lyrical subject as it engages with the historical, geographical, political ("freedom") and fantastic ("nightmare") dimensions of that space of belonging.

A second poem from the collection *Carré blanc* (1965) reinforces such a reading of Mansour's poetics. It is entitled "La porte de la nuit est fermée à clef":

Retrouver le désert	Finding the desert again
Mon pays desséché et secret	My desiccated and secret country
La vie la vie même	Life life itself
L'enchanteur endormi dans les mirages vert profond	The enchanter asleep in deep green mirages
5 Du tapis	Of carpet
Traverser la Judée le frais jardin clos	Crossing Judea the cool walled garden
Le cimetière	The cemetery
Ô vent de Galilée miroitement de la nostalgie	O wind of Galilee shimmer of nostalgia
Sous une lune de pierre	Under a stone moon
10 Fuir les tigrures des nuages sur le sol aveuglant	Escaping the tiger-striped clouds On the blinding ground
Fuir en dansant	Escaping while dancing
Un vent plaintif s'est levé dans mon cœur	A plaintive wind has risen in my heart
De pâles paroles tombées des tuiles ruissellent sur	Pale words fallen from the tiles trickle
ma peau sèche	on my dry skin
15 (Mer morte du souvenir au creux de l'après-midi)	(dead sea of memory in the hollow of the afternoon)
Viens enlace-moi	Come and hold me
Allons vers les forêts	Let's go to the forests
Les ravins	The ravines
Les blancs pommiers	The white apples

20 Je rêve consumée par une folie dangereuse	I dream consumed by a dangerous madness
L'horizon brûlant et impie	The burning and unholy horizon
Fait signe	Makes a sign
Et les pyramides s'érigent	And the pyramids are erected
Sur la plaque tournante	On the turntable
25 De midi	Of midday / Of the Mediterranean
Je rêve oui je rêve sans espoir de retour	I dream yes I dream without hope of return
Seul l'aveugle sait maudire la bougie échevelée	Only the blind knows how to curse the disheveled candle
Les tendres yeux étirés de l'amour sont cailloux pour toi	Tender drawn eyes of love are pebbles for you
Bijoux trous tanières	Jewel holes caverns
30 Luxure et putréfaction	Lust and putrefaction
Coutures et balafres de l'église	Seams and scars of the church
Nommée	Named
Orx	Gold

The first word, "retrouver" (to retrieve), renders the ambition of this poetic text explicit; the following words indicate that the object of the search is the space of the textual subject. The process of retrieving the secret, desiccated country is equated with the search for life itself. The objects of the search are the historical landscapes of Galilee and Judea; the method and the instruments of the search are the words of the French language. This echoes a similar practice in the poetry of Edmond Jabès. One example is Jabès's poem "Les rames et la voile" from the volume *Du Blanc des mots et du noir des signes* (1953–1956), in which a collage of fragments, aphorisms and quotes establishes a poetic space that seems to resonate with Mansour's poem, especially with regard to the following final section of Jabès's text:

Plages peuplées à midi de pensées nues; la nuit marges rendues aux sable.
[...]
Comme le ciel sur la mer, l'œuvre s'ouvre sur l'homme qui se cherche en elle.
Peuples et poèmes ont la voix de leurs mots.
    Pareille à la mer au moment du naufrage, l'histoire hausse le ton au chapitre des martyrs.
    L'expérience de la mort de l'homme et du mot est à la taille de leur audace.
    Le désert émet des mots arides.
    [...]
    La mémoire du poète est son temps.
    La poésie ne change pas la vie, elle l'échange.
    Nous sommes portés.
    Le poème est la ressemblance.

Beaches populated at noon with naked thoughts; the night margins returned to the sand.
[...]
Like the sky over the sea, the work opens on the man who looks for himself in it.
Peoples and poems have the voice of their words.
Like the sea at the time of the shipwreck, history raises the tone with regard to the martyrs.
The experience of the death of man and the word is the size of their audacity.
The desert emits arid words.
[...]
The memory of the poet is his time.
Poetry does not change life, it exchanges it.
We are worn.
The poem is the resemblance.

Mary Ann Caws has brilliantly analysed the trope of the desert in the writings of Edmond Jabès as a dialectical reflection of his distance from movements such as surrealism, as well as Jabès's intimacy with surrealist images.[18] Caws has also discussed the link between the imagery of the desert and the sense of nostalgia in the poetry of Jabès:

> A creative tension is so established: between speaking and silence, sand and water, mountain and utter flatness, nostalgia for the past and yearning for the future. [...] 'Non-appartenance' or non-belonging: the poet as nomad hears his questioning as it disturbs others, sensing his own separation, knowing his final disaggregation and the desert of 'diseternity,' as he calls it [...]. This desert wherein we all wander, this nothing, becomes, through the refinding of a hope once thought impossible, the place of a privileged inscription.[19]

In Mansour's poem, the "shimmer of nostalgia" (line 8) resonates with the imagery of the desert in Jabès, especially when this image of the desert is confronted with the affirmation that the lyrical speaker is dreaming "without hope of return". Nevertheless, in Mansour's poetry, this assertion is not desperate; on the contrary, the lyrical speaker consults different concepts and words in order to confront them with the existing reality of the text, exploring the character of different cultural formations without dismissing them altogether. The notion of belonging in Mansour's poem is translated into a conceptual quest seeking to grasp the contradiction between supposedly objective ideas and their linguistic expression. Via procedures reminiscent of surrealist automatism and the cut-up technique (of sentences and languages), a tendency of the French language is revealed: the tendency to eliminate all that is non-identical in concepts and

---

18 Mary Ann Caws. "Edmond Jabès: Sill and Sand", in: *L'Esprit Créateur* 32, 2, 1992, 11–18, here 11.
19 Caws 1992, 14.

words. In turning to herself as a source of plural linguistic thinking, the lyrical speaker subverts this tendency of the French language, opening it up to a heterogeneous, non-identical Mediterranean spatial imagery that is inhabited, even embodied by the lyrical speaker.

In its evocation of Jabès, but also in its own accentuations, Mansour's poem presents displacement as a mode of opening the poetic voice through the Judean/Galilean/Mediterranean "dream". In this poetical reflection, the historical landscapes are transformed into a poetical space in which belonging appears as a nexus beyond the laws of determinism. Belonging is not easy to capture in words, but it is connected to the unpredictable moments when incongruous elements encountered in everyday life combine to produce a kind of mystical insight, as in a waking dream; in other words, it is a kind of *hasard objectif*. However, in the kaleidoscope of spatial images in Mansour's poems, objective chance is not just the offshoot of a poetic technique, but the adequate mode of reflecting belonging.

"Sou caleidoscópica". The I-Narrator in Clarice Lispector's texts

While Joyce Mansour's texts reflect on belonging in the form of poetry, Clarice Lispector does so in the form of prose. In a short essay first published on June 15, 1968 in the *Jornal do Brasil*, Lispector links her reflections on the art of storytelling and narrative techniques with the question discussed here. The text is entitled *Belonging* (*Pertencer*), and it begins with a remark on the part of the I-narrator that a friend of hers, a doctor, has assured her that a child feels his/her environment from the very first moments of his/her life. After this first sentence, Lispector's essay continues as follows:

> Tenho certeza de que no berço a minha primeira vontade foi a de pertencer. Por motivos que aqui não importam, eu de algum modo devia estar sentindo que não pertencia a nada e a ninguém. Nasci de graça. Se no berço experimentei esta fome humana, ela continua a me acompanhar pela vida afora, como se fosse um destino. [...] Se meu desejo mais antigo é o de pertencer, por que então nunca fiz parte de clubes ou de associações? Porque não é isso o que eu chamo de pertencer. O que eu queria, e não posso, é por exemplo que tudo o que me viesse de bom de dentro de mim eu pudesse dar àquilo que eu pertencesse. [...] Pertencer não vem apenas de ser fraca e precisar unir-se a algo ou a alguém mais forte. Muitas vezes a vontade intensa de pertencer vem em mim de minha própria força — eu

quero pertencer para que minha força não seja inútil e fortifique uma pessoa ou uma coisa. Embora eu tenha uma alegria: pertenço, por exemplo, a meu país, e como milhões de outras pessoas sou a ele tão pertencente a ponto de ser brasileira. E eu que, muito sinceramente, jamais desejei ou desejaria a popularidade — sou individualista demais para que eu pudesse suportar a invasão de que uma pessoa popular é vítima —, eu, que não quero a popularidade, sinto-me no entanto feliz de pertencer à literatura brasileira. [...] Quase consigo me visualizar no berço, quase consigo reproduzir em mim a vaga e no entanto premente sensação de precisar pertencer. [...] A vida me fez de vez em quando pertencer, como se fosse para me dar a medida do que eu perco não pertencendo. E então eu soube: pertencer é viver.[20]

Lispector's essay explores what might almost be considered a negative dialectics of belonging which questions the relations and contradictions between the concept and the felt experience of its objects, putting forward the doubt that we can ever fully belong. Even more so, Brazil is depicted as a country where everybody yearns to become Brazilian — and in this yearning lies belonging. However, there is no need to fully belong, as this would amount to the reduction of human beings to a state of quantitative equivalence, in which their particular qualities would be lost or at least not taken to be important. It is striking that this essay also conceives of belonging as a belonging to literature. Two examples from different periods of Lispector's oeuvre may help to trace these experimentations.

---

20 Clarice Lispector, *A descoberta do mundo*, Rio de Janeiro 1999, 110–111. My translation: "I am sure that in the cradle my first wish was to belong. For reasons that do not matter here, I must have somehow felt that I did not belong to anything or anyone. That my birth was superfluous. If in the cradle I experienced this human hunger, it continues to accompany me through life, as if it were a destiny. [...] If my oldest wish is to belong, why then have I never joined any clubs or associations? Because that is not what I call belonging. What I wanted, and I cannot achieve, is, for example, to be able to give the best of what comes from within me to whatever or to whomever I might belong. [...] Belonging does not just come from being weak and needing to unite oneself to something or someone stronger. Often an intense desire to belong comes from my own inner strength – I want to belong so that my strength will not be useless and may serve to strengthen a person or a thing. But I do get some satisfaction out of life: I belong, for example, to my country, and, like millions of others, I belong to it in the sense that I am so close to being Brazilian. And I, who in all sincerity have never wanted or could want to be popular – I'm far too individualistic to be able to withstand the invasion of privacy that a popular person is subjected to –, I, who do not seek popularity, am nevertheless happy to belong to Brazilian literature. [...] I can almost see myself in the cradle, I can almost recreate in myself the vague and yet pressing need to belong. [...] Life has allowed me to belong from time to time, as if to give me the measure of what I am losing by not belonging. And then I knew: to belong is to live."

The novel *A paixão segundo G.H.*, published by Lispector in 1964 (one year before the publication of Mansour's poems discussed above), presents a female voice's first-person narrative using the stream of consciousness technique, evoking surrealist techniques such as automatic writing as well as the palindrome: each unnamed chapter of the novel begins with the last sentence of the previous one. These loops of the narrative thread are intrinsically bound to the metamorphosis of the female self. The reader never learns the full name of the first-person narrator – only her initials, G.H., as written on her luggage. The novel takes place in the maid's room in the back of the narrator's penthouse apartment situated above the noisy streets of Rio de Janeiro. In this room, the first-person narrator – a languid middle-class woman – struggles to see herself through the eyes of her former maid. The narrative space corresponds to the inside of the protagonist's apartment, where two distinct areas may be discerned: the first is the area usually inhabited by G.H.; the second is the maid's room, which turns into the space where the protagonist is haunted by a sense of deep interiority. G.H. enters the maid's room with the intent of putting it in order, given that her maid (named Janair) has stopped working at her home. Upon entering this space she has not visited in years, she is confronted – quite contrary to what she expects – with a very clean and tidy environment flooded with light. It is this unforeseen space that triggers G.H.'s contact with her self. When the protagonist sees the contours of a female body outlined by the former maid on one of the white walls of the room, she identifies this sketch as representing her own shape; triggered by this silhouette, she begins to experience an existential moment. When G.H. opens the door of the room's closet, she finds herself face to face with a cockroach – a being she identifies as an observer from an archaic past, dating back to the very origins of mankind. When the roach begins to creep forward, G.H. slams the door on the half-emerged body of the cockroach. The sight of the roach split in half on the floor of the maid's room, with its insides slowly oozing out, deepens G.H.'s existential moment.

This moment is not represented as an act of self-discovery on the part of the narrator, but as an act of abandoning the self. For the argument here, it is important to underline that the reflection of the self in this text is presented as a gradual detachment from one's roots. The narrator formulates this as follows: "A gradual desenraização de si mesmo é o verdadeiro trabalho que se labora sob o aparente trabalho, a vida é uma missão secreta".[21] This concomitant acceptance of every

---

[21] *A Paixão Segundo G.H.*, Rio de Janeiro 1998, 118. Idra Novey translates: "The gradual deheroization of oneself is the true labor one works at beneath the apparent labor, life is a secret

inheritance as an accident, of the self as nothing steady, nothing firm, nothing solid, but rather as an echo chamber for questioning and testing the limits of essential conceptions of identity constitutes, from my point of view, Lispector's most important contribution to the questions discussed here.

The various analyses and interpretations of this text have emphasized the dimensions of epiphany and violence, the relation to Kafka's *Metamorphosis*, the transition from the human to the non-human body, as well as the transition from a human body in general to the female body in particular.[22] Nelson Viera has interpreted the text as an allegory of the search for Jewish identity.[23] In her interpretation of *A paixão segundo G.H.*, Rosi Braidotti, the feminist philosopher of nomadic thinking, focuses on the moments of "being other than herself", consequently calling Clarice Lispector's novel "a tale about becoming".[24]

From my point of view, Braidotti's insight is an important reminder of the complexity that characterizes Lispector's narrative oeuvre in general and the narrative entities of her texts in particular. The metamorphosis of the narrator

---

mission". Yet the word "desenraização" does not mean "deheroization", but rather "uprooting" – clearly, the loss of this semantic dimension changes the sense of this passage completely.

22 Benedito Nunes, "Clarice Lispector Ou o Naufrágio Da Introspecção", in: *Remate de Males* 9 (1989), 63–70; Patricia Santos, "La Héroe Femenina Mística Regresa Del Desierto", in: *Languages Annual* 5 (1993), 506–512; Susan Martin, "A Paixão Segundo Peixoto: Uma Leitura Da Violência Em Clarice Lispector", in: *Revista de Crítica Literaria Latinoamericana* 21.42 (1995), 241-246; Kenneth Krabbenhoft, "From Mysticism to Sacrament in A Paixão Segundo G. H.", in: *Luso-Brazilian Review* 32.1 (1995), 51-60; Antônio Donizeti Pires. "Uma Barata Cheia De Espinhos: Leitura Intertextual De A Metamorfose, De Franz Kafka, e A Paixão Segundo G. H., De Clarice Lispector", in: *Itinerários: Revista de Literatura* 12 (1998), 165–175; Marianella Collette, "El Reconocimiento De La Identidad Corporal Femenina En La Pasión Según G.H., De Clarice Lispector", in: *Revista Canadiense de Estudios Hispánicos* 26.1–2 (2001), 211–223; Rosidelma Pereira Fraga and Jorge Alves Santana, "As Tessituras Psicanalíticas do Sujeito Feminino e a Linguagem do Desligamento Em A Paixão Segundo G. H., De Clarice Lispector", in: *Revista de Letras* 50.2 (2010), 507–523; Irving Goh, "Blindness and Animality, Or Learning how to Live Finally in Clarice Lispector's the Passion According to G. H.", in: *Differences: A Journal of Feminist Cultural Studies* 23.2 (2012), 113–135.

23 Nelson H. Vieira, "Clarice Lispector's Jewish Universe: Passion in Search of Narrative Identity", in: Marjorie Agosín (Ed.), *Passion, Memory, Identity*, Albuquerque 1999, 85–113.

24 "G.H. is a tale about women's 'becoming': it is about new female subjectivity. The first and foremost element for women's becoming, in both a political and existential sense, is time; [...] Lispector echo[e]s the century-old tradition of mystical ascesis, but also moves clearly out of it. G.H. symbolizes a postmodern kind of materialism: one that stresses the materiality of all living matter in a common plane of coexistence, without postulating a central point of reference or of organization for it". Rosi Braidotti, *Nomadic Subjects. Embodiment and Sexual Difference in Contemporary Feminist Theory*, New York 2011, 191.

in Lispector's *A paixão segundo G.H.* is a deliberate extension of the modernist stream of consciousness technique to programmatically reject a single narrative identity – not as a transformation of one self into another, but, more precisely, as the recreation of the narrated self as a polyhedral entity.

The specific aesthetic form of Lispector's text ushers in a self-transcendence rendered possible through the recognition of oneself as an active creator of various forms of meaning. The subject that thus emerges is, moreover, bound by various relations within and between herself and society. In a certain way, Lispector's de-essentialized narrator explores the possibilities of simultaneous accounts of different experiences with access to the framings of the social, of gender, of class, alongside access to broader narratives. Her mode of narration strives to become a means of finding the lived experiences of subjects. Her experiments with the limitations of the genre yield the level of the experiential with the proviso that every account is always partial and intersubjectively constituted, but these narrative experiments extend beyond this. The narrator of *A paixão segundo G.H.* offers a totality of experiences, whose order differs markedly from that of other, linear narratives. This places the reader within the heart of the text. 'I myself' – the reader – exist for the first-person narrator, in the sense that she is addressing me over and over again. In sharp contrast to Wayne C. Booth, David Goldknopf has interpreted this intrusion of the fictive world into the historico-factual one as a main feature of the first-person narrator.[25] Even so, he firmly tied this feature to the author ("At such times, it is really the author who is speaking, ventriloquially, through I"). In contrast to that notion, we discover in *A paixão segundo G.H.* an insistence on ethical self-transcendence through the narrative mode of the first-person:

> A deseroização de mim mesma está minando subterraneamente o meu edifício, cumprindo-se à minha revelia como uma vocação ignorada. Até que me seja enfim revelado que a vida em mim não tem o meu nome. E eu também não tenho nome, e este é o meu nome. E porque me despersonalizo a ponto de não ter o meu nome, respondo cada vez que alguém disser: eu.[26]

---

[25] David Goldknopf, "The Confessional Increment: A New Look at the I-Narrator", in: *The Journal of Aesthetics and Art Criticism* 28, No. 1 (1969), 13–21, here: 17.

[26] *A Paixão Segundo G.H.*, Rio de Janeiro 1998, 119. "The deheroization of myself is subterraneously undermining my building, coming to pass without my consent like an unheeded calling. Until it is finally revealed to me that life in me does not bear my name. And I too have no name, and that is my name. And because I depersonalize myself to the point of not having my name, I reply whenever someone says: I".

The specificity of Lispector's aesthetics is that this separation does not lead to a crisis of language, but rather to a language-immanent reflection on the overcoming of the self ("Me ultrapassarei"). The self, represented by the term "eu"/"I" in this text, becomes a cipher for the protagonist's tension between reality and inner experience in her struggle for freedom.

Clarice Lispector's modeling of the "I" in *A paixão segundo G.H.* has a cognitive character in implicitly suggesting a reflective hermeneutical praxis that slowly moves forward into the text by looking backwards on its own act. Already in 1979, Hélène Cixous had discussed this reflective praxis as an ethical literary endeavor.[27]

The concept of "passages" allows grasping the complexity of the textual subjects in Lispector because it favors plurality and interrelations rather than monolithic and essentialist reductions of belonging. In a recent essay, Johan Fornäs has described passages as "movements in both time and space with some intensified contrast between the moving subject and the surrounding contextual structures".[28] What characterizes Lispector's narrative selves is the high regard held for the self as a continuous movement between different fragments of belonging.

This can be demonstrated with regard to Lispector's novels, but also with regard to her short stories, which have recently been translated into felicitous English by Katrina Dodson. One of the collected stories illustrates how explicitly the above reflections on the narrative subject can become even the topic and structural basis of a narrative. Here, I would like to suggest a metapoetical reading of the story É para lá que eu vou, published in the 1974 collection *Onde Estivestes de Noite* (*Where were you at night*). The story begins as follows:

> Para além da orelha existe um som, à extremidade do olhar um aspecto, às pontas dos dedos um objeto – é para lá que eu vou. À ponta do lápis o traço. [...] É para mim que eu vou. E de mim saio para ver. Ver o quê? ver o que existe. Depois de morta é para a realidade que vou. Por enquanto é sonho. Sonho fatídico. Mas depois – depois tudo é real. E a alma livre procura um canto para se acomodar. Mim é um eu que anuncia.[29]

---

27 Hélène Cixous, "L'Approche de Clarice Lispector. Se laisser lire (par) Clarice Lispector", in: *Entre L'écriture*, Paris 1986, 113-138, here: 114f. "We are living in the time of the flat thought-screen, of newspaper-thinking, which does not leave time to think the littlest thing according to its living mode. We must save the approach that opens and leaves space for the other. But we live mass-mediatized[,] pressed, hard-pressed, blackmailed. Acceleration is one of the tricks of intimidation. We rush, throw ourselves upon, seize. And we no longer know how to receive. [...] Her approach is political, Clarice('s) approach: it is the living space, the between[-]us, that we must take care to keep. Having the humility, the generosity, not to jump over it, not to avoid it. Hurrying annuls".

28 Johan Fornäs, "Passages across Thresholds: Into the Borderlands of Mediation", in *Convergence: The Journal of Research into New Media Technologies* (8), 4, 2002, 89–106, here 90.

29 Beyond the ear there is a sound, at the far end of sight a view, at the tips of the fingers an object – that's where I'm going. At the tip of the pencil the line. [...] To me is where I'm going. And

"É para lá que eu vou" is a story without a plot line that sequences reflections of the self and challenges the reader to piece together the different components of the subject to make sense of it. But in doing so, the story does not emphasize content over form. It rather links the narrative reflections of the textual "I" ("Eu") with love, presented here as a mode of transgressing the restrictions of one self:

> À extremidade de mim estou eu. Eu, implorante, eu a que necessita, a que pede, a que chora, a que se lamenta. Mas a que canta. A que diz palavras. Palavras ao vento? que importa, os ventos as trazem de novo e eu as possuo. Eu à beira do vento. O morro dos ventos uivantes me chama. Vou, bruxa que sou. E me transmuto. Oh, cachorro, cadê tua alma? está à beira de teu corpo? Eu estou à beira de meu corpo. E feneço lentamente. Que estou eu a dizer? Estou dizendo amor. E à beira do amor estamos nós.[30]

According to my interpretation, the reflection of the narrative voice in this story emphasizes first and foremost the breaking down of a monolithic narrative identity. This, in turn, is central to the story's mode of pointing to the ethics of understanding and narrating the self as non-identical. The "narrating I" is presented as a kaleidoscope that is in touch with the other. Writing the self is presented as a mode of writing the other through love. It is only at the edge of love that a "we" can emerge. This move can be seen as the ethical nucleus of Lispector's narrative voices. The relation to ourselves, the other and the world is lived out in the narrative form. Lispector's ethic of self-representation speaks directly against the fashioning of identities. The textual subjects in her writings do not serve the function of self-identification, self-justification or self-criticism. The narrative voice is continuously explored in relational terms within a continuously changing and fluid configuration of relationships.

Clarice Lispector's experiments with narrative, with new ways of relating form and content and new ways of enlivening conventional storytelling techniques are closely intertwined with the question of belonging. That this question is not answered, but consciously left open, while our desire to belong is transformed into an innovative narrative voice – this defines the central role Lispector should play for our reflections on the modern Jewish literary canon.

---

from me I go out to see. See what? to see what exists. After I am dead to reality is where I'm going. For now it is a dream. A fateful dream. But later – later all is real. And the free soul seeks a place to get settled. Me is an I that I proclaim.

30 At the far end of me is I. I, imploring, I the one who needs, who begs, who cries, who laments. Yet who sings. Who speaks words. Words on the wind? who cares, the winds bring them back and I possess them. I at the edge of the wind. The wuthering heights call to me. I go, witch that I am. And I am transmuted. Oh, dog, where is your soul? is it at the edge of your body? I am at the edge of my body. And I waste away slowly. What am I saying? I am saying love. And at the edge of love are we.

Anastasia Telaak
Form and Language: Alejandra Pizarnik's Spatial Poetics of Un/Belonging

> Cuando a la casa del lenguaje se le vuela el tejado y las palabras no guarecen, yo hablo.[1]

To conceive of language in terms of a house means to trigger the whole chain of etymological figures related to genealogy and belonging – from Latin *genos* (family, descent, origin) and *genitivus* (of or belonging to birth; possession, source) to *genius/ingenium* (procreative divinity, innate quality), back to Ancient Greek *genike* (designing the general/generic case) and *gignesthai* (to become, to happen), whence English *gender*, *engender*, *genre* – biological and/or social sex; textual/literary form – derive from.[2] It is therefore not surprising that space, "my exile of language", and "my Jewish question" which vehemently emerges upon the father's death (1966) and prompts a fierce rejection of her birthplace, Argentina, appear as core preoccupations in Pizarnik's diaries and condense into the issue of form: "[...] mis cambios de formas, que yo llamaría cambios espaciales, tienen por objeto hallar un espacio literario como una patria o, si esto es demasiado, como la choza que encuentran en el bosque los niños perdidos" (Pizarnik 2014: 580, 765, 841).[3]

The house is one of the most ambivalent and unsettling of the spatial paradigms which inform, shape and structure the poetic oeuvre of Alejandra Pizarnik.[4] Figured as a sombre and asphyxiating dungeon, tomb or womb, or – as in the above quoted line from the prose poem *Fragmentos para dominar el silencio* [Fragments to dominate the silence, 1966; Pizarnik 2009: 223[5]] – devoid of its

---

[1] "When the roof flies off the house of language and words don't provide refuge, I speak." Translations of literary texts and critical studies other than in English are my own, unless otherwise stated.
[2] Online Etymology Dictionary; http://www.etymonline.com/index.php?allowed_in_frame=0&search=genus& searchmode=none (24.11.2015).
[3] "[...] my changes of forms, which I would call spatial changes, involve finding a literary space like a homeland or, if that is too much to ask for, like the cottage which the lost children find in the woods."; lunes/Monday [December] 1968. For the previous quotes: 5.4.1963, 23.11.1967.
[4] Equally crucial is the garden, both as a spatial paradigm feeding on relevant literary/cultural traditions, prominent (not only) in Judaism, and as a metapoetical concept.
[5] *Fragmentos para dominar el silencio* appears in Part I of the four-part collection of prose poems *Extracción de la piedra de la locura* [Extraction of the stone of madness, 1968] which Pizarnik dedicated to her mother.

sheltering roof, her writings more often than not entail an inversion of its most common metaphorical meaning: of safely being at home, *zuhause, chez soi*.

A critical reading of Pizarnik's oeuvre reveals that the conflict between the real territories Pizarnik inhabits during her lifetime – namely Buenos Aires, where she is born into in a Jewish family in 1936, a year after her parents' immigration from Volhynia to Argentina, and dies in 1972; from 1960 to 1964 Paris – and a self-conception committed to the paradigm of Jewish exile is shifted to a literary space. This paradigm in turn is presented as a Jewish legacy, a case of *genike*, and hooked in the paradigm of ethnos in several other entries of her diary, e.g. on 12.3.1965: "a long legacy of loners and isolated ones", the diarist notes in regard to the secluded life of her ageing parents in a gloomy family home, concluding: "Por mi sangre judía, soy una exilada" (Pizarnik 2014: 716).[6] Thus, "patria" – homeland –, the influential European 19th-century concept of identity and belonging linking the mother tongue to a national territory, is fundamentally challenged. Pizarnik's poetry is rather invested in the intermediary spaces between homeland and cottage, space and place, the national/cultural collective and radical individuality (separateness in terms of both tragic fate and self-assertion).

From the start, "patria" is divested of its concrete spatiality; a homeland is conjured and envisioned as an imaginary and/or abstract foundational place instead – literature, the "word of desire", the poem, the book.[7] Proving impossible, though, to translate life, the physical, creatural self into letters, to embody them, also the concept of a literary-literal existence is "de-founded"[8] and eventually transformed into a space the form, texture and imagery of which conveys uprooting and dislocation. Here, it is particularly the varied perspectives and material-related qualities of space and spatial changes affecting the figurative representation of corporeality as well as the cleavage between speech and writing/scripture (precisely in the religious, lawgiving sense of the word) which call attention: inside/outside – but also threshold or limit –, expansion/contraction, erection/immersion, surface/depth (palace, tower, cottage, coffin, stone, hole), as well as liquidity/density, fissures and fractures. Condensed in these spatial/textual patterns, Pizarnik's poetics of un/belonging not only interweaves with a writing/speaking constantly encircling its own suspension, thus

---

6 „For my Jewish blood I'm an exile."
7 The prose poem *La palabra del deseo* [The word of desire] and the one preceding it – *El deseo de la palabra* [The desire of the word] – were published in the (four-part) volume *El infierno musical* [The musical hell, 1971], Part I: *Figuras del presentimiento* [Figures of foreboding]; Pizarnik 2009: 271 and 269–270 respectively.
8 A prose poem titled *Desfundación* [Defoundation, 1966] is contained in Part I of *Extracción de la piedra de la locura* [Extraction of the stone of madness, 1968]

also tying in with the topos of the ineffable prominent in occidental poetry. Pizarnik's textures of un/belonging are equally and particularly hooked in an imagery of and discourse on the challenge of Judaism and an ambivalent nostalgia for East European Jewry, as much as they involve the aporias of representing the blind spots in a family history of traumatic loss, terror and displacement. Of all relatives of Pizarnik's parents' who had not emigrated but remained in their hometown Równe, only few survived the Shoah.

The following close readings focus on the different modes of un/belonging in Pizarnik's texts. They claim that within the complexity of these modes, we can discern the specificity of her aesthetic endeavor in its deep concern for the correlations between house, with its subtle connotation of *genos*, as well as language, and form, particularly in terms of genre.

I Genealogical places – house and temple, *HaMakom* and *Mishkan*

A closer look at *Fragmentos para dominar el silencio* shall initially provide a brief insight into the complex literary spaces and places reflecting the attempt of Pizarnik's poetic persona(e) to create a site – an origin – from where to speak.

Opening the second part of the tripartite prose poem and succeeded by a blank space before the "ladies in red" appear, the sentence "Cuando a la casa del lenguaje se le vuela el tejado y las palabras no guarecen, yo hablo" makes not only wonder if it is about a house which language inhabits, as if it were its possession, or if language itself is conceived of as a house, harboring words unable to provide refuge or to heal. Even more disconcerting in view of a spatial orientation is the question as to what or who causes the house to fall into ruins – is it the "powers of language" identified with the "solitary, desolate ladies singing through my voice which I listen to from afar"? If so: Where to locate, in the same segment, a lyrical I oscillating between self-assertion (it listens to "my voice"), a phonic, thus physical permeability insinuating dispossession (it is someone else, the ladies, who sing "through my voice"), and an exteriority to the 'proper' voice ("my voice which I listen to from afar") shattering the traditional concept of identity? And above all: What kind of language could "yo"/ "I" possibly speak, when the "house of language" is falling into ruins? If "I" is to count among the living, endowed with the gift of speech, it can't be situated but inside the metaphor, with all its allusions to a collective site (family, lineage, house of prayer). Following this line of reflection, the lyrical I experiences the collapse of language, yet is paradoxically born out of its ruins, born to language after the exile of language.

Collapse, ruins, language; the impossibility and the necessity to speak: elements which – given Pizarnik's prominent transposition of sacred Jewish paradigms, ranging from the Pentateuch to Talmudic and Kabbalistic sources, to poetological concepts – bring to mind the destruction of the Temple of Jerusalem, the house of God and the holy language, as the core of Judaism, and engender a radical form of diasporic writing here. Yet, not only the pervading images of death, but also the blanks between the three parts of the poem as well as those in its second segment tell that the language projected in the first person singular ("I speak") after the collective catastrophe sees itself threatened by and at the same time fascinated with a twofold silence: there is, on one hand, the singing silence of death ("No es muda la muerte") the fissures of which are sealed by "the mourners", the weeping and sobbing of the "ladies in red" (a multiplied Madame la Mort and most prominent figure in Pizarnik's poetry), and there is, on the other hand, "my grey silence" being flourished by the "sweet weeping" of a "you" whose identity is not disclosed. Be it death or, by contiguity, one of the mourners/the red ladies, or the girl which "nestles in me" in the poem's first part - the impression of a reciprocal contagion and intertwining of death and the poetic persona in a zone of uncanny, literally restless silence(s) is crucial here.

The ambiguous, threatening and spellbinding quality of the audible silence of death is sustained by the orphaned girl located in a somber space of desert/exile in the first part of the poem ("far away, in the black sand"), or rather by its poetic image situated in a context of *genos*: as a body/vessel "dense of ancestral music" erupting into the question: "¿Dónde la verdadera muerte?", thus prefiguring the collapse of the house of language. Lacking the verb (está/is), the question's quality of a cry for a death beyond the phantasmatic sounds permeating and dissociating the lyrical I is intensified. According to this reading, "true death" can't mean but absolute, pure silence – a silence, as Slavoj Žižek aptly states, like that preceding creation or synonym with the Edenic language: "disturbing [...] the constant murmur of the real and thus opening a glade where words may be said" (Žižek 2006: 247).

Also the "ancestral music" is ambiguous: Preceding the outcry, it might be implicitly linked to the "the powers of language" allegorised by the "desolate ladies" singing through my voice", and also to the dirges, the singing of the mourners in the middle part of the prose poem, as a manifestation of a specific cultural tradition. In either instance the line following the invocation suggests a related reading: Stated in the present perfect,[9] the sentence "I have wanted to illuminate myself in the light of my lack of light" stresses the desire articulated here, while the element of light/(spiritual) illumination subtly supplements the

---

9 The present perfect tense would be the English equivalent to the pretérito perfecto compuesto in the original "He querido iluminarme a la luz de mi falta de luz."

metaphorical nexus 'dense body/vessel' – 'eruption/shattering' reminiscent of the Kabbalistic notion of God's creation of the world: According to the Lurianic Kabbalah, upon creating the world, God (*En Sof*) contracted parts of himself into vessels of light (*tzimtzum*), whereupon they shattered (*Shevirat ha-kelim*), their shards turning into sparks of light enclosed "within the material creation", proving its imperfection or even the existence of evil.[10]

Regarding the remembrance of "ancestral music" as a potentially inspiring one, empowering to poetic creation, the very end of the first part of the *Fragments* phonetically takes up and modifies the moment of eruption: "La que no pudo más e imploró llamas y ardimos"[11] shows the reclining girl, the lyrical I and the wolf in one figure indicating an extreme emotional limit, on the verge of collapse; indeed, the act of imploring bears a subtle contiguity to the experience of imploding. The metaphorics of fire, ardor, and burning again, exceptionally pronounced in Pizarnik's poetics, obviously alludes to the myth of Prometheus here. It transmits, on the one hand, the transgressive intensity of the desire of poetic creation, of "transcribing ardent relations" ("transcribir relaciones ardientes") by "entering inside the music so I could have a homeland" (Pizarnik 2009: 265), as it reads in the prose poem *Piedra fundamental* (Foundation stone, 1971).[12] An early poem with the telling title *Orígen* [Origin, 1958] explicitly links the poetic element of fire/ardour to the liquid, smooth quality of an "ancient melody" – "hot, wise like the sea,/ trembling from within my blood/ renewing my fatigue of other ages [...]" (Pizarnik 2009: 88)[13]. The word "wise" and the ethnic marker ("from within my blood") proves connatural to the "ancestral music", which in turn, and considering the manifold subtexts derived from Judaism in Pizarnik's oeuvre, conceivably echoes Jewish liturgical music or traditional Yiddish folk songs. The metaphorics of fire however equally signifies madness, destruction, death – in Pizarnik's oeuvre: the total consumption of the poetic persona in the act of desiring/creating a pure language/an undivided voice in its own right, hooked in an imagery of devastation cyphering the inaccessible memory of the distant, vanished world of parents, grandparents and their ancestors.

In this prose poem, the lyrical I gives the impression of being as dispossessed from the ardour of fire as from its voice. After the silence following the

---

[10] This concept follows the Lurianic Kabbalah; cf. https://en.wikipedia.org/wiki/Tikkun_olam, and https://de.wikipedia.org/wiki/Schvirat_ha-Kelim, 22.04.2018.
[11] "Who could not take it any longer and implored the flames and we burnt."
[12] Contained in the volume *El infierno musical* [The musical hell, 1971], part I : Figuras del presentimiento [Figures of foreboding].
[13] The poem is contained in the volume *Las aventuras perdidas* [The lost adventures], 1958; Pizarnik 2009: 88.

collapse of the house of language and its statement "I speak", the "ladies in red" – "the desolate ladies"/"powers of language" – return weeping and (by way of the metaphorics of flowers/blooming) flourish the grey silence of the poetic I as if it were a grave. The originally sacred source of linguistic/poetic inspiration thus turns into a language/music precisely the lethal quality of which becomes a source of fatal fascination. This fascination superimposes itself on the "house of language" as the sacred site/site of sacred language par excellence, and in the sense Heidegger – and, to a certain extent, also Pizarnik in her early work – conceived of it: as the "house of being" (*Brief über den Humanismus*; 1946/47), with the voice of the (illuminated) poet as its sentinel. Similarly, another subtext belonging to the religious heritage of Judaism is being eclipsed: the belief in the arrival of the Messiah as depicted in the Tanakh, particularly in the Book of Isaiah and Jeremiah. For neither a rebuilding of the temple and, by implication, the restoration of the sacred/poetic language – thus also of the creator-poet –, as foretold in Isaiah, turns into a (poetic) reality here, nor does "the Branch of David"/"of Jesse"/"of the Lord" "bear fruit"/ "spring forth" to the "pride and the adornment of the survivors of Israel".[14] Instead, "the branches die in memory".[15]

The above mentioned intertextual references to the main tenets of Judaism, mystic/kabbalistic beliefs included, encourage the impression that a fundamental cleavage traverses Pizarniks prose poem, i.e. the very site of poetic language formally, structurally and metaphorically represented in the incurable shattering of its voice, its 'vessel'. This cleavage can be understood as an aporia regarding a commitment to Judaism and Jewishness. An acute awareness of it is particularly manifest in Pizarnik's diaries, whereby the diarist adopts as ambiguous an attitude as Kafka, whom she declares to be "my house, my race" (Pizarnik 2014²:424). In the prose poem, the commitment to the "ancestral music", in particular to the imperative of memory and Messianic thought, is mirrored in so far as by a poetic re-enactment of the destruction of the Temple of Jerusalem, an immemorial

---

14 Cf. Jeremiah 33:15-16, Isaiah 11:1-5, and 4:2, https://bible.knowing-jesus.com/topics/Branches,-Illustrating Messiah, 2304.2018.
15 Given the image of the reclining figure nestling inside the poetic I "with its wolf-mask", the intertextuality concerning Isaiah in *Fragmentos para dominar el silencio* might even extend to the (negativized) "vision of a messianic age in which *the wolf shall dwell with the lamb* and the calf with the young lion" (Isaiah 11:6; my italics), which Maimonides understood as a metaphor, meaning that upon the arrival of the Messiah "enemies of the Jews, likened to the wolf, will no longer oppress them"; cf. http://www.jewishvirtuallibrary.org/the-messiah, 23.04.18. In the short prose text *La verdad del bosque* [The truth of the woods; 1965], a transcription of *Little Red Riding Hood* within the context of postmemory, the wolf acts as an aggressor from outside damaging a Jewish (and markedly feminine) genealogy, and as a corrosive within the narrative I which, seeing itself to be trapped in a damaged life, claims revenge.

catastrophe deeply anchored in Jewish collective memory is evoked. What motivates this evocation and transports its traumatic dimensions into the text: this, the prose poem doesn't *say* but performs it in a fragmented space pervaded by the presence of absence: the phantasmal real gaping in the language experienced by those who count among the generation of postmemory. "Perdida en el silencio/de las palabras fantasmas./Si vivir es memoria cerrada/quién me pierde/en el silencio fantasma/de las palabras" (Pizarnik 2009:319) reads a six-line stanza written between 1956 and 1960.[16] In the prose poem *Los poseídos entre lilas* [The obsessed among lilacs] from the volume *El infierno musical* [The musical hell, 1971], the lyrical I is more explicit:

> Yo estaba predestinada a nombrar las cosas con nombres esenciales. Yo ya no existo y lo sé; lo que no sé es qué vive en lugar mío. Pierdo la razón si hablo, pierdo los años si callo. Un viento violento arrasó con todo. Y no haber podido hablar por todos aquellos que olvidaron el canto. – Alguna vez, tal vez, encontraremos refugio en la realidad verdadera. Entretanto ¿puedo decir hasta qué punto estoy en contra? [...] Las palabras hubieran podido salvarme, pero estoy demasiado viviente. No, no quiero cantar muerte. [...] (Pizarnik 2009: 295)[17]

Against this background, the issue of belonging in *Fragmentos* is rendered in the aporia of committing oneself to a genealogical chain/tradition as a text(ure) which, marked by irreparable death and loss, harbors the self in the uncanny silence of "bewitching lure", tempting it to surrender to singing death. At stake is the freedom to not "sing death", to have a voice, a language and a silence of one's own, or rather to be one's own voice. Thinking of the Latin *ex-sistere*, it is this word's dynamic quality of meaning – to step forth, to emerge – what the lyrical I, after ceding its very textual ground to the "powers of language" possessed by the "solitary, desolate ladies" in the first fragment, endeavours to achieve at the beginning of the second fragment: by presenting the self as an impossible paradoxon. And it makes another attempt to let its proper singular voice – the poem – ex-sist in the last fragment: here, however, the act of saying "my poem", articulated as a command(ment) for the future ("yo he de decirlo"),

---

[16] "Lost in the silence/of phantom words./ If living is locked up memory/ who loses me/in the phantom silence/of the words." As is the case with several texts in the edition of Pizarnik's *Collected Poetry*, also the context which these lines are taken from – a succession of short poetic fragments – is not indicated in it.

[17] „I was predestined to name things with essential names. I do not exist anymore, and I know it; what I don't know is what lives in my place. I lose my mind if I speak, I lose the years if I fall silent. A violent wind devastated everything. And having been unable to speak for all those who forgot the chant. – Sometimes, perhaps, we will find refuge in true reality. Meanwhile: can I say up to which point I oppose? [...] Words could have saved me, but I am all too alive. No, I do not want to sing death. [...]".

not only contends with its denial in one and the same sentence. Put in brackets, enclosed in what seems to last but a single breath – "(here, now)" –, the possible sense and destiny of "my poem" is doubted, too. In the original version, the uncertain poem-to-be vouches for a poetic voice in an anagrammatic constellation which semantically, and in opposite to the Kabbalistic practice of permutation, doesn't promise divine splendor; it locates the "here and now" of the lyrical I/the poem in the suspension of exile. Thus, it reminds of the *HaMakom* which denotes an attribute of God after the loss of his material dwelling (the Temple), signifying "a topos with and without topology" (Völkening 2007: 86) in rabbinical thought. Here, it coalesces with that of the transient, diasporic Mishkan (tabernacle), in the middle of which dwells a holy absence whose character as a "space of possibility" defines itself by means of borders (Bark 2007: 178–179).

II *Genos* and genre – poem and prose poem

The (inter-)textual literarization of genealogical issues, as well as their transfer into spatial terms and images directly correlate with Pizarnik's outmost concern for "the choice between verse and prose", for "literary containment and expansion" (Pizarnik 2014: 429)[18] in her desire to forge "my new, unknown voice" (Pizarnik 2009: 355, 436). This interrelation in turn favors fragmentariness as a formal, structural and poetic mode, as much as it mirrors a powerful tension between the symbolic and the imaginary. This is not surprising, given that Pizarnik was strongly influenced by German Romanticism, French Symbolism and Surrealism. However, the issue of genre notably interlocks with questions of generation and birth, of the law "in a natural and symbolic sense", as Derrida has elaborated in his essay *La loi du genre* (1980; Derrida 2015).[19] In Pizarnik writings, this becomes manifest in an ongoing struggle with the poem from the outset – she fervently cherishes the idea of of a book yet turns to less canonical forms: "cuento o novela o poema en prosa. Un libro como una casa donde entrar a calentarme, a protegerme" (Pizarnik 2014: 499).[20]

---

18 Here and for the immediately following: 25.07.1962; from an untitled prose poem, dated May 1972, and the poem *"Casa de la mente"* (14.4.1970) respectively.
19 "The issue of the literary genre is no formal issue: it interlocks with the motive of the law altogether, with the motive of generation in a natural and symbolic sense, of birth in a natural and symbolic sense, of generational differences, of the sexual difference between the male and the female gender (genre) [...]."
20 "Story or novel or prose poem. A book like a house I could enter to warm myself, to protect myself" (27.9.1962).

Pizarnik seeks to transgress the canonical laws of genre and *genos*, her writing thus underscoring, "re-marking" belonging, in an ambivalent way. Particularly in the years during which she gains access to the literary scene of Buenos Aires and then consolidates her reputation as a refined and fascinatingly sombre lyrical voice, she aspires "to participate in a genre" and sets herself the highest standards in regard to formal, grammatical and lexical rigour. At the same time, she seems to increasingly challenge generic rules: by dissolving boundaries in an "anarchic productivity" difficult to classify, and by seeking for an escape route from conventions, from simulacra of meaning.

Until about 1962, Pizarnik almost exclusively engages in (free) verse; for her, it is the genre which traditionally operates within generic laws, enabling "to contain what overflows". "Recién hoy comprendo que la rima y la métrica tienen sentido pues defienden del terror a los grandes espacios", it reads on October21th 1962; on May 24th 1966: "[...] ¿Aprender qué? Formas. Mis contenidos imaginarios son tan fragmentarios, tan divorciados de lo real, que temo [...] dar a luz nada más que monstruos. Yo 'civilizo' mis poemas al detenerlos y congelarlos" (Pizarnik 2014: 616, 511, 743).[21] In her "perfect small poems", Pizarnik focuses on belonging through form, demanding "intensity, not extension": "My discontinuity demands sparks of light, small luminaries to last for an instant" (Pizarnik 2014: 859, 577, 859).[22] This conceptual desire echoing Kabbalistic patterns and a tenet of modern poetry, the reconstitution of the divine (Pizarnik 2012: 234)[23], also remarkably mirrors the "diasporic constellation" of Jewish lifeworlds characterized by "spatial suspension", "territorial transgression" and – contrary to the "geometrical axiom of surface and expanse" specific to majority cultures – by "the axioms of the unprotected spot" (Diner 2011). "Cada poema *está* solo", Pizarnik writes on November 25th 1966. "Además de cada poema, cada verso es en su ser. Digo que todo es en sí, a solas, aislado y fragmentado. Dura faena la de unir los fragmentos. Eso se llama curar el poema como una herida" (Pizarnik 2014: 767).[24] To this adds her assertion that "[I]n opposition

---

[21] "Only today I understand that rhyme and metre make sense for they give protection against the terror of big spaces." "To learn what? Forms. My imaginary world is so fragmentary, so divorced from reality that I fear [...] to give birth to nothing but monsters. I 'civilize' my poems by restraining and freezing them." First quote: 7.6.1963.
[22] "Mi discontinuidad exige destellos, pequeñas luminarias que duran un instante" (31.3.1963). Previous quotes: 11.5.1969.
[23] In her essay on modernism: *Una tradición de la ruptura* (1966).
[24] "Every poem *stands* alone. [...] Aside from each poem, each verse is in its being. I say that everything is in-itself, all alone, isolated and fragmented. Hard drudgery to join the fragments. This is what healing the poem like a wound means" (italics in the original).

to the sense of exile, to a perpetual expectation, there is the poem – Promised Land" (Pizarnik 2012: 299).²⁵

At the same time, a break with genre and *genos* concerning structure and discourse stirs in the "unconscious energy", in the "*affective automatism*" Pizarnik declares to be "my authentic form" (Pizarnik 2014: 652/5.1.1964): the poetic voice appears as fractured, the idea of a native/generic tongue is denied as much as "a language I inherited from some strangers [...] 'a net of holes'" is deplored (Pizarnik 2012: 61). Haunted by a mad queen, a blind or mute king and the dead, intermeshing oedipal and suicidal figures with darc romantic vampirism and the image of Ahasver, the fractured space turns into a site within which the "errant verbal matter" (Pizarnik 2009: 415) becomes entangled in an ongoing "exorcism" and "restauration" (Pizarnik 2009: 251²⁶).

In Pizarnik's diaries, several entries in the context of her father's death (1966) give an insight into the acute struggle for a determined sense of belonging which involves the issue of genre and *genos*. "I am not Argentine. I am Jewish", the diarist writes, continuing: "Este descubrimiento me obliga a impedir movimientos esenciales de mi naturaleza: buscar verdugos. [...] Mi padre y el sufrimiento de mi raza me avisan que los desafié, que, si hace falta, me vuelva yo verdugo. No puedo prolongar la cadena de esclavitud, de suavísima sumisión" (Pizarnik 2014: 772).²⁷ The self-analysis Pizarnik's diarist presents here reveals her profound conflict regarding an understanding of Jewishness which, even in view of the devastating blows suffered by "my father" as member of "my race", the Jewish collective singled out for vilification, persecution and murder, appears to demand submissiveness and thus proves irreconcilable with the wayward "nature" of a "judía rara" (a "strange Jew", as she calls herself elsewhere) searching for henchmen. This dilemma is exacerbated by a "new terror" emerging from what the diarist believes to be an "absolute impossibility", "a trap": To commit herself to a Jewish collective and thus to conceive of herself in terms of a belonging based on the concept of (Jewish) genealogy/ethnicity equates to bow to the "suffering of my race" and to seal a symbolic contract identified with the Jewish house-as-exile. Yet to disclaim that contract not only implies to relinquish the "crown" deemed to be bestowed

---

25 „En oposición al sentimiento del exilio, al de una espera perpetua está el poema – tierra prometida."; in her essay *El poeta y su poema* (1968).
26 In the prose poem *Extracción de la piedra de la locura* (1964).
27 Here and for the following quotes: "This discovery obliges me to restrain essential stirrings innate to me: to search for henchmen. [...] My father and the suffering of my race admonish me that I have defied them, that, if need be, I turn into a henchman myself. I can not prolong the chain of slavery, of gentle submissiveness." – "Maybe I want to ascribe to my being Jewish this absolute impossibility of entering the Argentine community which I belong to nominally" (19.- 6.11. [sic] 1967).

upon her by "el invisible pueblo de la memoria más vieja" (Pizarnik 2009: 247)[28]. Apart from execrating Argentina as culturally dull and even baleful in the relevant diary entries, the symbolic national space in her country of birth constitutes a "nominal" belonging at most: "Acaso quiero adjudicar a mi ser judío esta imposibilidad absoluta de entrar en la comunidad argentina que integro nominalmente." To that impasse may add the challenge of Jewish self-conception in a country where the struggle for national identity (*argentinidad*) in various regards went along with positivist racial and anti-Semitic discourses.[29]

Three texts from 1971 – *Poema para el padre*, *Casa de Citas*, and *Sala de psicopatología*, the first published as a poem in January 1972, the other two published posthumously under (short) prose and poetry respectively, and all three staging the house – paradigmatically illustrate the expounded intricate interleaving of genre, *genos*, and the issue of belonging.

Poema para el padre is a poem dedicated to the most waveringly idealized figure in Pizarnik's writing. It largely poetises the Wandering Jew and Mosaic exile in an elaborate elegiac form conceivable of as an epitaph and as the "house of the world" (*beitolamo*), a place of rest. The house is also present, if tacitly, in the tongue of the father by which he is introduced and highlighted immediately after an opening suggesting a tale of epic dimensions ("Y fue entonces"): It quotes the "little house" the poetic voice, a "tiny rose-coloured marionette", makes "in his/her tongue" in the prose poem *Extracción de la piedra de la locura* (1964; Pizarnik 2009: 250[30]): a temple *en miniature* imagined as a fatal pathway to a homelike language through self-sacrifice. "Cold and dead", the father's tongue in the poem rises to a chant from a tower the poem reproduces. The tongue's chant on top and the lyrical writing I's hand at the lower end of this vertical – here we have the desire for the word and its tradition cast in a classical genealogical mould.

Of all the sacred topologies the poem reflects – thus reflecting a fascination of the law –, two are pivotal: the Kaddish, a musical site to mourn a dead and praise God in his celestial heights, and, as the change form "canción" to "canto"

---

[28] "the invisible people of the oldest memory"; in the prose poem *Extracción de la piedra de la locura* (1964).

[29] Pizarnik's ambivalence towards Argentina also relates to a European conception of her Jewishness (in Paris, she writes in 1965: "exile is natural, is a homeland, whereas here [in Argentina] it hurts"; Pizarnik 2014: 716), and to her writing in a space where many intellectuals already before her lifetime regarded themselves as "marginal citizen[s] of the West" (Borges in Graff Zivin 2008: 11).

[30] In the phrase „yo hago mi casita en su lengua yo habito en la palma de su mano", the possessive "su" can refer to a female or a male figure. The passage in Isaiah 49,16 alluded to here allows for both references.

in the second part of the poem recommencing with "Entonces" indicates, the biblical scene at Mount Sinai, staged in a highly ambiguous way.

First, it is significant that almost the entire poem is rendered in a non-diegetic mode; it is not until the last word which brings the chain of tradition and the poem to an end, "escribo", that the poetic voice 'reveals' itself – in written words like "quicksand hollows". Thus, it not only places itself outside and inside a poem actualizing a crucial moment of Jewish cultural memory; it literally disperses the foundational act implied in the shift from sounds to signs, the site of transmission as transcription: from an "aphonic" name, a "promised God", to the promise of "doing" "all things 'God' speaks about". Hence, what Moses allegedly performed, a "transmission into memory" (Blanchot 2010: 224), is evoked and at the same time suspended in an oscillation of meaning.

Also the effects of the musical element are telling: The poem audibly suggests a recreation of the chant it encloses and emulates. It features a specific rhythm and chromaticism marked by consonantal alliterations, dark vowels and caesurae ("entonces"), by a distinct set of recurrent, semantically interwoven words and locutions (particularly "canción/canto/cantar" and its contrapuntal "ausencia") which emphasize the act of remembering and simulates an acoustic space of romantic-liturgical closeness. Moreover, the "commemorative listening" the poem suggests implies a "precondition for the perception of sounds as a meaningful coherence" (Bielefeldt 2001, 389); since the poem also reflects the phenomenon that "there are no limits around the sound", thus suggesting "a tendential suspension or reduction of time" (McLuhan/Powers 2013: 181), it effects the quality of a temporal lapse coherent with the moment of divine revelation in its second part. This lapse is doubly remarked in a historical (non-biblical) context in the first part of the poem: In relation to the divine chant the challenge of which the poem displays by means of the gap between (divine) pneuma and (Mosaic) gramma, the poem transmits the experience of a father whose song equally lacks an intelligible content, despite of being sung. Additionally, the heterogeneity between speech and voice is annulled: the latter is absent, too. That *something* seems audible, though, makes the song/singing father appear as present-absent, as a sensation/manifestation insisting on a phantasmal level: the signifier "song" is merely a symbolic representation, its real essence proves elusive.

This subtle essence makes the father the object of apotheosis in the second part and involves the poetic voice in a writing which canonically "generates and perpetuates the Jewish awareness of living in exile through centuries – for preparing the children to overcome exile and enter the Promised Land means to establish the experience of exile" (Bodenheimer 2012: 33). However, the presence-absence of the father's song relates to an experience of exile as inaccessible as the song he saved – in an absent body, through prohibitions in a profaned world "of obscene gardens", without the possibility of transmission – , a song his descendant seeks to trace up to its source, to the chants the young father is imagined to have shared with a community of which only shadows remained. Here, the temporal lapse of revelation is transferred to a blank space resisting all attempts to harbour an incommunicable trauma.

In its formal rigour and structural complexity, this poem becomes a paradox monument of belonging: If it appears to dismantle the "metaphysics of presence" (Derrida 1974: 26) and the reality of a stringent law through "significate-effects" (Bennington/Derrida 1994: 42), both prove literally fascinating and thus indispensable for the poem. Hence, the poem confirms itself as a law, validated but by its form: the transient, uncertain space of pneuma inspires the song of the father for its own sake, for the sake of the poem.

Pizarnik sets a full stop after "escribo", as if wanting to prevent the silent chant to pass beyond the limits of the poetic architecture. *Casa de citas*, by contrast, displays the decomposition of silence outside the (law of the) poem, inside a haunted house of a language of exile. Already the title evokes language, law and *genos* by making use of its own ambiguity: One of its possible meanings, "house of appointments", refers to the *Mishkan*, pitched by Moses in the desert (Ex 25, 9) and prefiguring the later Temple (*bajit* – house) as a spiritual centre. This house represents, as Franziska Bark points out, a "space of possibilities" already in the Torah: the "fragmentary", "incoherent" construction plan rendered in Exodus – "the dialogue between God and Moses [...] on Mount Sinai, "the re-narration of an acoustic event" (re-enacted in the poem) – thwarts a proper notion of the *Mishkan*; its "immediate reality is thus the space unfolding in analogy to the narration/the act of reading", leaving its midst, the space of God, vacant (Bark 2007: 172–178). This is the path that Pizarnik's text exemplarily follows, as reveals the second meaning of *Casa de citas*: by haphazardly arranging quotes from the works she has read and from her own writings which in turn quote from yet other works of hers, as well as from works of other authors, Pizarnik literally presents a "house" of quotations.[31] Last but not least, *Casa de citas* also means brothel in Spanish.

The expectations pinned on the house in each of its positive meanings – similar to those riveted on the poem: a sheltering frame within which to "transcribe ardent relations" (Pizarnik 2009: 265)[32] – are dashed in a text whose author appears to seek to communicate with his own absence: Statements in a babel of

---

[31] As to her own works, Pizarnik quotes from the prose text *El hombre del antifaz azul* (1972) referring to Lewis Carroll's *Alice in Wonderland*, and from her only play *Los perturbados entre lilas* (1969), itself abundantly quoting from her (prose) poems. Other quotes are from Lichtenberg, Benn, Bachelard (from his book on Lautréamont) and Konstantin Kavafis.
[32] In the prose poem *Piedra fundamental* (1971).

voices, some of which may constitute parts of a dialogue or a monologue, most often don't match or, if so, are declared to be as real and coherent as an entry registered among others in a dictionary, a profane surrogate for the Scriptures. The experience of revelation is now the "empty inside of its [the language's] own irreality" (Blanchot 2010: 48), a place where love, liberty, truth don't reveal themselves, don't 'happen', but where their elusive presence is indicated through an eerie fascination, as already the epigraph to the text, a quote from Bataille's short prose piece *Le Petit* (1943), suggests: "J'en parle afin de traduire un état de terreur"[33] – with "traduire" significantly replacing the original "révéler" (Moskoviz 2004: 1163) and followed by the lines: "A la place de Dieu… / il n'y a / que / l'impossible, / et non Dieu." The intended meaning of "le Petit" – God-anus – subtly floating about, the impossible divine marks also the absent centre of *Casa de Citas*. In fact, the narrative strategies we find here resemble those applied in the fragmentary reference text: "aphorisms, logic hiatuses and parodies namely of Kantian imperatives" organized around an "undecidable referent" (Moskoviz 2004: 1142–1143). They circumscribe a "space where the sign of the reflection of a thought emanating screams is written", at the expense of the body, of "the unadjectivable power of primitive desires" (Pizarnik 2012^3: 69). Coherently, a collapse of Kant's "critique of the reason-of-a-bitch" is asserted: "[T]he house – the 'metaphysical square'" – is "left in ruins" (Pizarnik 2012: 178[34]), profaned, vulgarized, haunted by shadows threatening with madness. A corresponding suicidal impulse rejecting the concept of belonging based on genealogical bonds is openly stated, in a language no more seeking to be poetic, but adopting the colloquialisms of the Argentine idiom: "Dijiste que me fuera. Intento hacerlo desde que me parió mi madre. – Vos no existís, ni tu madre, ni nada, salvo el diccionario."[35]

While claiming the validity any individual assertion claims, also this statement figures as a quote among others. Similarly, the biblical paradigm of exile and dispersion alluding to *Poema para el padre* ("A lo lejos sonaba indistintamente la voz de una muchacha que cantaba canciones de su tiempo de muchacha"), and the modified quote from Genesis 11:8 ("Dispersados serán por el mundo las mujeres que cantan y los hombres que cantan y todos los que cantan."[36]) represent quotes among others and are thus divested of a substantial,

---

[33] I am grateful to Tomasz Swoboda (University of Gdańsk) for his quick localization of the text.
[34] *Los perturbados entre lilas*, Pizarnik, Prosa Completa, 178.
[35] "You told me to go away. I am trying to do that since my mother gave birth to me. – You don't exist, nor your mother, nor anything, save for the dictionary."
[36] Here and for the following: "In the far distance resounded indistinctly the voice of a girl singing songs from her girlhood. [...] Dispersed all over the world shall be the women who sing and the men who sing and everyone who sings."

authentic meaning on the level of discourse. Structurally, though, they prove indispensable for the text itself to 'happen'. In other words: In a text widely performing by means of 'mere' quotes designed to disclaim authenticity, to dismantle the transcendental house-as-genre, *genos* and law are maintained as a phantom trace – in the shadow(s) haunting the desperate voice at the end of the text. Hence, the house-as-genre is not crossed out, but altered in regard to the expectation invested in it. *Casa de citas* not only mirrors disillusionment with joining Moses and Ahasver in a habitable dwelling. It is a house where those commemorated in the *yizker-bykher* (memorial books) blur in the spectrality of language – "I no more find a name for this. [...] I don't find a name for that."

"mi querida niña que no has tenido madre (ni padre, es obvio) [...]" (Pizarnik 2009: 414).[37] According to that assessment from *Sala de psicopatología*, the text – issued much later than those published posthumously in 1982[38] – fiercely defies a generic definition both in regard to discourse and structure. Stretching over seven pages and manfesting a theatricality already perceptible in *Casa de Citas*, it presents an autofictional poetic voice alternating between passages of coherent prose and unities increasingly displaying structures proper to a poem. Moreover, the text opens with a poetic voice sarcastically exhibiting itself as the protagonist of a diasporic condition, enumerating different transient places in Europe and the USA and eventually finding herself in a psychiatric ward. Thus, the sacred house of language is mockingly parodised, while the presentation of "una señora originaria del más oscuro barrio de un pueblo que no figura en el mapa" (Pizarnik 2009: 411)[39] suffering from severe heartache unleashes a raging stream of invective against a birthing mother along with a provocative display of diasporic lesbian erotism debasing rabbinic tradition.[40]

Hyperbolic figures of abandonment and obliteration in an other's voice are intensified in a passage relating to suicide: "Que te encuentres con vos misma – dijo./ Y yo le dije:/ Para reunirme con el *migo* de *conmigo* y ser una sola y misma entidad con él tengo que matar al *migo* para que así muera el *con* y, de este modo, anulados los contrarios, la dialéctica supliciante finaliza en la fusión de los

---

37 "my dear girl who has never had a mother (nor a father, it's obvious) [...]" (*Sala de psicopatología*, 1971).
38 Pizarnik wrote this text during her stay in the Hospital Pirovano in Buenos Aires, in 1971.
39 „a lady native of the darkest quarter of a village uncharted on the map".
40 *Sala de psicopatología* counts among the texts in which Pizarnik explicitly, albeit with utter scepticism shows her familiarity with still another tradition she considered to be Jewish: psychoanalysis. [Wilhelm] Reich, [Theodor] Reik, and Sigmund Freud – referred to also as a poet – are mentioned by name in the text.

contrarios" (Pizarnik 2009: 414).⁴¹ The pun is not only a mocking demonstration of Hegel's dialectics and the illusions of self-identity; it is also concerned with the inextricable conflict between exile/dispersion and a law grounded in the transcendental: *migo* – echoing the ego and reminiscent of Spanish "miga", crumb, and "migar", to crumble⁴² – appears as opposed to *con* – an agglutinating prefix cut off from the already scattered ego; besides, it is reminiscent of Batailles's *Le Petit* and the impossible divine, god assisting his own absence: the asshole (le con) as the utmost irrevocable and irremediable wound. The subsequent lines, reproducing an aphorism of Lichtenberg, underscore the unachievable appropriation of an autonomous reality under an injured heteronomous law, and, as the vision of the garden quoted from a poem in the prose poem *Extracción de la piedra de la locura* (1964) shows, also the impossibility of countering this aporia other than with a sarcastic quote of the romantic paradigm: "El suicidio determina/ un cuchillo sin hoja/ al que le falta el mango./ Entonces:/ adiós sujeto y objeto,/ todo se unifica como en otros tiempos, en el jardín de los cuentos para niños lleno de arroyuelos des frescas aguas prenatales;/ ese jardín es el *centro* del mundo, es el lugar de la cita, es el espacio vuelto tiempo y el tiempo vuelto lugar, es el alto momento de la fusión y del encuentro [...]". Increasingly shifting towards free verse, *Sala de psicopatología* ends with the lyrical I saying a poem which denotes a dead-end, and yet – as if somehow believed to offer refuge like a sheltering house – displays a feature of classical poetry unusual in Piazrnik's oeuvre: rhymes.

III Towards a recognition of diasporic writing: Pizarnik's "kleine Literatur"⁴³

"Que me dejen con mi voz nueva, desconocida." Given Pizarnik's endeavour to allow for a humor she conceived of as innate – subtle, acute, and subversive –,

---

41 Here and for the following: "You should meet yourself – she said./ And I said to her:/ In order to reunite myself with the *me* of the *with-me* and be one and the same entity with it I have to kill that *me* so that the *with* dies and, in this way, the contrasts nullified, the torturous dialectics ends with the fusion of the contrasts. Suicide determines/ a knife without a blade/ lacking a handle./ So:/ goodbye subject and object,/ everything unites as in other times, in the fairy tale garden full of brooklets of fresh prenatal waters,/ that garden is the *centre* of the world, it is the place of encounter, it is the space turned into time and time turned into place, it is the high moment of fusion and encounter [...]".
42 In his analysis of *Sala de psicopatología* focusing on the patterns of subjectivity in Pizarnik, Jaime Rodríguez-Matos points out the "miga"/"crumb" to the same effect (Rodríguez-Matos 2011: 576).
43 From Gilles Deleuze's and Félix Guattari's famous book *Kafka. Pour une littérature mineure* (1975), the expression coined by Kafka in his diaries.

her so-called *Textos de humor* can be considered to be an attempt to realise both "my new, unknown voice" and a new form. Undated, these texts most probably belong to her works written "[F]rom the mid-sixties onwards" (Mackintosh 2010: 509) and were in part published posthumously, among them several ones destined to appear as a whole in a (no more ascertainable) order. Here, Pizarnik's concern with genre and *genos*, thwarted encounters and miscarried unifications continues in an open 'diasporic' space akin to the concept of the 'rhizome' (Deleuze/Guattari) and difficult to define as a story or another traditional genre of fiction. The multilayered *Historia del Tío Jacinto* [Story of Uncle Jacinto], based on the *"Idiotishe gesichte von Alejandrishe Argentinian genialishe fraulein"* allegedly found in the "National Library of Minsk", renders, along with the parody of German language with Yiddish inflections, the image of confused and confusing sadomasochistic family relations disguised as a burlesque nonsensical fiction. A humor considered to be hurting by Pizarnik herself is still stronger in the texts collected under *La Bucanera de Pernambuco o Hilda la polígrafa* [The buccaneer of Pernambuco or Hilda the polygraph], published in 1982, displaying a spectacular babel of voices and linguistic registers largely left out in her writing until then.[44] Moreover, in these so called "textos de humor" during the conception of which Pizarnik particularly studied Freud's *Der Witz und seine Beziehung zum Unbewussten* [Jokes and their Relation to the Unconscious, 1905], as well as the parodic/satiric style of Cortázar and Bustos Domecq (the invented author of Borge's and Bioy Casare's literary collaborations), we don't find a narrative proper, but verbal puppets acting as a kind of theatrical language-automatons called "persopejes". Thus, and apart from debasing the dramatis personae by means of the pejorative Spanish suffix "-eje", Pizarnik makes plain her intentions by dissonantly hybridizing them with the term "herejes" – heretics.

Regarding the issue of belonging in the context of space, form/genre, and language, the heresy staged in *La Bucanera de Pernambuco o Hilda la polígrafa* proves extraordinarily polyvalent. In this space, Pizarnik makes use of multiple voices under the surface of which displacement, confusion, and vengefulness respect to *genos* continue to be at work. The display of truisms and romantic irony, the ambiguity and potential of puns inherent to language, the emission of a libidinous language of the subconscious and vulgar slips of the tongue, as

---

[44] The word "polígrafa" denotes: (1) a person writing about different topics in a secret, ciphered or extraordinary way; (2) an ancient automatic machine for printing copies; (3) a lie detector applied to persons suspected of a crime. These meanings correspond to the predominantly cryptic representation of parental (particularly mother-) figures holding their daughter hostage in the context of a traumatic family history. They also tie in with the figure of the *Golem* prominent in Pizarnik's writings.

well as parodic misunderstandings, elliptical sentences and silences sometimes including a cryptical author/narrator acting as another verbal puppet – all that amounts to the production of an "excess of signifiers in the text [...] that cannot be contained" (Graff Zivin 2008: 92) and cross out the illusion of (a 'sameness' of) the Self, hence also the traditional 'repository' of belonging.

Other textual elements and literary strategies additionally contribute to the specific form of expression in *La Bucanera de Pernambuco*: The puppets/voices resound in different languages (French, English, Italian, German, Russian, Yiddish), as well as in a variety of idiomatic, morphological and phonetic modes characteristic of these languages and of Argentine Spanish, both standard and vernacular, and particularly including the register of the obscene. Furthermore, the range of quoted spaces, places and intertextual levels is considerably widened: from European, Latin American and Spanish (philosophico-erotic) cities, regions, and literature, Jewish/Yiddish religious and psychoanalytical sources to Far Eastern as well as popular culture and own works. Together with the 'diasporic' condition conveyed hereby, Pizarnik's "persopejes", involved in verbal errantry, also remind of Ahasverus, a figure she repeatedly and ambivalently dealt with in her literary self-fashionings from the outset.[45]

That the 'director' of the "persopejes" might create this complex and highly educated linguistic and cultural space of errantry also in order to heretically mock a lethally injured East European Jewry seems probable: although the published texts are far from being discreet, it is only in some of the (to date unreleased) manuscripts stored in the Department of Rare Books and Special Collections in Princeton that in particular a maternal voice is overtly shown speaking a defective, 'yiddishized' Spanish and thus a Jewish language depreciated as a 'corrupt' jargon in Western- and Central Europe is exposed.[46]

Considering the transtextual presence of the books which Borges and Bioy Casares wrote together between 1940 and 1946[47] – vivid satires on a preposterous *criollo*-patriotism in Argentine society and politics, on the glorification of a pure Spanish descent –, it becomes patent that in the "textos de humor", Pizarnik's does more than break with the image of the acclaimed Argentine "poeta lírico

---

[45] According to the Christian legend condemned "to never gain a foothold in any place" and having "[usurped something] [F]rom every nation [...], every random place, every tip of the world", Ahasver appears as the prototypic (Western-bred) other whom Pizarnik's diarist identifies her ancestors and herself with (Pizarnik 2014²: 55).

[46] This has been established by Fiona J. Mackintosh (2010) on the basis of the mentioned manuscripts.

[47] *Seis problemas para don Isidro Parodi* [Six problems for Isidro Parodi, 1942], *Dos fantasias memorables* [Two memorable fantasies] and *Un modelo para la muerte* [A model for death].

amenazado por lo ineffable y lo incomunicable" (Pizarnik 2003: 413[48]) she had forged herself and responded with to the expectations of contemporary literary critics and readers.[49] Above all, she "does something" (Derrida) to the Spanish language a brilliant command of which she longs for and denies herself. Having eventually remained 'loyal' to it despite her fascination with French, here her voices unsettle the textual, formal and linguistic territory/space they had used to uneasily occupy form within and make the Argentine-Spanish 'madre patria/lengua' promiscuous[50], thus honouring Kafka's concept of the "kleine Literatur" in their own way: speaking up for an existence and a writing against the grain, the norm of homogeneity, and speaking from within a minority whose right to belong to manifold cultures, languages and traditions has always been contested and brutally crushed. From the interstices of this excessive linguistic firework, the cryptic progenitors-protagonists of "the tragedy of the pygmies' destiny" (the speechless "last Rex Pigmarum" and a monstrous she-wolf in *La Bucanera de Pernambuco o Hilda la polígrafa*) still emerge, but also Pizarnik's undiminished, challenging vision of a language as a liquid, breathing space, smooth, diaphanous, open to openings, coincidences, contingencies, bourgeoning to a law harboring its own wound:

> [...]? y ese lenguaje como una mano ahuecada llena de agua riquísima? Lo soñé todos estos días [...] algo totalmente opuesto al NO, a la severidad [...] como la boca llena de risa, como el sexo lleno de semen, como un sí afirmado sin cesar, una danza ni lenta ni veloz, un moverse con infinita facilidad y docilidad. Ese idioma era el que soñé hace unos días y fui feliz pues creí que había puesto un nombre a mi extraño estar aquí, en este mundo anguloso, rectilíneo, cuyas aristas fueron corroídas por el ácido del sueño. (Pizarnik 2014: 713–714)[51]

---

48 "the lyrical poet threatened by the ineffable and incommunicable".
49 Mackintosh (2010) also mentions the predominantly and point-blank negative reactions to some of the texts Pizarnik herself submitted for critical reading, as well as the negative reviews *La Bucanera de Pernambuco o Hilda la polígrafa* received upon its posthumous publication.
50 Accordingly, in a diary entry temporally coincident with the work on *Textos de humor*, a trait ascribed to the Jews by a voice presenting itself as Jewish is "adultery"; Pizarnik 2003: 847 (16.1.1969).
51 "[...] and this language like a cupped hand full of delicious water? I have been dreaming of it all these days [...] something completely opposed to NO, to severity [...] like the mouth full of laughter, like the sex full of semen, like a yes affirmed incessantly, a dance neither slow nor fast, like moving with infinite lightness and litheness. That idiom was the one I dreamt about some days ago, and I was happy, for I thought that I had found a name for my strange being here, in this angular, straight-line world the edges of which were corroded by the acid of the dream." (12.3.1965).

IV Texts

Fragmentos para dominar el silencio

I
Las fuerzas del lenguaje son las damas solitarias, desoladas, que cantan a través de mi voz que escucho a lo lejos. Y lejos, en la negra arena, yace una niña densa de música ancestral. ¿Dónde la verdadera muerte? He querido iluminarme a la luz de mi falta de luz. Los ramos se mueren en la memoria. La yacente anida en mí con su máscara de loba. La que no pudo más e imploró llamas y ardimos.

II
Cuando a la casa del lenguaje se le vuela el tejado y las palabras no guarecen, yo hablo.

Las damas de rojo se extraviaron dentro de sus máscaras aunque regresarán para sollozar entre flores.

No es muda la muerte. Escucho el canto de los enlutados sellar las hendiduras del silencio. Escucho tu dulcísimo llanto florecer mi silencio gris.

III
La muerte ha restituido al silencio su prestigio hechizante. Y yo no diré mi poema y yo he de decirlo. Aun si el poema (aquí, ahora) no tiene sentido, no tiene destino.

Poema para el padre

Y fue entonces
que con la lengua muerta y fría en la boca
canto la canción que no le dejaron cantar
en este mundo de jardines obscenos y de sombras
    que venían a deshora a recordarle
    cantos de su tiempo de muchacho
en el que no podía cantar la canción que quería cantar
la canción que no le dejaron cantar
sino a través de sus ojos azules ausentes
de su boca ausente
de su voz ausente.
Entonces, desde la torre más alta de la ausencia
su canto resonó en la opacidad de lo ocultado

Fragments to dominate the silence

I
The powers of language are the solitary, desolate ladies singing through my voice which I listen to from afar. And far away, a girl lies in the black sand, tense with ancestral music. Where is true death? I have wanted to illuminate myself in the light of my lack of light. The branches die in memory. The reclining girl nestles in me with her wolf-mask. Who could not take it any longer and implored flames and we burnt.

II
When the roof flies off the house of language and words don't provide refuge, I speak.

The ladies in red went astray within their masks, though they will return to sob among flowers.

Death is not mute. I listen to the singing of the mourners sealing the fissures of silence. I listen to your sweetest lament flourishing my grey silence.

III
Death has restituted to silence its bewitching lure. And I will not say my poem and I am to say it. Even if the poem (here, now) doesn't make sense, doesn't have a destiny.

Poem for the father

And it was then
that with the dead and cold tongue in his mouth
he sang the song they did not let him sing
in this world of obscene gardens and of shadows
untimely coming to remind him
of songs from his boyhood
in which he could not sing the song he wanted to sing
the song they did not let him sing
but through his absent blue eyes
his absent mouth
his absent voice.

en la extención silenciosa
llena de oquedades movedizas como las palabras que escribo.

Casa de citas

> *J'en parle afin de traduire un état de terreur.*
> Georges Bataille

- Hay como chicos mendigos saltando mi cerca mental, buscando aperturas, nidos, cosas para romper o robar.
- Alguien se maravillaba de que los gatos tuvieran dos agujeros en la piel, precisamente en el sitio de los ojos.
- "Odio a los fantasmas"– dijo, y se notaba claramente por su tono que sólo después de haber pronunciado estas palabras comprendía su significado.
- Abrí la boca un poco más, así se notará que estás hablando.
- Me siento como si no fuera capaz de hablar más en la vida.
- Hablá en voz muy baja. Y sobre todo, recordá quién sos.
- ¿Y si me olvido?
- Entonces bramá.

- Estoy pensando que.
- No es verdad. Cosas desde la nada a ti confluyen.

- A lo lejos sonaba indistintamente la voz de una muchacha que cantaba canciones de su tiempo de muchacha.
- ¿En qué pensás mientras cantás?
- En que aquel sueño de ir en bicicleta a ver una cascada rodeada de hojas verdes no era para mí.
- Sólo quería ver el jardín.
- ¿Y ahora?
- Siento deseos de huir hacia un país más hospitalario y, al mismo tiempo, busco bajo mis ropas un puñal.
- Como vos, quisiera ser una cosa que no puede sentir el paso de los años.
- Supongo que el envejecimiento del rostro ha de ser una herida de espantoso cuchillo.
- La vida nos ha olvidado y lo malo es que uno no se muere de eso.
- Sin embargo, cada vez nos va peor.
- Entonces la vida no nos ha olvidado.

- Perras palabras. ¿Cómo han de poder mis gritos determinar una sintaxis? Todo se articula en el cuerpo cuando el cuerpo dice la fuerza inadjetivable de los deseos primitivos.

Then, from the highest tower of absence
his chant resounded in the opacity of what is concealed
in the silent extension
full of quicksand voids like the words I am writing.

Casa de citas

> *J'en parle afin de traduire un état de terreur*
> Georges Bataille

- There are like beggar boys jumping my mental fence, searching for openings, dens, things to break or to steal.
- Somebody marveled that cats had two holes in their skin, precisely in the place of the eyes.
- "I hate ghosts" – she said, and it was perfectly clear from her tone of voice that only after she had pronounced these words she understood their meaning.
- Open your mouth a bit more, thus it will be obvious that you're speaking.
- I feel as if I won't ever be able to speak in my life.
- Speak very low. And most of all, remember who you are.
- And if I forget?
- Then roar.

- I'm thinking about what.
- That's not true. Things from nowhere join you.

  In the distance resounded indistinctly the voice of a girl singing songs from her girlhood.
- What do you think about while singing?
- About that dream of going by bike to see a waterfall surrounded with green leaves. It wasn't for me.
- I only wanted to see the garden.
- And now?
- I feel the desire to flee to more welcoming a country, and at the same time I am looking for a dagger under my clothes.
- Like you, I'd like to be a thing insensitive to the passing of the years.
- I suppose that the ageing of the face must be a wound of horrible knife.

- Life has forgotten us and the trouble is that you don't die of it.
- Still, we're going from bad to worse.
- Then life hasn't forgotten us.

- Bastard words. How should my screams be able to determine a syntax? Everything is articulated in the body when the body says the inadjectivable power of the primitive desires.

– Apenas digo el espacio donde se escribe el signo del reflejo de un pensar que emana gritos.

– Soy real– dijo. Y se puso a llorar.
– ¿Real? Andate de aquí.
– Algo fluye, no cesa de fluir.
– Dije que te fueras.
– Dijiste que me fuera. Intento hacerlo desde que me parió mi madre.
– Vos no existís, ni tu madre, ni nada, salvo el diccionario.

– Alcancé el maravilloso poder de simpatizar con cualquier cosa que sufriese.
– No entiendo. Fui al prostíbulo, y esa bella constelación de divinas difuntas.

– Entiendo. La crítica de la puta razón.
– Quedé asombrada con cantidad de asombro pues vi a una mujer montada sobre un animal en estado bruto.
– Mi miedo al dar a la vida un solo adjetivo.
– Siempre tropiezo en mi plegaria de la infancia.
– Siempre así: yo estoy a la puerta; llamo; nadie abre.
– Le dije cuanto había en mi corazón.
– Por eso huyó, ¿verdad?
– A la hora de morir uno canta para sí, no para los demás.
– Sólo en su canto podía reconocerse al amante silencioso.
– Dispersados serán por el mundo las mujeres que cantan y los hombres que cantan y todos los que cantan.

– Y entonces se vestirá tranquilamente con el hábito de la locura.
– De nuevo la sombra.
– Y entonces me alejé o llegué. ¿Tendré tiempo de hacerme una máscara para cuando emerja de las sombras?
– La sombra, ella está aquí. Casa de sal volcada, de espejos rotos. Yo había encontrado un pequeño lugar solitario, propicio para llorar. Esta vez la sombra vino a la tarde, y no como siempre por la noche. Yo ya no encuentro un nombre para esto.
– Esta vez vino por la tarde, y no como siempre por la noche. Volvió a venir, más ya no hallé, aun siendo día, un nombre para aquello. Esta vez parecía amarillo. Yo estaba sentada en la cocina con un fósforo quemado entre los dedos.

– I barely say the space where is written the sign of the reflection of a thinking emanating screams.

– I'm real – she said. And she started to cry.
– Real? Get away from here.
– Something flows, doesn't stop flowing.
– I told you to go away.
– You told me to go away. I'm trying to do that since my mother gave birth to me.
– You don't exist, nor your mother, nor anything, except for the dictionary.

– I reached the marvellous power of sympathizing with anything that suffers.
– I don't understand. I went to the brothel, and this beautiful constellation of divine deceased girls.
– I understand. The critique of the reason-of-a-bitch.
– I was amazed with considerable amazement, since I saw a woman riding a brute.
– My fear to give to life an only adjective.
– Always I trip over my childhood prayer.
– Always like that: I'm at the door; I knock; nobody opens.
– I told him how much there was in my heart.
– That's why he fled, right?
– When it comes to dying one sings for oneself, not for the others.
– Only in his/her chant she could declare herself to the silent lover.
– Dispersed all over the world shall be the women who sing and the men who sing and everyone who sings.

– And then she will calmly dress in the habit of madness.
– Again the shadow.
– And then I moved away or arrived. Will I have time to make myself a masque by the time I emerge from the shadows?
– The shadow, it is here. House of spilled salt, of broken mirrors. I had found a small lonely place, fit for crying. This time, the shadow came at noon, and not, as always, at night. I no more find a name for that.

– This time it came at noon and not, as always, at night. It came again, but even being day, I no more found a name for that. This time it seemed yellow. I was sitting in the kitchen with a burnt match between my fingers.

Sonja Dickow
Architectures of Absence: Nicole Krauss's Novel *Great House*

Presence/Absence

> A story is not like a road to follow ... it's more like a house. You go inside and stay there for a while, wandering back and forth and settling where you like and discovering how the room and corridors relate to each other, how the world outside is altered by being viewed from these windows. And you, the visitor, the reader, are altered as well by being in this enclosed space, whether it is ample and easy or full of crooked turns, or sparsely or opulently furnished. You can go back again and again, and the house, the story, always contains more than you saw the last time. It also has a sturdy sense of itself of being built out of its own necessity, not just to shelter or beguile you. (Munro 1997, xx–xi)

To perceive a story like a house, to inhabit its empty or filled rooms for a while, to move through its corridors, to look out its windows, or to discover something new in each reading –Alice Munro's notion of the dynamic spatiality of literature bears further consideration. However, the components of the house are not the only literary topoi; by using spatial metaphors, Munro also appears to be interested in the making of a literary world, or in the architecture of literature's unique spatiality as a concrete end in itself (Dünne and Mahler 2015, 3). This unique spatiality is dynamic; it opens new paths with each reading and changes the person reading, or visiting, the story. In this essay, I employ Munro's idea of architectural topography as the basis for an analysis of the novel *Great House* (2010), by the Jewish-American writer Nicole Krauss.

In Krauss's novel, a multitude of different lives, times, and places are interwoven through the travels and changes of ownership of a gigantic desk. The desk is introduced into the narrative when a Chilean poet, Daniel Varsky, loans it to Nadia, a writer from New York who is identified only by her first name. Soon after Varsky is murdered by the Pinochet regime, his furniture becomes Nadia's possession. From this point on, the desk appears as an object of memory, inclusion, and desire, circulating across the novel's different narratives of violence.

Note: The topics considered in this paper are part of a comprehensive analysis of Nicole Krauss's Great House. This larger analysis is one component of a dissertation about figurations of the house and home in contemporary Jewish literatures. Quotations from the novel will be cited here with corresponding page numbers within parentheses.

https://doi.org/10.1515/9783110525519-015

In addition to these different accounts, the desk also exists as a dense and dynamic site of literary potentiality:

> Nineteen drawers of varying size, some below the desktop and some above, whose mundane occupations (stamps here, paper clips there) hid a far more complex design, the blueprint of the mind formed over tens of thousands of days of thinking while staring at them, as if they held the conclusion to a stubborn sentence, the culminating phrase, the radical break from everything I had ever written that would at last lead to the book I had always wanted, and always failed, to write. [...] Or am I making too much of it? (16)

Nadia's characterization of the drawers of the desk as a "blueprint of the mind" and the "conclusion to a stubborn sentence" is symptomatic to its effect as a screen onto which its owner can project his or her fears and wishes.

The discovery and loss of this inanimate protagonist, as well as its erratic movements and complicated exchanges of ownership, propel the plot of the novel. With a heavy heart, Nadia gives the desk to a young woman from Jerusalem who poses as the daughter of the murdered poet. All traces of the desk and its new owner from Jerusalem are subsequently lost. The next fragment of the desk's biography transpires in England, where it is now in the hands of Arthur Bender, an emeritus professor; it had been owned by his wife, Lotte Berg, a Jewish writer who fled from Germany as a girl. Before she bequeathed it to Daniel Varsky, the "tremendous body of furniture" (84) had once stood in her office. "To call it a desk is to say too little" (248), Bender recalls. He describes it as a room-dominating, almost living object which threatens to devour the other objects in the room, greedy as a "Venus flytrap" (248). Bender eyes the desk jealously, as it shares a secret with his wife. The narrative then shifts to Isabel, an American student who meets two siblings, Leah and Yoav Weisz, in London. The siblings grew up in London and in Jerusalem. Isabel gradually unravels the family's mysterious and disturbing history, which includes the origins of the desk. Leah and Yoav's father, George Weisz, has made it his life's work to find the desk and place it in the replica of his long-dead father's office from prewar Budapest, which he has re-created from memory in Jerusalem. George's father, a scholar of Jewish history, was the desk's first owner, before the National Socialists stole it, destroyed his house, and murdered him and his wife. George Weisz survived the Holocaust, having been sent on a children's transport to England. Later, as an antiques dealer, he devotes himself to finding the scattered plunder of the Nazis "[o]ut of the ruins of history" (285). The only remaining piece of furniture he cannot acquire is his father's desk. "My father died fifty years ago on a death march to the Reich," he explains. "Now I sit in his room in Jerusalem, a city he only imagined. His desk sits locked in a storage room in New York City, and my daughter holds the key" (287–288).

The desk's absence leads to my thesis in this essay, namely, that a diegetic and poetological inspection of the Kraussian literary house reveals a prominent "architecture of absence," which differs from Munro's more general view of the house of storytelling. Furthermore, this architecture can only be detected against the backdrop of Jewish literature and history. The term "architecture of absence" may seem slightly paradoxical; therefore, I would like to offer the image of a house-like structure, which encapsulates something that is missing and longed for. In Krauss's complex and subtle novel, absence is conceived as a potential space for possibility, a space in which something fundamentally productive and aesthetic can come into being. The central argument of my reading is that in *Great House*, loss and absence are the elements which inspire the processes of remembering and storytelling. These processes can be understood as substitutes for the loss of physical place; ultimately, they attribute self-reflexively to the power of literary space, aiming to protect memory and to facilitate belonging. Here arises the question regarding the extent to which *Great House* presents loss and absence as a poetological premise for the creation of this space of textual belonging. At the same time – and this becomes particularly clear in terms of the historical circumstances of absence – Krauss's novel never reduces what is missing into something completely positive. Against the backdrop of twentieth-century Jewish history, the desk's biography and its travels are linked to violence and flight, and to the sufferings of the Holocaust, which are presented by means of transgenerational traumatic dynamics, as the novel tells of the damage these events wreak across generations.

Great House consists of two parts, each divided into four chapters; in three of the eight chapters, the names of the characters reappear, giving the impression of a kaleidoscopic reflection. Each chapter highlights a different fate, until, at the end, the fragments cohere into a fragile yet comprehensive picture. The five different narrating voices, their retrospectives and prefigurations – in addition to the sudden movements in setting and narrated time – make it difficult to determine the actual timeframe of the narrative. Thus, when exploring the novel, readers must continually reorient themselves. In the many otherwise positive reviews of the novel, some critics expressed the feeling that this complexity overburdened the text. Here, however, I interpret this overburdening as a correlation between structure and content, considering the antique dealer's overloaded houses: as George Weisz collects more and more belongings of Holocaust victims in his rooms, it becomes clearer to the readers that those objects cannot eliminate the absence that is caused by death.

In keeping with Munro's spatial metaphor of the house, the branched narrative network of strands and perspectives represents the different rooms through which the desk passes in its biography. The corridors, i.e., the connections between the rooms, become clearer as the desk emerges as a common theme in each specific narrative; in this labyrinth, the mobility of the desk structures the seemingly unrelated narrative strands.

In Krauss's interviews we find statements regarding her process of writing the novel which echo Munro's image of the story as a house. Krauss compares writing literary fiction to gradually exploring a house, to opening doors and discovering new rooms (Voigt 2011). "You live in them over the course of a long period, both as a reader and as a writer," she explains in another interview: "The feeling I have when I write of putting all these pieces together, and noticing how they create a shape, and then knowing that I have built something and that it will stand up; it's so satisfying to me" (Cooke 2011). As she moves from room to room, the floorplan of a "ghostly Great House" eventually emerges (Cooke 2011). Krauss's description is informative. She does not seem interested in building a place of homeliness; rather, as is hinted at by the word "ghostly," she seems to work towards something uncanny. Sigmund Freud developed his concept of the uncanny [*Unheimlich*] from the etymology of the word "homey" (*heimlich*, in German), which, semantically, is similar to home [*Heim*] and to house [*Haus*]. Hence, this negation of "homey" describes something being simultaneously trusted and familiar, yet also strange and uncanny (Freud 1970 [1919], 248).[1] The literary house is uncanny, as it denies the reader any comfortable stability and confuses him with its "strangeness" – and, one could say, with its artistic autonomy or its own life as text. "Ghostly" also refers to the structure of the novel house, as some things are not addressed explicitly, but only intimated to as subtext. Of this stylistic decision Alan L. Berger and Asher Z. Milbauer have noted that Krauss's novels indirectly engender pain over absence and over the horror of the Holocaust (Berger and Milbauer 2013, 67). This observation is also true of *Great House*, in which the stolen and later dispersed items of furniture serve an important function as "thing[s] of exile" (Bischoff 2016, 78), in that they refer to the injustices and sufferings that have been inflicted on their Jewish owners.

In terms of the literary representation of spatiality, we can speak of an interconnection of thematically and semantically nested spaces which continually increase in size and are, at their core, empty, thus encompassing an absence which drives the plot.

---

[1] Freud's wordplay here does not work in English. I have included the German so that the reader can appreciate what he was addressing.

Jewish Perspectives or the Great House in Exile

In *Great House*, Krauss breaks with the general notion of literature as a house, in that her "architecture of absence" and cartography of Jewish experiences of localization and delocalization both refer to mobile and endangered belongings and affiliations. Her novel highlights the concrete and abstract houses that are preserved not only in cultural memory, but also in the personal recollections of the protagonists. The different layers of cultural memory are summoned through the catastrophic events of the twentieth century, which are imbedded in the protagonists' personal memories, and through the destruction of the Second Temple in Jerusalem in 70 CE. The legend of Yochanan ben Zakkai, who greatly contributed to the establishing of a text-based religion through the Talmud after the destruction of the Second Temple and the beginning of the Jewish exile, functions here as a *mise en abyme* for the relationship between absence and presence.

In this context, the values of absence and presence are radically reassessed. Thus, for example, George Weisz recalls that "my father, a scholar of history, taught me that the absence of things is more useful than their presence" (287). In the passage regarding ben Zakkai, absence triggers reflections on the transformation of concrete physical places into abstract narrative spaces. In describing the teachings of ben Zakkai, Krauss writes: "Turn Jerusalem into an idea. Turn the Temple into a book, a book as vast and holy and intricate as the city itself" (279). The house of the text takes the place of the Temple, thereby portraying abstraction and mobility as important facets of a textual experience of space in exile.

In the story of ben Zakkai, which has been handed down from father to son, the central question is how one can contend with existential loss. "Bend a people around the shape of what they lost," says the father, quoting ben Zakkai, "and let everything mirror its absent form. Later his school became known as the Great House, after the phrase in Book of Kings: *He burned the house of God, the king's house, and all the houses of Jerusalem; even every great house he burned with fire*" (279, italics in original). With the destruction of concrete places, the work of memory and tradition begins. "Two thousand years have passed, my father used to tell me," George Weisz remembers, "and now every Jewish soul is built around the house that burned in that fire [...]" (279). The complex experience of situatedness which had developed in the Diaspora – utterly tangible in each specific country yet spiritual in its orientation towards the absent Jerusalem – is passed from one generation to the next through the novel's protagonists.

Krauss recognizes the potential of the legend of ben Zakkai in its central theme of re-imagination as a reaction to existential loss. "[T]he answer to catastrophic loss was absolute reimagination. It's a Jewish story, but it's a very universal idea." (Krauss in Rothenberg Gritz 2010). As Sidra DeKoven Ezrahi writes on the subject of re-imagination and the emergence of Jewish culture from the Diaspora: "For some two thousand years after the second destruction in 70 CE, in the absence of a temple, a republic, or any form of territorial or political sovereignty and at variable distances from the ruined shrine, Jewish poets managed to preserve Jerusalem in its symbolic state" (DeKoven Ezrahi 2007, 222). This preservation of a symbolic Jerusalem in writing represents a form of creative, cultural substitution for the absent, physical Jerusalem, a simulacrum which originates in the experience of exile (DeKoven Ezrahi 2007, 223–224). DeKoven Ezrahi's "diasporic aesthetics" (225) resonates in Krauss's novel in the figuration of Leah Weisz, who keeps absent her father's object of longing, the desk, and prevents it from being placed in his office-replica as the last key piece of the puzzle.

On a self-reflexive level, we can understand *Great House*, i.e., the novel itself, as a substitution through which the physical and immovable house yields to the mobile house of the text. As George Weisz explains, "Two thousand years have passed, my father used to tell me, and now every Jewish soul is built around the house that burned in that fire, so vast that we can, each one of us, only recall the tiniest fragment: a pattern on the wall, a knot in the wood of a door, a memory of how light fell across the floor" (279). Through the fragments of memory mentioned here, the house is implicitly named as a mnemonic topos known since Simonides and as a rhetorical piece. The contents of remembered speech are imagined as objects that are deposited at various locations throughout the house. Like objects, these contents can then be accessed, albeit mentally, in order to be collected and memorized. For the young George and his father, however, only the preservation of the fragmentary is possible. "But if every Jewish memory were put together, every last holy fragment joined up again as one, the House would be built again, said Weisz, or rather a memory of the House so perfect that it would be, in essence, the original itself" (279). Here it seems as though the emphasis shifts from the original to the practice of remembering itself, which is then granted the central meaning; thus, the original yields to the substitution of communication and transmission of an almost perfect memory as a performative and constitutive act, so that only the simulacrum can be handed down.

Indeed, Weisz's quotation evokes an observation made by Yosef Hayim Yerushalmi in his work *Zachor*, concerning Jewish memory and historical writing. According to Yerushalmi, "the question of the meaning of history has played a decisive role with Jews at all times," yet "the writing of history either [had no role] at all or, in the best case, [played] a subordinate one" (Yerushalmi 1988, 10). To explain this discrepancy, Yerushalmi points to the importance of historical orientation and the transgenerational transfer of a "living past" which are crucial in Judaism and stem from the commandment to remember (Yerushalmi 1988, 39).

In Krauss's novel, it is chiefly George Weisz who dedicates his life to the task of remembering by means of collecting things of belonging. However, his way of remembering seems to be an ambivalent one as he attempts, unavailingly, to rebuild a lost space of the past. Hence, the difference between remembering the past by abstract, textual, and verbal means and reconstructing it by spatial means becomes apparent.

Nevertheless, Weisz is aware of the failure inherent to his spatial engagement with remembrance as the collection of "every last holy fragment." In Krauss's novel, these "holy fragments" evoke an extension of the Kabbalistic concept of world healing, *Tikkun Olam*, though in a revised state. Known since rabbinic Judaism and adapted through medieval Kabbala, *Tikkun Olam* refers to the notion that every individual is obliged to repair (heal) the world through his or her righteous behaviour, presupposing that all inhabitants of Earth are, since a time before creation, inherently broken and flawed.[2] Throughout the novel, in an inversion of this concept, the fragmentary becomes the most important facet of Weisz's architecture of memory, which he establishes for the time after the destruction of the great house. The fragmentary also accompanies Jewish and non-Jewish protagonists alike into the present, as seen in the search for the desk, whereby the losses that are suffered question the existence of any wholeness or continuity. Thus, Weisz's statement, that "We live, each of us, to preserve our fragment, in a state of perpetual regret and longing for a place we only know existed because we remember a keyhole, a tile, the way the threshold was worn under an open door" (279), also brings to light a keenly personal level. His reference to completely ordinary components of a concrete house possibly points to his childhood home. The abstract holy space and a concrete family house can no longer be clearly distinguished, and they now enable the notion that culturally transferred memory and very personal memory are both articulated and formed by concrete and abstract spaces, either inhabited or imagined.[3] In Krauss's novel, concrete and abstract spaces are evoked by "architectures of absence" that span

---

2 Following the Lurian Kabbalah, the so-called breaking of the vessels, *Shvirat ha-Kelim* precedes the *Tikkum Olam*. This complex model of thought describes how the divine omnipotence, *Ein Sof* [infiniteness], moved into a room [*Tsimtsum*], and collected all of the divine rays of light, the *Sfirot*, into vessels. Some of the vessels could not accommodate the beams and broke, whereby divine sparks of light were dispersed across the world. Since then, everyone bears a sign of this rupture within, which can only be healed in the Messianic Age (Scholem 1957, 291–292).
3 Barbara Mann likens this complexity of space to the Hebrew term *makom*, meaning either place or space, as well as divine authority. Mann suggests that *makom* "may also be productively considered in relation to what has been called the spatial turn in the academy, a reference to the emerging importance of space as a critical category in the humanities and social studies" (Mann 2012, 17). Her plea to "think [...] about space through the lens of text" (2) calls to mind Dan

from ben Zakkai's great house to the Weisz's family home, and are, in terms of the novel's composition, an aesthetic device and main theme.

The House as Still Life

Not only are places absent in Krauss's novel, but also people, in particular those who were murdered, such as Weisz's parents and the poet Varsky. "It's true, I can't bring the dead back to life," George Weisz states. "But I can bring back the chair they once sat in, the bed where they slept" (275). Whereas the previous section of this article discussed, among other things, the potentiality of absence and the inversion of *Tikkun Olam* in the context of cultural memory, this quotation makes manifest that, after the Jewish history of the twentieth century and the incomprehensible anguish of the Holocaust, absence is in fact something exceedingly present. Philippe Codde perceives the attention to *absent presences* and to the tension between absence and presence as an ontological structure in the literature of the third generation of Jewish writers in the United States. Codde points to an ethical imperative to remember and think in these writers' texts – an imperative originating in the growing historical distance from the Holocaust. This ethical stance is distinguished by its communication of the past through indirect representation.

In *Great House*, the traces of the Holocaust, of which Codde speaks (Codde 2011, 677), are present in the furniture: "Leah remembered the arrival of certain of these long-lost pieces at the house on Ha'Oren Street, tense and somber events that had terrified her so much that as a small child she would sometimes hide in the kitchen when the crates were pried open, in case what popped out were the blackened faces of her dead grandparents" (115). These pieces of furniture, according to Leah and Yoav Weisz, are only seemingly inanimate and occasionally reappear, like the revenants of the murdered relatives. "*Sometimes I think that had he allowed himself to live as he wanted to,*" Leah believes of her father, "*he would have chosen an empty room with only a bed and a chair. […] He was burdened with a sense of duty that commanded his whole life, and later ours*" (115, italics in original). Instead of an almost empty room, however, the Weiszes' premises are filled with the furniture of people who fled or were murdered, which form a collection of secondary witnesses to a violent and painful history.

Miron's *From Continuity to Contiguity*, a work which illustrates literary scholarship's focal shift, from the previous category of time to perceptions of space.

Leah's view of her father discloses his own ambivalent attitude. He deeply desires to collect the fragments of his father's possessions, yet he is simultaneously burdened and "occupied" by them, as manifested in his inclination for an empty room. The empty room is interpreted as a space of possibility for one's own autonomous existence, a space not already filled by another person's history. As discussed in relation to the legend of ben Zakkai, loss and absence in *Great House* represent something which is not entirely negative; they contain the possibility of a productive force, that of a "diasporic aesthetics," in the words of DeKoven Ezrahi. This perspective shapes *Great House* as a generational process, primarily expressed in the father-daughter relationship between George and Leah Weisz. The burden of an extreme sense of responsibility is also passed to one's children. The loss of a homeland and of parents, the suffering experienced at a young age – these life events live on in George's children, though they are never spoken of. The siblings are described as "prisoners of their father's, locked within the walls of their own family, and in the end it wasn't possible for them to belong to anyone else" (113). The varied meaning of the English verb "to belong," which can signify affiliation as well as ownership, points here, in its ambiguity, to a conflict between the siblings: they feel as though their father and his past have taken possession of them, resulting in a loss of autonomy. The "walls of their own family" refer both to prison, i.e., the Weiszes' house, as well as to the effect the father has on his children, even after his death. "*It can't go on like this or we really will stop living,*" Leah confides in her friend Isabel. "*One of us will do something terrible. It's as if my father is luring us closer to him every day. It gets harder to resist*" (116, italics in original).

This overpowering dynamic could be described as "postmemory," a term coined by Marianne Hirsch that describes the "uneasy oscillation between continuity and rupture," which comes to light when traumatic knowledge or traumatic experiences are passed down through the generations (Hirsch 2008, 106–107). In *Great House*, Krauss continually returns to her protagonists' interior spaces and inner lives, which, for most of them, have been severely disrupted by murder, forced displacement, and loss of homeland. These experiences remind us of the term "trauma," which etymologically, in Greek, indicates a wound. As Hirsch explains, the connection between postmemory and the past arises not from one's own memory, but rather from "imaginative investment, projection, and creation," which are accompanied by generational distance. Thus, it is entirely possible for inherited memories to exert overwhelming force and for the parents' life history to repress the experiences of the children (Hirsch 2008, 106–107).

The house that George Weisz has built, which is simultaneously a museum of his family, becomes a still life of the past with overwhelming inherited memories (in Hirsch's words) in which the children themselves have no place. The more the house is filled with objects from the past, the more it also exposes an absence, an absence of the present as well as the absence of any orientation towards the future. In spatial imagery, it may be pictured as a ruin: though it is physically present in its remnants, it refers to a place and a time that are past.

Ruins possess an uncanny character which enables them to haunt subjects and to distort their linear sense of time. Analogous to the spatial structure of a trauma, in which the significant event must be expunged from consciousness, thereby rendering memory inaccessible, ruins accommodate something absent, which establishes their negative spatiality, "a location defined not only by what has ceased to exist, but also by what cannot be accommodated spatially" (Trigg 2009, 96). In line with Dylan Trigg's assertion, and by implementing the connection between architecture and trauma, we can read the Jerusalem replica of the destroyed office in Budapest as a traumatic ruin, one which mirrors what is absent – represented by the missing desk – rather than what is present.

George Weisz's tireless efforts to recreate his father's office exactly as it exists in his memory, before its plunder by the Nazi Gestapo in 1944, illuminate the emotional meaning bestowed upon the spaces of childhood. Gaston Bachelard speaks in this context of the house of our childhood as a frame for the images we remember later on: "In short, the house we were born in has engraved within us the hierarchy of the various functions of inhabiting. We are the diagram of the functions of inhabiting that particular house, and all the other houses are but variations on a fundamental theme" (Bachelard 1994 [1957], 15). The house of George Weisz's parents is engraved upon his memory as such a fundamental theme, such that he uses it as an original floorplan to build his later houses.

> [E]verything in his study in Jerusalem was laid out exactly as my grandfather's study in Budapest had once been, down to the millimeter! [...] For forty years my father labored to reassemble that lost room [...]. As if by putting all the pieces back together he might collapse time and erase regret. The only thing missing in the study on Ha'Oren Street was my grandfather's desk – where it should have stood, there was a gaping hole. Without it the study remained incomplete, a poor replica. (115–116, italics in original)

Where the narration of the past fails, explains Trigg, the place of the trauma comes to light, "with an indirect language, blocked from interpretation and displacing the certainty of self, memory and place" (Hornstein 2011, 99). The fictitious subjectivities of George and Leah Weisz differ in how they grapple with the dislocation of "self, memory and place." For George Weisz, the discrepancy between the lost historical place of childhood and his replica, between "memory" and "place," is a painful and ultimately deadly experience. Leah Weisz, on the other hand, is perceived as a figure whose identity and autonomous life are expressed in this exact discrepancy and in the maintenance of absence: while the search for the missing desk provides George his life-long objective, Leah consciously withholds this piece of furniture from him and thereby precludes any completion of the Jerusalem ruin.

Thus, George Weisz's study, forever closed to other people, is consequently more than a visible, physical place. It is also Weisz's attempt to make the emotional space, which stands behind the concrete place, habitable once again; an attempt to recover his lost childhood, and a failure to do so. Whereas almost all the furniture has been recovered, the aura of his parents' home cannot be recaptured. The Jerusalem replica does not allow itself to be filled with the previous life of the murdered father, even though George Weisz tries to create, out of these memories, an "architectural imaginary world" (Hornstein 2011, 5). The way in which *Great House* conceives such an "architectural imaginary world" in literary terms connects it to the theme of absence; its completion remains in the realm of memory and postponement, as represented by the missing desk.

In *Great House*, we find places that are physically present and complete, yet they are simultaneously *im*mobile, and thus fundamentally dead; these include the replicas of destroyed places of the past. Yet the novel also consists of spaces that are either incomplete, or absent, or completely imaginary. It is precisely this incompleteness or absence that causes the protagonists to engage, productively, with their past and with questions of belonging, a process which helps to determine the mobility of these spaces. Leah, for instance, sends an envelope containing the key for the storage room in New York to her brother's son, thereby bequeathing it to the next generation (289). Thus, the key, an everyday object, acquires a symbolic dimension: although, theoretically, it enables access to the desk, it also marks the desk's absence, which is thereby passed on to the descendants.

The Drawer

The theme of inaccessibility develops throughout the novel and seeps into its smallest spaces, such as the locked drawer in George Weisz's childhood desk:

> Only one drawer had a lock, and for my fourth birthday my father gave me the little brass key. I couldn't sleep at night, trying to think of what to put in the drawer. The responsibility was crushing. In my mind I went over my most prized possessions again and again, but all of them suddenly seemed flimsy and grossly insignificant. In the end I locked the empty drawer and never told my father. (284)

Young George believes that none of his childish possessions deserve the honor of being housed in this special drawer of his venerated desk. Here, the smallest mysterious space in the novel appears as a moment of blank space, an encapsulation or expression of a mysterious inaccessibility. The drawer remains empty and locked, never to be opened again, not even by any of the desk's future owners; it persists as a "veritable organ of the secret psychological life" and of an "esthetics of hidden things" (Bachelard 1994 [1957], 78, xxxvii). The boy's fantasies that encircle the drawer ultimately articulate the emotional significance invested in a mundane piece of furniture which is so closely tied to the figure of the father.

The drawer becomes a "house of things" (Baschelard 1994 [1957], xxxvii) for the boy. It implies personal, psychological and imaginative depths, which contrast with the desks multitude of drawers that store supra-individual history. "My father was a scholar of history," George Weisz reports. "He wrote at an enormous desk with many drawers, and when I was very young I believed that two thousand years were stored in those drawers the way Magda the housekeeper stored flour and sugar in the pantry" (284). In this passage, the starkly mundane ingredients of everyday domestic life – "flour and sugar" – are mixed with the historical dimension of the two thousand years of Jewish exile, thereby bringing about an overlapping of time and space in the desk.

All the different spheres that connect the young George to the desk are united in his father's literary activity; textuality manages to bring together the most disparate areas in the boy's imagination. Once again, recalling the image of interlinked spaces of absence, the empty drawer presents an absence or negative spatiality that corresponds to the absence of the lost desk in the replicated office in Jerusalem.

Conclusion

"[W]e lose sight/site of places when we are no longer before them," writes Shelley Hornstein. "Yet the images of them are waiting to be retrieved: remembered, or imagined, in another place" (2011, 6). The many layers of physical presence and visibility, in conjunction with evoked emotional-abstract images and imaginative forces, shape Krauss's complex and dense novel. These varied yet related spatial elements are linked to one another – from the largest and most abstract room, which concerns the legend of Yochanan ben Zakkai and the destruction of the Second Temple in Jerusalem, to George Weisz's closed office in his museum-like family home in Jerusalem, which he has constructed as a replica of his father's lost office in Budapest, and from the gigantic desk to the smallest space, its empty, locked drawer. Furthermore, the destroyed and absent great house inspires the legend of ben Zakkai, as well as the transgenerational transfer of written tradition and memory, within the Weisz family; it is then taken up once again, in the office in Jerusalem, and in microcosm, in the empty drawer. Thus, my aim here has been to reveal the novel's architecture of absence as it reproduces itself in the structure of this article, beginning with Jewish cultural memory and ending with individual recollection.

Violence and pain, which are bound to the loss of places of belonging and, much more so, to the loss of loved ones, shape an experience that confronts the creation of new spaces of memory, which are characterized by their incompleteness and postponement. Ultimately, these new spaces facilitate an understanding of belonging that, in the absence of the concrete physical places or objects of desire, emerges in the narrative of remembering. Both the complexity and the intellectual and spatial mobility of belonging are considered in the novel, and can be discerned in its intertextual architecture.

The desk itself is central within the postmemorial constellation of the novel, with specific reference to the multi-layered configuration of belonging. It simultaneously represents continuity and a violent break in genealogy. Additionally, as a miniature of the wandering, imagined great house, this inanimate protagonist and aesthetic agent contains all the living protagonists' memories and fantasies, through which the potential of absence is expressed: in the respective biographies of these protagonists, it is the desk's absence that motivates the narrative of memory about it. Consequently, the mobile place within the text is highlighted, emphasizing its potential to create abstract places of belonging that survive loss and that subsequently refer via self-reflection to the great house of the novel, where memories are preserved.

References

Bachelard, Gaston. *The Poetics of Space*. Boston: Beacon Press, 1994.
Berger, Alan L., and Asher Z. Milbauer. "The Burden of Inheritance." *Shofar. An Interdisciplinary Journal of Jewish Studies* 31.3 (2013): 64–85.
Bischoff, Doerte. "Vom Überleben der Dinge. Sammlung und Exil in Edmund de Waals *Der Hase mit den Bernsteinaugen* und Nicole Krauss' *Das große Haus*." *Sprachen des Sammelns. Literatur als Medium und Reflexionsform des Sammelns*. Ed. Sarah Schmidt. Paderborn: Wilhelm Fink, 2016. 59–80.
Codde, Philippe. "Keeping History at Bay: Absent Presences in Three Recent Jewish American Novels." *Modern Fiction Studies* 57.4 (2011): 673–693.
Cooke, Rachel. "Nicole Krauss: 'I take great pleasure in thinking.'" https://www.theguardian.com/books/2011/feb/13/nicole-krauss-great-house-interview (27 February 2017).

DeKoven Ezrahi, Sidra. "'To What Shall I Compare You?': Jerusalem as Ground Zero of the Hebrew Imagination." *PMLA* 122.1 (2007): 220–234.
Dünne, Jörg, and Andreas Mahler. "Einleitung." *Handbuch Literatur & Raum*. Eds. Jörg Dünne and Andreas Mahler. Berlin: de Gruyter, 2015. 1–11.
Freud, Sigmund. "Das Unheimliche (1919)." *Sigmund Freud Studienausgabe, Band IV, Psychologische Schriften*. Eds. Alexander Mitscherlich, Angela Richards, and James Strachey. Frankfurt am Main: S. Fischer Verlag, 1970. 241–274.
Hirsch, Marianne. "The Generation of Postmemory." *Poetics Today* 29.1 (2008): 103–128.
Hornstein, Shelley. *Losing Site. Architecture, Memory and Place*. Farnham: Ashgate, 2011.
Krauss, Nicole. *Great House*. New York and London: W.W. Norton & Company, 2010.
Mann, Barbara E. *Space and Place in Jewish Studies*. New Brunswick: Rutgers University Press, 2012.
Munro, Alice. "Introduction to the Vintage Edition." *Selected Stories*. New York: Vintage Books, 1997. xiii–xxi.
Rothenberg Gritz, Jennie. "Nicole Krauss on Fame, Loss, and Writing About Holocaust Survivors." https://www.theatlantic.com/entertainment/archive/2010/10/nicole-krauss-on-fame-loss-and-writing-about-holocaust-survivors/64869/ (27 February 2017).
Scholem, Gershom. *Die jüdische Mystik in ihren Hauptströmungen*. Frankfurt am Main: Suhrkamp Verlag, 1957.
Trigg, Dylan. "The place of trauma: Memory, hauntings, and the temporality of ruins." *Memory Studies* 2.1 (2009): 87–101.
Voigt, Claudia. "Der schreckliche Schreibtisch." http://www.spiegel.de/spiegel/print/d-76397428.html (27 February 2017).
Yerushalmi, Yosef Hayim. *Zachor: Erinnere Dich! Jüdische Geschichte und jüdisches Gedächtnis*. Berlin: Verlag Klaus Wagenbach, 1988.

Part III

Masha Gessen
Introduction to Svetlana Boym's "Remembering Forgetting"

The story Svetlana always told about her emigration went like this: She was nineteen, standing in line to buy dried Caspian roach from a food vendor in Crimea when a man standing behind her asked if she wanted to go to America. To her, "America" was shorthand for "the West," and the West was expressed in a single image: Maria Schneider in Antonioni's "Passenger," riding in the back of a convertible, her hair blowing back, the road receding behind her as she sets off – the embodiment of freedom. Svetlana said that yes, she would like to go to America, and in short order she and the man in the dried-roach line were married and off to America.

The sculptor Konstantin Boym, the husband in question, remembers the story differently. But the difference in narratives is perhaps no greater than the difference between any two persons' recollections of events that date back more than three decades. Crimea and Maria Schneider figure in both of their stories. Svetlana and Konstanin met in Crimea, that is, they married, they emigrated together – albeit nearly two years later – and later still, when they were living in Boston, Svetlana told Konstanin that the kind of freedom Maria Schneider's hair symbolized was incompatible with marriage.

The light-hearted story of a flight to freedom fits well in the general narrative of emigration from the Soviet Union – give or take the Caspian roach stand. It is a story of ambition, opportunity, and hope. It is never but never a story of hardship. Sure, Soviet Jews left as stateless persons and arrived in the United States on refugee visas. The reasons for the refugee visas were well articulated: Jews were subjected to systematic discrimination and occasional violence in the Soviet Union, and this discrimination and violence drew upon a centuries-long tradition, to which the Soviet state had added a legal ban on the Hebrew language and the effective prohibition of Judaism. Still, these grievances hardly set the Jews apart from millions of other Soviet citizens. Numerous ethnic and religious groups faced similar discrimination, or worse – consider the Crimean Tartars, who had been deported from their land, or Jehovah's Witnesses, whose religious practice had been criminalized. What really made the Jews different was that, thanks to lobbying from the American Jewish community and the vagaries of international politics, they had a way out. A refugee visa was a winning lottery ticket.

As refugees journeys go, our passage was charmed (I say "our" because Svetlana and I took the same route from the Soviet Union to Boston, during the same months of 1981, though we didn't meet for another decade and a half).

There were no long foot marches or tent camps for us, and our life in limbo lasted but a few months. Still, there were cramped quarters, there was the experience of people being herded like cattle, and there was the unmistakable refugee condition of time suspended in uncertainty.

The way Svetlana told the story of her revision of personal history was that one day, about thirty years after leaving the Soviet Union, during a visit to Vienna she was reminded of the circumstances of her first meeting with the city (if such a meeting could be said to have occurred). This inspired her to study the Camp. I suspect the way she recast her story was also influenced by her beloved Hannah Arendt's 1943 essay "We Refugees," in which Arendt took Second World War-era Jewish refugees to task for passing themselves off as cheerfully ambitious economic migrants.

Svetlana was the only person I ever heard use the words "refugee camp" to describe the compound to which she, and I, had been briefly confined in February 1981. It was jarring. But we had been refugees, and it had been a camp.

Her project, though, was not to establish a better, more accurate memory. Rather, it was to remember the forgetting. It was an exercise in storytelling – that is, in telling a story that had been present all along, silent. Svetlana was taken with the idea of parallel stories, indeed entire parallel lives that continued after the people who had lived them had forgotten them. She wrote about the life her old self was leading back in Russia while the new Svetlana was living as an emigre in America, about the lives of other names she might have been given, and, in the camp project, about the life Svetlana the photographer had led in the shadow of Svetlana the literary scholar.

She undertook a kind of research – a mixture of historical digging and investigative journalism – that was unusual for the kind of academic she had been. This was not the first time she ventured into a new field and quickly excelled. She found the camp and excavated its archival history.

She then turned to oral history, interviewing artists and writers who had been in the camp. She had them draw sketches of the camp on napkins. Some, it turned out, thought that the interior courtyard had been square, some that it had been rectangular, some that it had been round. I no longer remember what I remembered, but I do remember that I had been wrong. I do not, however, remember what I had forgotten – the correct shape of the courtyard. I do remember that to me, at the time, if felt like a prison courtyard, and that because of it I had always told people that I hated Vienna – and when I was a fellow at the same institute as Svetlana, a few years before she was a guest there, I didn't venture out in search of the camp either.

I went to Vienna to give several talks in May 2015. Svetlana asked me not to go to the camp without her. At the time, she was finishing a film about the camp, which was going to be part of an exhibit she was planning at the Jewish Museum of Vienna. Another part of the exhibit would be what she referred to as the "camp reunion": those artists and writers who had been in the camp would reconvene in the city of their misery, or their refugee-dom, or their forgetting. At the time, I was helping Svetlana work on her book of autobiographical stories, which was helping her forget her illness, if only for a few minutes at a time. I looked up the camp address in the manuscript and bicycled to Simmering. But I rode past the site – to stop and walk the grounds would have violated the ban. Svetlana died several weeks later, in August. The following summer, I was again a guest at the institute, and once again I biked to Simmering. This time I stopped and walked the grounds. Later that summer the film she made about the camp was screened at the Jewish Museum. But there was no reunion.

Svetlana Boym
Remembering Forgetting. *Tale of a Refugee Camp*

The little that remains of the memory of my refugee camp *circa* 1981 is in extreme close-up: a breach in the concrete wall with barbed wire, a foot in a darned sock dangling from the upper bunk bed, an unzippable suitcase filled with obsolete things, a roll of the foreign toilet paper, pink like the fairy in *The Wizard of Oz*. And no establishing shot.

To tell you the truth, none of these things bothered me for twenty-seven years. I happily forgot my forgetting. My immigration from Leningrad to Boston had a few detours, gaps, and loose ends. But the point was not to travel down memory lane but to move on, to begin again. Why remember the unmemorable?

In the Soviet Union of the 1980s, *leaving* was a code word. If you whispered it with mysterious gravitas, there would be no need to ask further questions. To leave meant to flee once and for all. You knew well your point of departure but not

Note: "Tale of a Refugee Camp" © Estate of Svetlana Boym. The editors of this volume gratefully acknowledge Musa and Yuri Goldberg (Svetlana's parents) for granting copyright permission for "Tale of a Refugee Camp." The essay first appeared in Tablet magazine, at http://www.tabletmag.com/jewish-arts-and-culture/books/176945/camp-tale, and is reprinted here with permission. The essay was subsequently published by Bloomsbury Press.

https://doi.org/10.1515/9783110525519-017

necessarily your destination. To leave was an intransitive verb that marked a break in space and time. You might as well have been going to the moon or to the underworld. Farewell parties in the 1970s and 1980s resembled funerals in their finality.

I decided to emigrate at the age of twenty and had to leave the country without my parents. I met my future husband, Moscow architect Constantin Boym, in Koktebel, Crimea in 1979. After a ten-minute conversation while we waited in line for beer and sundried roach, he asked me if I cared to join him in emigrating to America. So goes the family legend, but the truth is a bit more complex. Constantin was a well-known "paper architect" and had applied to leave the Soviet Union permanently a year earlier; he was looking for a companion, for it was rumored in Moscow that there was a shortage of nice Jewish girls in America. After an impulsive non-deliberation, which combined my ardent desire to leave the country and a somewhat less ardent desire to teach a lesson to my non-responsive Leningrad boyfriend, I applied for a marriage license three weeks after Constantin and I met. A year and a half later, in January 1981, after a grueling process of exclusion and harassment, our much more grown-up selves received permission to depart permanently. This was not a romantic story, but an emigrant one. We were stripped of citizenship and were told that we would never be able to return, even to see our families. The "personal search" to which we were subjected at Soviet Customs lasted many hours and included intimate parts of our bodies and of our personal belongings. The customs officers enjoyed the procedure. They fingered every scratch on the few family pictures, counted the number of permitted individuals in the group photos, penetrated every seam in our clothes, patted the linings of our oversized, rusty-zippered suitcases in search of false bottoms. Since then I always travel light, but more often than not, the zipper on my carry-on bag does not come together till the last minute.

My father remembers the moment of my departure with cinematic clarity. It took place at a Moscow airport, at the gate reserved for those who were "leaving for permanent residency." I said my last goodbye and moved behind the glass, through which my parents could still see me go through the next customs gate. A family standing in line behind me consisted of a young couple with a baby and a baby carriage and a grandfather carrying a large manuscript that was clearly invaluable to him. "Either the manuscript or the baby carriage," said the customs officer. Whatever that manuscript was, it was something the older man could not part with. "To hell with you," the young mother shouted and pushed away the baby carriage. At that moment I disappeared behind the glass. The baby carriage rolled slowly into the empty corridor and down the steps. An uncanny afterimage, courtesy of Sergei Eisenstein.

It was another seven years before my parents saw me again. In my family we generally leave longing behind with our personal belongings, and we treat nostalgic tales with a grain of salt.

My "journey to freedom" was short in time and cosmic in proportion. This was one of the first times in my life that I traveled by plane across the border. At the Vienna airport I caught a glimpse of the spring sky framed by the ramp and a frivolous sign ("Duty Free") which I couldn't decipher. We were greeted by the representative of a refugee assistance organization and quickly herded onto unmarked buses with darkened windows and transported to the outskirts of Vienna, or someplace else. We had no idea where we were and didn't ask indiscrete questions.

My first impression of the camp was disappointing. The place resembled a provincial military hospital or a monastery. Is this what the West looks like? Neither terrifying nor exhilarating, just banal. Among the transient residents of the camp were Soviet Jews from Central Asia to Leningrad, Poles, Crimean Tartars, and a Russian Protestant escaping religious persecution. The camp was operated by several Jewish philanthropic agencies and guarded by Austrian soldiers with friendly German shepherds. The latter were supposed to protect us from attacks from the outside. From what I remember, we worried little about that and just wanted to catch some rest and dream about the future. We took walks in the camp yard but never went outside the walls. Men shared past erotic dreams to fall asleep; women kept their dreams to themselves. We ate plenty of comfort food and Austrian sweet breads and filled out many forms that itemized our hyphenated identities. Movies were shown all the time, and they mixed with our scarce memories.

I would like to give you a more detailed description of the camp, to provide you with snippets of conversation between the emigres on the upper bunkbeds and emigres on the lower bunkbeds, their tired jokes and discussions of the meaning of existence, to convey the anxious whispers of the social workers and armed guards, to provide lifelike images of narrow beds with broken springs, the archives of classified documents next to the trash storage, ruined warehouses in the walled monastic yard where brown pigeons pecked at the cones of the local evergreens. I'd like to share with you the taste of the sweet bread soaked in weak tea, the homey camp pasta with Viennese sausage, and the flickering image onscreen of sun-kissed athletic men and women building a city on the sand with song and dance. Only I don't remember any of that, and I'd rather not fill the gaps with plausible fiction.

We never saw the Vienna that we dreamed about, the city of Mozart and Sigmund Freud. We remained extraterritorial. Like the Freudian unconscious, our transit camp had no outside; it was a place out of place and a time out of time. I don't know how long we stayed there. It felt like we were in a time capsule, a place where there was no present, only the repressed past and the unknown future. Actually, I had a good camera with me, probably a Zenith, with a high precision lens and a long zoom. It never occurred to me to use it. The camera was meant to be sold at the flea market in Rome together with Ukranian linens, nesting dolls, and caviar, to make some money for rainy days "in the West." I had studied photography as a teenager, experimenting with reflections on rippling water and urban panoramas. It never occurred to me to photograph anything in the camp. There was nothing there "to write home about." New immigrants like to take cheerful pictures next to other people's houses and bright cars. The camp didn't seem worthy of a photograph.

******

Fifteen years after leaving the camp, I became a photographer. I returned to photography as suddenly as I had dropped it. My digital camera has a few special effects that imitate the old Leica, but I don't use them. Since the late 1990s I've been documenting my travels through the world, collecting errors, overexposures, chance encounters. I have been taking pictures of the places that I would otherwise not remember.

Once, during my presentation at the Vienna Kunsthalle commemorating the twentieth anniversary of the fall of the Berlin Wall, a man in the audience asked me: "Why do you photograph the same landscape in different places?"

"I don't know," I said. "These are just transits, warzones, afterimages of something we see and forget."

"So is this your first time in Vienna?" he continued, changing the subject.

"No. The first time was in 1981. In a refugee camp," I said, surprising myself.

"Really? What was it like?"

"I don't remember much."

"Where was it?"

"Nobody knew."

It was then, during my second visit to Vienna, that I decided to find the address of my former camp. Just to take a picture of it, to fill the gap. This would be a photographic project, not a nostalgic trip down memory lane.

Curiously, my former husband Constantin – we had gone our separate ways in 1986 – shared the excitement of my quest. Ironically, it was the break up of my second, American marriage that sent me back to retrace my emigration.

My initial research into the location of our camp proved futile; the more I prodded, the more mysteries I encountered; they hid, one inside another, like the nesting dolls that we had carried in our overburdened suitcase. It was clear that the break in my personal memory went together with a lacuna in collective history. The extraterritorial refuge for extralegal immigrants was not to be found on Viennese maps or in archival records. Our story was deeply embedded in the inconvenient histories of the Cold War well as in the improbable adventures and acts of courage of many individuals who brushed that history against the grain. The city of Vienna that we didn't get to visit in the 1980s was a magnificent sleepy capital of the fallen Hapsburg Empire, which had disintegrated after the First World War and after the Second World War became a small "non-aligned" country at the crossroads of East and West. Vienna carried its war scars quietly, observing a code of silence when it came to confronting its recent history. Black-and-white documentary footage showing the Viennese happily greeting Hitler, a native son, in 1938 were not very popular during the 1980s, when Austrians preferred to see themselves as victims of Nazism and avoided going through the "management of Nazi memory," as did the Germans. Equally not addressed were the years of the occupation of the city by the Red Army, which liberated Vienna from the Nazis in 1945 and remained there until 1948, almost turning

Austria into one of the Eastern Bloc countries. It was no coincidence that postwar Vienna became a stage-set for many Cold War movies, from the shadowy black-and-white *Third Man* to the Technicolor James Bond of *The Living Daylights*. Sometimes when film directors could not secure a permit to film in the Soviet Union, they would film the backdrop for Petersburg-Petrograd-Leningrad in the baroque squares of Vienna. In the 1970s through the 1990s, Vienna became an inconspicuous transit point for the many refugees from Eastern Europe.

I began to understand what our Vienna transit might have looked like from the outside with the help of the article "Tales of the Vienna Airport," written by the journalist Joe Nocera for *Harper's Magazine* (May, 1982). In trying to make sense of the dramatic transport of refugees from the Soviet Union, Nocera came to a paradoxical conclusion. Each country involved in our transit was creating its own diplomatic half-fiction. This included the Soviet Union, the United States, Israel, and Austria. These half-truths didn't impede the process of emigration but actually enabled it. In other words, if there had been a hypothetical classified information leak, or if a particularly enterprising investigative journalist had revealed all the arrangements made between the Soviet Union, Austria, the United States, and Israel, our transit might not have taken place.

First and a foremost a humanitarian shelter, the camp was also a site of awkward political arrangements. The Austrian chancellor at the time, Social

Democrat Bruno Kreisky, agreed to take a humanitarian role in the passage of the Soviet Jews, but did so obliquely. The first transit camp organized by Kreisky's government with the assistance of Jewish philanthropic agencies, including the Jewish Agency, the American Jewish Joint Distribution Agency, and the Hebrew Immigrant Aid Society (HIAS), was at Schoenau Castle, near Vienna. This camp was closed after the terrorist groups Black September and the Eagles of the Palestinian Revolution attacked a train carrying Jewish emigres from Ukraine via Bratislava to Vienna in September 1973. To make a long and controversial story short, the terrorists took hostages, and in order to secure their release the chancellor of Vienna agreed to close the camp at Schoenau Castle. But Kreisky kept his commitment to house the refugees, moving them to undisclosed and heavily guarded locations, first to the military barracks in Woellersdorf and then to a Red Cross facility in the district of Simmering.

Since I didn't have the exact address of the camp, I began to wander through Simmering with the help of Google Earth. After all, the family of the co-founder of Google, Sergei Brin, had followed the same immigrant route as I had. Simmering harks back into history; it was a medieval village with a famous brewery and a church. Later, it became an industrial district of Vienna known for its material recycling industries and for the Gasometer featured in the exemplary Cold War film *The Living Daylights*. I came across several local newspaper articles from the time reporting on protests against placing a transit camp for Jewish refugees in Simmering: "We will not cease to protest against this camp which is a danger for all of us, particularly for our children," stated Angelika Kneth, aged thirty-four, mother of four children, who objected to the presence of armed guards and barbed wire near a kindergarten. The Interior Minister of Kreisky's Social Democratic government, Otto Roesch, had tried to reassure local residents: "We have to fulfill a humanitarian task. Everybody must understand that it is our duty to help other people." As ironies of history go, it was later disclosed that Roesch had once been a Nazi stormtrooper; as a minister in the Social Democratic government of Bruno Kreisky, however, he played a humanitarian role in the transit of Soviet Jews.

My main lead in my search for material traces of the camp was an Austrian documentary filmmaker with a Russian last name, Alexander Schukoff, who made a film about the district of Simmering in 1977–1978, a few years after the camp opened. I had hoped that Schukoff, having filmed for a year in the neighborhood, might have the camp's address. "This is what you would have seen if you had been allowed to leave the camp. I give you a bigger window now," he said, graciously offering me his film as a gift. The film is a poetic meditation on the metropolitan city's working class district that the Viennese rarely visit. Located between the cemetery and the airport, it was home to the Viennese fiakers who do nostalgic horse-carriage tours of Vienna and at night return to unspectacular Simmering, which looks like Eastern Europe. Local residents, young and old, complain of boredom, that nothing has ever happened in Simmering.

Schukoff's film makes no mention of the refugee camp that existed for ten years on the street around the corner. The director confessed that he had no information about it. What about the neighborhood protests in 1974? He was doing *cinema verité*, not investigative journalism, he explained. While being faithful to the ebb and flow of local daily life, he might have missed the biggest Cold War story to have unfolded in Simmering, and in Vienna, at the time. Or perhaps he got the story right: the camp remained extraterritorial; it existed "off" the Viennese map, disconnected from the rest of the city. *Cinema verité* captured the site's eerie invisibility.

I decided to look for more history in the archives of the HIAS, one of the organizations that supported our transit and resettlement in the United States. The associate director greeted me with open arms but warned me that he didn't have the address of the camp. He ordered the Vienna files from the 1980s. They contained everything that had been declassified, excluding personal files. Among the documents that caught my attention were a check from an Italian man who wanted "to support the Jewish people after World War II," a passionate letter from a caseworker who advocated allowing refugees to choose their ultimate destination, a letter documenting the mysterious disappearance of the HIAS Hungarian translator who turned out to be a double-agent and escaped with a large sum of money, and a telefax from the Austrian Interior Ministry that demanded that the refugees in the camp be informed about their rights to request political asylum. Since I already knew that at the time most Western European countries had tried their best not to offer political asylum to Soviet Jews, I copied the telefax and buried it in my folder as another example of half-truth practiced by the Austrian government. As for the Hungarian double-agent, apparently he remained at large. And the passionate caseworker was in the right. Apart from those few intriguing documents, most of the HIAS files were tantalizingly unrevealing. They contained the minutes of the organization's administrative meetings, requests for new furniture for the HIAS offices, and instructions on how to handle the "noshrim," or *dropouts*, whose numbers were growing. I was puzzled by the terminology.

"Who were those 'dropouts'?" I asked the associate director of HIAS.

"You," he answered, smiling.

Dropouts in the files always came in the plural, while we, the refugees, wanted to think of ourselves only in the singular. Over the span of seven years I graduated from a *dropout* to a *refugee*, from a *non-resident* alien to a citizen. Dropouts were those of us who "dropped out" of going to Israel, the destination listed on our exit visas, choosing instead the limbo of the refugee camps and hoping to get across the Atlantic. The HIAS files revealed that the *dropouts* didn't always follow orders, tried to outsmart their superiors, and deviated from instructions. Yet they remained well protected, taken care of, and nourished in the camp with no address somewhere off the Viennese map, between the airport and the train station.

I looked up a few of my fellow *dropouts* whom I hadn't known at the time but who had subsequently become my friends. None of them were particularly interested in finding the location of the camp. The idea of a "camp reunion" left them cold. They approached the conversation with a dose of healthy skepticism.

Why revisit the camp now? We were very tough then because we knew how to forget; if we start remembering now we could risk our immigrant resilience. Obsession with the past might short-shrift our future. "Is there is a change in your life now that makes you look back at that first big break?" one friend asked.

"I just want to take a picture of it," I said, not too convinced myself.

My former camp mates had their own blind spots next to vivid memories. Most interviews happened surreptitiously, in transit or in between other important tasks; they were not fully recorded. I asked my witnesses to draw pictures of the camp as they remembered it, on napkins. Now this strange collection of paper ephemera, stained with garlic oil and cappuccino, offers a collective memory map of what the camp might have looked like.

Masha Gessen, political journalist, aged fourteen at the time of emigration, recalls her disappointment at the sight of Austrian guards with German shepherds: "I thought I was emigrating to the 'West' and then I found myself in the camp. I thought that my parents had deceived me; the West was the camp." By contrast, Masha's younger brother, writer and editor Kostya Gessen, aged six at the time, enjoyed his stay "It wasn't a camp," he said. "More like a hotel, yes, a nice hotel with a yard. I had a good time there." The singer Regina Spektor, also aged six at the time, didn't think it was a nice hotel: "There was no floor there, just bunk beds everywhere," she recalled.

My witnesses couldn't agree on the geometrical shape of the camp yard. Anna Wexler-Katznelson, an historian of Russian art, was aged six at the time of emigration; she claims that the camp yard resembled a black square, just like the famous painting by Kazimir Malevich. Artist Vitaly Komar, who passed through the camp as an adult, said that the yard had the shape of a mandala. At present Vitaly is working on the artistic project of transforming and sometimes reconciling symbols of different religions. The shape of the yard echoed the speaker's artistic psychic geography. "Of course, I was keeping records in the camp," said Vitaly. "My notebooks with little squares were with me. Only my records had nothing to do with the place I was in. I was putting down my thoughts on art."

Curator and artist Anton Vidocle, aged fifteen at the time of emigration, commented that the camp looked like a high school, sort of like PS1 in New York. He had no recollection of his departure from Moscow, but held a "photographic memory" of the camp's movie theater and the new suit with red stripes that he wore there. He knew all along that the dogs and the armed guards were on our side and were protecting us from the outside. He wasn't scared of them. He remembers most fondly an erotic conversation he eavesdropped on in the collective ward. "It must have been the retelling of the famous Story of O, the erotic classic. I was completely taken by it." My former husband Constantin noticed the unusual shape of the pre-war window in the camp ward. Unable to fall asleep, he peered through it, chasing glimpses of the outside world. He saw a stranger walking on a dark street. "That's the West, I thought," said Constantin. "All I wanted was to be that man strolling somewhere outside the camp." "Look, maybe it doesn't matter what actually happened in the camp," he added at the end. "What matters is the camp of memory. Or art."

Indeed, why seek physical confirmation of our unbelievable stories? The immigrant is a bit of a trickster, who moves laterally, like a knight in the game of chess, in order to survive. Maybe it would have been more accurate to recreate the camp of our escape dreams that had transported us beyond the thick concrete walls. Such a camp would not require a precise address.

It dawned on me that my campmates and I might have been afraid of a question that I never dared to ask. Why did you leave? Or worse: Did you ever imagine what your life would have been without emigration?

I always believed that I couldn't. My emigration began long before my actual departure and has lasted long after my arrival. I might have started expatriating myself as a teenager when I still lived in Leningrad, or earlier, when I first heard my grandmother's story about her time in the Gulag.

My grandmother Sara (Sonya) Goldberg, a secondary school teacher in Leningrad, was rounded up in 1948 during Stalin's so-called anti-cosmopolitan campaign, aimed largely at Soviet Jews, including atheists and those who had changed their names and claimed other ethnicities in their documents. Grandma Sonya considered herself "lucky" after she had been released; thanks to Stalin's death, she spent only six years in the Gulag, instead of ten. Fifteen years later she was "rehabilitated" for the "absence of the content of the crime."

My grandmother's story had many blank spots because for twenty or so years nobody in the family talked to her about her life in the camps. Without conversations, memories turn into stones or fairy tales. I inherited her blind spots and her fears and have carried them with me through life. She didn't know where her camp was located within the vast zone of the Gulag. She never talked about how she had resisted arrest and tried to cut her veins. Instead, she remembered tricking the informants in the camp who wrote reports to the authorities, and mostly she loved to recall her friendship with the actress Tatyana Okunevskaya and how at difficult moments they had talked to each other with the help of Chekhov: "One day we will see diamonds in the sky. You will see that day will come."

What I gathered from the fragmented tale of the camps that she told me when I was eleven was that there was another unwritten history and another secret territory outside the official maps, a camp zone where millions of Soviet citizens were detained without having committed any crime. In the 1970s my grandmother became a kitchen dissident. While cooking her soup, made with the skinniest and cheapest chickens that she got in the market for one ruble and five kopeks, she listened to Voice of America. For years she cried over the death of Kennedy and the Soviet tanks in Prague in 1968. Sometimes she imagined what they were saying on the radio, since the sound was jammed. She would just stand there, whispering something to a faraway addressee, a prayer or a poem, as she looked through the unwashed window into our dark Leningrad yard.

My emigration can be considered political, since I had taken part in several demonstrations protesting human-rights violations, yet at the age of twenty my understanding of the political was rather vague. It was a blend of the existential dreams of liberation that we saw in foreign movies and a rebellion against the local coercion and claustrophobia of the Brezhnev era, known as the Era of Stagnation, that threatened to destroy our teenage ideals of justice.

I could blame the great Italian director Michelangelo Antonioni for seducing me with his long cinematic takes that promised an unforeseen freedom of movement. My father organized a film club in the Palace of Culture in the Petrograd district of Leningrad, and this club became his cozy little homeland. In his words, it was a state within a state that also provided good babysitting for the club-goers' children, rebellious Leningrad pre-teens like myself. Almost no American films were shown in such film clubs, but there were plenty of Polish and Czech existential tales as well as films by Italian communist filmmakers, filled with existential mysteries and wonder. I loved Michelangelo Antonioni's

Passenger (the Italian title was *Professione: Reporter*) more than the others. It was the story of a journalist (played by Jack Nicholson) who chooses to radically change his life and adopt the identity of a dead man. At the end he encounters a beautiful and mysterious woman (played by Maria Schneider) and finds his match in the existential adventure of life and death. I watched the film not for the complex plot of mistaken identity but rather for the long takes and eccentric vistas into a foreign life. I was particularly taken by the free-spirited and edgy Maria Schneider, who criss-crosses borders somewhere in the Pyrenean mountains, just to study architecture or to meet strangers. I never saw women and borders like that. The film was explained to us as a "Marxist critique of bourgeois alienation," but it felt more like a cultural luxury, a quest for freedom and creative living. There was a breeze in the heroine's hair and the long duration of a non-obligatory time that shaped my dreamscape. I had to emigrate, go through several transit camps, and work hard for years before I could enjoy that kind of artistic wanderlust.

My first border crossing didn't resemble anything I had seen in the movies. Yet movies remain among my most vivid memories of the camp. The camp's film collection included Holocaust movies and various comedies on Jewish subjects. We were extremely ignorant, since any study of Jewish culture was effectively prohibited in the Soviet Union, condemned as either "cosmopolitan" or "Zionist propaganda" – the two contradictory terms were used interchangeably. We knew that we didn't want to try on the exotic Eastern European Jewish attire from another time, which appeared foreign or even kitschy to us. When the representative of the Jewish Agency asked me in the camp if I planned to go to Israel, I answered that I didn't want to go to the country of *Fiddler on the Roof*. This was an embarrassing mixture of ignorance and chutzpa. I didn't realize that I had just left one of the film's homelands, Russia, and was about to arrive for permanent residency in the United States, where the poor fiddler found his cinematic home. All pain apart, some of our camp experiences had an element of absurdity to them and resembled a chance encounter between *The Fiddler on the Roof* and *The Third Man*.

In 2012, I decided to go back across the border, to go to Vienna for the third time and to properly scout the location in Simmering. Before my departure I nervously looked through copies of the "Vienna files" that I had obtained with the kind permission of HIAS. I reread the article from the *New York Times*, perused the case of the cunning Hungarian spy, unfolded the telex message from the Austrian Minister of the Interior who suddenly seemed to care about the plight of the refugees. Just as I was ready to put this paper back into my drawer, I spotted a few faint typewritten letters in the fold at the bottom of the page: *Transit Camp,*

XX Dreherstrasse, Vienna 11. I couldn't believe my eyes. I had possessed the exact address of our transit camp for a year. It was hidden in plain view, in the fold of the Xerox copy in my desk drawer .

A chance encounter in Vienna brought the last key witness in my investigation. During the first week of my stay I met a local journalist who was married to a Russian artist. I told him about my investigation.

"Yes, the camp on XX Dreherstrasse," he said, looking into my eyes. "It was an ugly place."

This was not small talk. The man had done his civil service there in 1985, when it again became an office of the Red Cross. We both remembered cracks in the concrete wall with the barbed wire, anonymous hospital rooms, a "prison yard" with sickly trees.

"Have you ever asked what was there before?" I prodded.

"No. In Vienna, we don't do that," he said quietly.

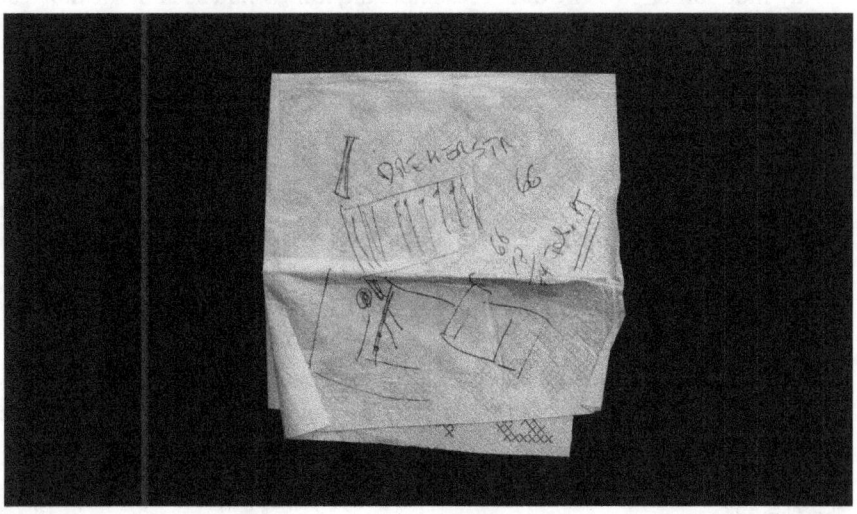

He drew a picture on a napkin of the narrow bunk bed with broken springs that had left scars on his body. There was something else there that haunted him even more than those springs: the blank forms and signs written in Cyrillic, instructions that he couldn't understand. Unreadable, they became the stuff of his dreams. By 1985–86 the former transit camp ceased to exist, as emigration from the Soviet Union fizzled. That stained napkin with its drawing of springs protruding from bunk beds might have been the last afterimage of our unphotographed transit.

Remembering Forgetting. *Tale of a Refugee Camp* —— **229**

XX Dreherstrasse, it said on the napkin. On a sunny wintry day in January 2012, I returned to the camp. From the window of an old car I got an oblique glimpse of the village church and lacy curtains on dark windows, as evocative as they were unrevealing. The journey felt like a road movie with long takes and no denouement.

"Sorry, there is not much here," said my Viennese friend who had driven me to Simmering. He left me alone to wander along the deserted Dreherstrasse.

The main building that housed the camp hadn't survived, but the territory did, complete with fences, warehouses, packaging from recycling machines, archives of trash. I found a shopping cart filled with evergreen pinecones, a moving altar to an emigrant genius loci.

In 2006 a part of the former camp territory had been developed into an ecological housing project. The new buildings bore the Italian names of exotic fruits: *Melanzana, Pera, Melone*, turning the history of the site into a delicious pastoral. The new buildings were surrounded by an ecologically correct fence behind which was an abandoned territory with high grass, weeds, and withered dandelions growing next to the thick concrete wall circa 1970. There was still occasional barbed wire visible and the rusting remains of the old infrastructure for the security cameras. Between the ecological fence and the concrete walls of the former camp, Simmering teenagers were playing a ball game, oblivious to the past and the future, the way teens are.

The adults were not so different. Nobody working or living on the site had any knowledge of what had been there before. "A military hospital? A monastery? Something like that." I was stopped and questioned by local residents when I took out my camera. I quickly excused myself, claiming to be an architectural photographer interested in the former Carmelite monastery. The owner of a new lighting design firm working at the site politely invited me into a building and guided me through its recently redesigned interiors, newly remade to "evoke some history." The office had a nice retro feel of the mid-century modern style, with a few historicist echoes. It preserved the unusually shaped windows that Constantin had recalled. Once again I was struck by the intimate proximity of the refugee camp and the ordinary residences of Simmering; yet even in memory they occupied non-contiguous and incommensurable spaces of experience. I was tempted to tell the retro-loving designer that his office was on the site of a former camp, but I was afraid that he might ruin my camera's memory card.

Did I recognize anything when I revisited the camp territory? To be honest, no new reminiscence came to me; no taste of sweet bread soaked in camp tea could breach my forgetting. Yet photographing the former camp territory was strangely ecstatic. It felt like quenching an old thirst. It wasn't for the sake of recovered memory or history, just for its own sake.

Upon my arrival back in Boston, I found myself staring at the images of the camp, rescuing and highlighting the cracks in the wall.

Everything I had photographed all over the world was there: the stains on the concrete walls, sickly poppy flowers and dandelions, half-readable signs, the pinecones in a disowned shopping cart, and a dove, the color of urban ruins, finishing her comfort food, in haste. Wandering through the invisible ruins of the camp I discovered the landscape of my own photographs that traveled with me from one continent to another.

I didn't know until then that I had been a subject of my photographs and not only the photographer. I stumbled upon an uncharted emotional geography mapped over the inconvenient history. Somehow the walls of the camp stood both for liberation and for confinement, for memory and for forgetting; they became a canvas for our improbable hopes.

After many turns and returns I recognized my point of departure. It was not my house in Leningrad but this forgotten refugee camp that I carried with me, even as I traveled light. Unmemorable and unmonumental, the camp became a ruin in reverse, a palimpsest of my future transits, a hidden backdrop to my second home. T. S. Elliot described such departure in the last of his *Four Quartets:*

> We shall not cease from exploration
> And the end of all our exploring
> Will be to arrive where we started
> And know the place for the first time.

Sasha Senderovich
Svetlana Boym Remembers Forgetting

When we met for what would be the last time, at Hi-Rise Bakery near her home in Cambridge, Massachusetts, in early August of 2014, Svetlana Boym had just published her essay "A Soviet Drop-Out's Journey to Freedom." The author of *The Future of Nostalgia*, she had written elsewhere on topics of displacement, nostalgia, and estrangement. This essay in *Tablet Magazine*, however, was Svetlana's first substantial piece of writing about the process of remembering her own experience en route from the Soviet Union to America in the early 1980s. The timing was important: the author of four scholarly monographs as well as various creative works including fiction, drama, and visual art, Svetlana had earlier that summer traveled to Vienna to shoot her film "Remembering Forgetting," about the transit camp where she had spent time as a refugee; her essay in *Tablet* was a kind of blueprint for the film and an indication of further autobiographical writing still to come.

Over coffee, Svetlana told me that she was upset that her editors at *Tablet* had insisted on changing her essay's proposed title, "Remembering Forgetting," which she wanted to be the same as the title of her film. The editors proved impervious to her pleas to drop the title that ultimately went to press: she felt that it needlessly concretized her experience of searching through the recesses of memory for traces of an experience, which had no discernable beginning or end and which, as she had discovered, continued to linger uneasily as a kind of faint screen for much of her life after immigration. As the author of a book on artistic and philosophical conceptions of freedom, she felt that *Tablet's* title designated freedom as a port of unambiguous arrival rather than a lifelong endeavor, the results of which were less certain.

When the conversation turned to me, whose dissertation Svetlana had advised a few years earlier, she – wearing her mentor's hat – was also not particularly impressed with my excitement that her writings about her own immigration would now be joining the growing bookshelf of works by some of the Russian immigrant authors that I had begun writing about. Like Gary Shteyngart and David Bezmozgis, who had written about the immigrant journeys of Soviet Jews to America in, respectively, *Little Failure* (2014) and *The Free World* (2011), Svetlana had spent time in Vienna and Rome. These were places where Soviet Jews who, during the Cold War, having exited the USSR on Israeli visas without the slightest intention of traveling to Tel Aviv, had to wait for up to a year for their passes to North America, uncertain about the eventual outcome of their quest. However, as Svetlana reminded me, the new cohort of Anglophone immigrant writers, whose growing literary output had been captivating the American reading public for more than a decade, had been young children when they made the journey, whereas she had been in her early twenties. In reconstructing their memories of transit in memoirs and autobiographically inspired fiction, she ventured, they filled their narratives with recollections that could not have been their own. "I don't remember any of that," she wrote, referring to the transit camp where she lived in Vienna, "and I'd rather not fill the gaps with a plausible fiction."

For Svetlana, the starting point of remembrance was the absence of any clear personal memory. This absence of memory, in turn, itself became lodged in the gap in collective memory, where it lingered for more than three decades. As Svetlana eloquently put it in her essay, the central question animating her personal and artistic quest was "Why remember the unmemorable?" Why remember the uneasy circumstances of initial displacement from her home in Leningrad, when her subsequent life in the theretofore mythical "West" had, by all accounts, proven to be a success? Her desire to reinvent herself, as it were, overshadowed the space of transit where reinvention was not easily possible.

Collective memory did not aid Svetlana's personal recollection, either: "the break in my personal memory went together with lacuna in collective memory," she explained. American Jewish organizations, Western diplomats, and refugee agencies were all involved in arranging the passage of Soviet Jews through the transit camp where Svetlana had stayed in Vienna. And yet, the whole experience was overlaid with a patina of uneasiness for all involved. Soviet Jews did not easily fit Western Jews' image of people in need of rescuing. And, contrary to popular belief, they were not ardent Zionists. They could have gotten to Israel very quickly, of course, had they so wished; instead, they stayed in Vienna and Rome for long periods of time, waiting to get to the United States or Canada. A constellation of issues made the narrative that could have emerged from the process of remembering inconvenient at best: what remembering disclosed was the story of statelessness and transit, of the absence of any clear destination, and of the false pretenses under which many Soviet Jews managed to exit the USSR to seek asylum in North America (in particular, "family reunification" with non-existent relatives invented by Israel's Jewish Agency in order to circumvent Soviet laws that did not acknowledge the right to emigrate as such).

Svetlana's essay about the Viennese site that she referred to as "my camp" belongs compellingly and beautifully to the elegiac celebration of transit itself. Svetlana's camp, as she discovers, had long ago ceased to exist as a physical space. However, as she explores in her essay – published here with, for the first time, Svetlana's preferred title and edits – the camp's faint image in the crevices of her memory had strangely determined more of her life's work than one would have thought possible for a place never considered worthy of recollection.

Notes on Contributors

Almog Behar is a poet, novelist, and postdoctoral fellow at the Van Leer Jerusalem Institute's Polonsky Academy, and one of the founders of the Judeo-Arabic Cultural Studies program at Tel-Aviv University. Born in 1978 in Netanya, he now lives in Jerusalem. He is the author of three books of poetry – "Zim'on Be'erot" (Well's Thirst, 2008), "Chut Moshekh Min Ha-Lashon" (A Thread Drawing from the Tongue, 2009), and "Shirim Le-Asirei Batei-HaSohar" (Poems for the Prisoners, 2016), a collection of short stories entitled *Ana Min Al-Yahoud* (I am one of the Jews, 2009), and the novel *Chahla ve-Hezkel* (Rachel and Ezekiel, 2010). In his scholarly work, he focuses on questions of Mizrahi literature in Israel, and on the influence of liturgical traditions from the Muslim world on new Mizrahi literature. His current postdoctoral research examines movements between Hebrew and Arabic in twentieth-century Jewish literatures from the Arab world.

Svetlana Boym (1956–2015) was the Curt Hugo Reisinger Professor of Slavic and Comparative Literatures at Harvard University and a Faculty Associate of the Graduate School of Design. She studied Hispanic literatures at Leningrad State Pedagogical Institute and at Boston University and received her PhD in Comparative Literature from Harvard University. A native of St. Petersburg, Russia, Boym was also a writer and media artist. Her experimental photographs have been exhibited in Berlin, Madrid, Ljubljana, Copenhagen, Glasgow, New York, and Cambridge, MA, and at the Venice Architectural Biennial (2010).

Stephanie Bung is Professor of French and Spanish Literature at the University of Duisburg-Essen. Her research focuses on modern poetry, salon culture of the seventeenth century, postcolonial studies, and the literature of the *extrême contemporain*. With Jenny Schrödl, she published *Phänomen Hörbuch. Interdisziplinäre Perspektiven und medialer Wandel* (2016). Her most recent book is *Spiele and Ziele. Französische Salonkulturen des 17. Jahrhunderts zwischen Elitendistinktion und belles lettres* (2013), which was awarded the Kurt-Ringger-Prize in 2012. Her monograph *Figuren der Liebe. Diskurs und Dichtung bei Paul Valéry und Catherine Pozzi* appeared in 2005.

Hélène Cixous was born in Algeria in 1937, to a Sephardic Algerian father and an Ashkenazi German mother. She moved to France in 1955, where she quickly became Professor of English literature. In 1968, she created the experimental *Université Paris VIII* and, in 1974, the first French doctoral program in Women's Studies. Now Emerita, she teaches at the *Collège International de Philosophie*. She has received honorary degrees from universities around the world; her literary prizes include the *Prix Médicis* (1969), the *Prix des Critiques* for best theatrical work (1994), the *Prix Marguerite Duras* (2014), the *Prix de la langue française* (2014), and the *Prix Marguerite Yourcenar* (2016). She has been "house playwright" at Ariane Mnouchkine's *Théâtre du Soleil* for more than thirty years. The translations into a wide range of languages attest to the international recognition of her oeuvre. As a writer, Cixous consistently breaks down the boundaries of genre (and of gender). She poses many intellectual challenges with her texts that, while rooted in the practices of fiction, theory, and criticism, also depart from them.

Sonja Dickow holds an MA from the University of Hamburg, where she studied German literatures. She recently submitted her doctoral thesis, "Configurations of House and Home. Diaspora Narratives and Transnational Perspectives in Jewish Literatures of the 21st Century," at the University of Hamburg. This study examines modalities of representations of home and of houses in contemporary Jewish literatures against the backdrop of Jewish history, on one hand, and within the context of universal migration and globalization, on the other. Dickow is an alumna of the *Ernst Ludwig Ehrlich Foundation* and a former Visiting Research Fellow at *Da'at Hamakom* Center for the Study of Place in the Modern Jewish World at the Hebrew University, Jerusalem.

Alex Epstein was born in Leningrad (St. Petersburg) in 1971 and moved to Israel when he was eight years old. He is the author of ten collections of short stories and three novels; his work has been translated into English, French, Spanish, Russian, Greek, Dutch, Croatian, and Italian. In 2003 and 2016, he was awarded Israel's Prime Minister's Prize for Literature. In 2007, he participated in the International Writing Program at the University of Iowa. In 2010, he was writer in residence at the University of Denver. He teaches creative writing in Tel Aviv.

Masha Gessen is John J. McCloy Professor at Amherst College, a journalist, and the author of ten books of nonfiction. Her most recent book, *The Future Is History: How Totalitarianism Reclaimed Russia*, won the 2017 National Book Award for Nonfiction. Gessen is also the author of the national bestseller *The Man Without a Face: The Unlikely Rise of Vladimir Putin* (2012). Gessen is a staff writer at *The New Yorker*.

Ruth Ginsburg, since retiring from the Department of Comparative and General Literature of the Hebrew University, has been a frequent translator of Freud from German into Hebrew. She has published translations of *The Interpretation of Dreams* (2002), *Moses and Monotheism* (2009), *The Uncanny* (2012), and *Totem and Taboo* (2013). She recently completed a translation of a collection of previously untranslated essays by Erich Auerbach. She is currently working on a translation of Freud's *Beyond the Pleasure Principle*. Her recent publications include essays on trauma and theoretical considerations of translation.

Natasha Gordinsky is Lecturer in the Department of Hebrew and Comparative Literature at the University of Haifa, and a member of *The Israel Young Academy*. She is the co-author, with Susanne Zepp, of *Kanon und Diskurs. Über Literarisierung jüdischer Erfahrungswelten* (Vandenhoeck & Ruprecht Verlag 2009) and the author of *In Three Landscapes: Lea Goldberg's Early Writings* (in Hebrew; Magnes University Press 2016). She has published articles on multilingualism, nostalgia, and post-memory in modern and contemporary literature.

Carola Hilfrich is Senior Lecturer in the Department of General and Comparative Literature at the Hebrew University of Jerusalem, the founder of the University's Graduate Program in Cultural Studies, and a founding member of the I-CORE *Da'at Hamakom* Center for the Study of Cultures of Place in the Modern Jewish World. She is the author of *Living Script* (2000; in German), a book on representation and translation in Jewish German modernity, and the co-editor, with Stéphane Mosès, of *Between Cultures* (1997), a volume on the theory and practices of cross-cultural exchange. Her articles explore mediations and circulations of Jewish and other modernities in postmodern and contemporary literatures. Most recently, she has collaborated with Matteo Pericoli and Jonathan Charley for the chapter on literary architecture in *The Routledge Companion on Architecture, Literature, and the City* (2018).

Yael Kenan is a PhD candidate in the Department of Comparative Literature at the University of Michigan, Ann Arbor. She is also working toward a graduate certificate from the Frankel Center for Judaic Studies. Her research focuses on interconnections between Hebrew and Arabic, and between literature, ethics, and politics in the contemporary Levant. Her dissertation project examines the reciprocal construction of mourning and nationalism in Israeli and Palestinian literatures after 1948. She has published articles about mourning black bodies in the U.S., and about addressing Mahmoud Darwish in Hebrew.

Vivian Liska is Professor of German Literature and the Director of the Institute of Jewish Studies at the University of Antwerp, Belgium. Since 2013, she is also Distinguished Visiting Professor in the Faculty of the Humanities at the Hebrew University of Jerusalem. She has published extensively on literary theory, German modernism, and German-Jewish authors and thinkers. She has been editor or co-editor of numerous books, including the two-volume ICLA publication *Modernism* (2007), which was awarded the Prize of the Modernist Studies Association in 2008; *Contemporary Jewish Writing in Europe: A Guide* (2007); *What does the Veil Know?* (2009); *The German-Jewish Experience Revisited* (2015); and *Kafka and the Universal* (2016). She is the editor of the book series "Perspectives on Jewish Texts and Contexts" (De Gruyter, Berlin) and co-editor of the *Yearbook of the Society for European-Jewish Literature* and *Arcadia: International Journal of Literary Studies*. In 2012, she was awarded the Cross of Honor for Sciences and the Arts from the Republic of Austria. Liska's recent books include *Giorgio Agamben's Empty Messianism* (2008); *When Kafka Says We. Uncommon Communities in German-Jewish Literature* (2008); *Fremde Gemeinschaft. Deutsch-jüdische Literatur der Moderne (2011)*; and, most recently, *German-Jewish Thought and its Afterlife. A Tenuous Legacy* (2017).

Eric Prenowitz teaches in the School of Fine Art, History of Art and Cultural Studies at the University of Leeds. He is the executive editor of *Parallax*, a quarterly journal of critical cultural theory published by Routledge (Taylor & Francis). He has published widely on the writings of Hélène Cixous, and has translated a number of her works into English. He is currently preparing a translation of Cixous's book on the painter Luc Tuymans, *Relevé de la mort*.

Shlomith Rimmon-Kenan is Professor Emerita of English and Comparative Literature at the Hebrew University of Jerusalem and a member of the Israel Academy of Sciences and Humanities. She is the author of *The Concept of Ambiguity – The Example of* James (1977), *Narrative Fiction: Contemporary Poetics* (1983), and *A Glance beyond Doubt: Narration, Representation, Subjectivity* (1996), as well as of numerous articles on literary theory and on specific authors, including James, Faulkner, Nabokov, Brooke-Rose, and Morrison. She has also worked in interdisciplinary junctions: literature and psychoanalysis, historiography, law, and medicine. She is currently engaged in a collaborative project with Professor Susan Lanser, Brandeis University, exploring narratives of the Israeli-Palestinian conflict from a narratological perspective.

Sasha Senderovich is Assistant Professor of Slavic, Jewish, and International Studies at the University of Washington, Seattle. Together with Harriet Murav, he translated, from the Yiddish, David Bergelson's *Judgment: A Novel* (Northwestern University Press, 2017). He has published on Russian Jewish writers Isaac Babel and Moyshe Kulbak, as well as on contemporary works by Soviet-born American Jewish emigré authors, including Gary Shteyngart and Anya Ulinich. He is working on his first monograph, *How the Soviet Jew Was Made: Mobility and Culture after the Revolution*.

Anastasia Telaak is a DAAD Lecturer at the Institute of German Philology at the Jagiellonian University in Kraków. She wrote a dissertation on Jewish topographies in Argentine literature and has published several articles on Jewish literatures. Her research interests include Jewish thought, history and culture, Modernist literature, German-Jewish literature since 1945, and (prose) poetry. Having recently worked on borders, translation, and transgression in Uljana Wolf's prose poetry and on Tomer Gardi's poetics of "broken German," she is currently preparing an essay on the correlations between the concept of mother tongue, the intertextual transfer of Kafka and Freud, and the figures of Moses, the Golem, and Ahasver in Alejandra Pizarnik's oeuvre.

Cécile Wajsbrot is a French writer and translator and was born in Paris in 1954. She writes mostly novels but happens also to write essays. She just concluded a five novels cycle about art, creation and reception – on which she has been working for twelve years. The last one, Destruction, appears in 2019. Her work is translated into several languages, among which German and Spanish. She is a translator from the English (Virginia Woolf) and from the German (Peter Kurzeck or Marcel Beyer). Living both in Paris and Berlin, she received the prize of the Académie de Berlin in November 2016. Since 2017 she has been a member of the Deutsche Akademie für Sprache und Dichtung.

Susanne Zepp is Professor of Spanish, Portuguese, and French Literatures, the Director of the Gulbenkian Doctoral Program for Portuguese Literature and Culture, and Principal Investigator at the Friedrich Schlegel Graduate School for Literary Studies at the Freie Universität Berlin. From 2003–2015, she served as the Deputy Director of the Simon Dubnow Institute for Jewish History and Culture at Leipzig University. She received her PhD with a work on Jorge Luis Borges and skepticism in 2002, and completed her Habilitation at the University of Cologne with a *venia legend* in Romance Literatures and Cultures. She teaches literary and historical texts in Spanish, Portuguese, and French that range from the sixteenth to the twentieth century. More recently she has written on representation and time and on the writings of Peter Szondi. Her most recent books are an introduction to Portuguese and Brazilian literary studies and the first critical essay collection on Claude Lanzmann, a monograph on Early Modern Jewish literary creativity (Stanford University Press), and an edited volume on German as a Jewish language (Leipzig University Press).

www.ingramcontent.com/pod-product-compliance
Lightning Source LLC
Chambersburg PA
CBHW061938220426
43662CB00012B/1944